The New Iranian Cinema

THE NEW
IRANIAN CINEMA

Politics, Representation and Identity

Edited by
Richard Tapper

I.B. TAURIS
LONDON · NEW YORK

Published in 2002 by I.B.Tauris & Co Ltd
London and New York
www.ibtauris.com

In the United States and Canada distributed by Palgrave Macmillan a
division of St. Martin's Press
175 Fifth Avenue, New York NY 10010

ISBN   hardback 1 86064 803 7
       paperback 1 86064 804 5

A full CIP record for this book is available from the British Library
A full CIP record for this book is available from the Library of Congress

Library of Congress catalog card: available

Typeset in Garamond by Dexter Haven Associates, London
Printed and bound in Great Britain by MPG Books Ltd, Bodmin

Contents

List of Illustrations

Acknowledgements

This book arose from a conference held at the School of Oriental and African Studies (SOAS) in London, in association with the major Festival of Iranian Films screened at the National Film Theatre, London, during June and July 1999.

Seven chapters (those by Devictor, Farahmand, Haghighi, Varzi, Saeed-Vafa, Lahiji and Sadr) are revisions of those presented at the conference. Naficy's excellent presentation, useful in the conference context, was marginal to the theme of the book; in its place he kindly agreed to revise and update an important published paper. Rahimieh's chapter has also appeared elsewhere. The remaining chapters (those by Ghazian, Dabashi and Mir-Hosseini, as well as the editor's introduction and Mulvey's afterword) were written specially for the book.

The editor is most grateful to Farhad Hakimzadeh for the impetus to convene the conference, to Ziba Mir-Hosseini for co-convening the conference, and to Rose Issa and Sheila Whitaker (who also edited the most valuable and stimulating accompanying book, *Life and Art*, British Film Institute, 1999) for organizing the festival. Efficient conference organization was provided by Sarah Stewart and Regina Miesle at the SOAS Centre for Near and Middle Eastern Studies. The conference was supported generously by the Iran Heritage Foundation, the British Institute for Persian Studies, the SOAS Research Committee and Iran Air (travel costs of some participants), and the Iran Heritage Foundation has also contributed to the cost of publication.

The editor is also grateful to the editors of *CEMOTI* and *Thamyris* for permission to reprint, in modified form, the chapters by Naficy and Rahimieh respectively; and to Hamid Dabashi for providing illustrations 4 and 5 (courtesy of Mohsen Makhmalbaf), to Kim Longinotto for illustration 7 and to Hamid Reza Sadr for the others.

Notes on Contributors

HAMID DABASHI is Professor of Iranian Studies, Chairman of the Department of Middle East and Asian Languages and Cultures, and Director of Graduate Studies at the Center for Comparative Literature and Society at Columbia University, New York. His books include *Authority in Islam: From the Rise of Muhammad to the Establishment of the Umayyads* (Transaction, 1989), *Theology of Discontent: The Ideological Foundation of the Islamic Revolution in Iran* (New York University Press, 1993), *Staging a Revolution: The Art of Persuasion in the Islamic Republic of Iran* (with Peter Chelkowski, Booth-Clibborn, 2000) and *Close-Up: Iranian Cinema – Past, Present, Future* (Verso, 2001).

AGNES DEVICTOR has a doctorate in political science from the Institut d'Etudes Politiques in Aix-en-Provence, France. She did field research between 1994 and 1998 for her thesis on 'The cultural politics of the Islamic Republic of Iran, with reference to cinema (1979–97)'. She teaches political science at the IEP in Aix and Iranian cinema at Université de Paris III, has directed the programme on contemporary Iranian cinema in the Festival d'Automne 2000 and writes regularly for *Le Monde*.

AZADEH FARAHMAND is a doctoral candidate in the Department of Film and Television, University of California at Los Angeles; she has a Bachelor degree in philosophy and a Masters in Critical Studies. Her current research engages in theoretical debates on national and transnational cinemas, as well as roles and impacts of international film festivals, taking the recent Iranian cinema as a model. Her articles include 'Recent Iranian Cinema: a re-view', in *Intersections* and 'Weaving through cultures, transpassing broken bridges: an interview with Rafegh Pooya', in *Jusur: UCLA Journal of Middle Eastern Studies*. She has also published poetry and prose in both Persian and English in various journals and anthologies, including *A World Between: Poems, Short Stories and Essays by Iranian-Americans* (ed. Persis M. Karim and Mohammad Mehdi Khorrami, George Braziller, 1999).

HOSSEIN GHAZIAN is Director of the Ayandeh Research Group, an influential social science institute close to the reformist tendency in Iran. He also acts as advisor to the journal *Zanan*, to the National Institute for Research on Public Opinion and to the Centre for Media Studies and Research. He has recently been conducting various research projects relating to the 2001 presidential elections, and to social and family issues in Tehran. He has a doctorate in Political Sociology. One of the founders of the journal *Kiyan*, he has over 15 years of experience in journalism, and has published numerous articles in academic journals and edited books.

ALI REZA HAGHIGHI works as a consultant for a number of reformist newspapers and for the foreign media in Iran, and has been a researcher for television programmes such as *People's President* (CNN) and *444 days* (BBC). He also teaches at the Azad University. He did his BA, MA and PhD in Tehran University in the Faculty of Political Science and Law. His 1993 MA thesis was on 'Obstacles to the Growth of Civil Society in Iran'; his PhD thesis was on 'Changes in Cognitive and Behavioural Models of the Religious Intellectuals in Iran', a subject on which he has presented papers at conferences outside Iran. His publications include *Ravand-e Islamgera'i dar Torkiye* (*The Process of Islamization in Turkey*, 1994).

SHAHLA LAHIJI is Director of Rowshangaran Publishing and the Women's Studies Center, Inc. in Tehran. Before the Revolution, Lahiji was active in social and cultural activities and journalism in Shiraz and Khuzistan. Since the Revolution, she has been politically active and outspoken on women's rights and conditions. The first woman publisher in Iran, she herself is the author of numerous books in Persian of original research, compilation and translation, including *Portrait of Women in the Works of Bahram Beyzai, Filmmaker and Script writer* (Rowshangaran, 1989).

ZIBA MIR-HOSSEINI is an independent researcher, writer and consultant on Middle Eastern issues, specializing in Islamic law, gender, family and rural development. She obtained her PhD in Social Anthropology in 1980 at the University of Cambridge; between 1990 and 1993 she held a Research Fellowship at Girton College, Cambridge. She is currently Research Associate at the Centre for Near and Middle Eastern Studies, SOAS, University of London. She is the author of *Marriage on Trial: A Study of Islamic Family Law in Iran and Morocco* (I.B. Tauris, 1993) and *Islam and Gender: The Religious Debate in Contemporary Iran* (Princeton University Press, 1999 and I.B. Tauris, 2000), and co-director (with Kim Longinotto) of two feature-length documentaries for Channel Four: *Divorce Iranian Style* (1998), and *Runaway* (2001).

LAURA MULVEY is Professor of Film and Media Studies at Birkbeck College, University of London and Director of the AHRB Centre for British Film and Television Studies. She has been writing about film and film theory since the mid-1970s. As reflected in her books *Visual and Other Pleasures* (Macmillan, 1989) and *Fetishism and Curiosity* (British Film Institute, 1996), her work has been influenced by and involved with feminism, avant-garde cinema and psychoanalytic theory. In the late 1970s and early 80s, she co-directed 6 films with Peter Wollen, including *Riddles of the Sphinx* (BFI, 1978) and *Frida Kahlo and Tina Modotti* (Arts Council, 1980). In 1994 she co-directed a documentary with artist/filmmaker Mark Lewis, *Disgraced Monuments*, which was broadcast on Channel Four.

HAMID NAFICY is Professor of Film and Media Studies and Chair of the Department of Art and Art History, Rice University, Houston, Texas. He has published many studies on theories of exile and displacement, exilic and diasporic cultures, films and media, and Iranian, Middle Eastern and Third World cinemas. His books include *An Accented Cinema: Exilic and Diasporic Filmmaking* (Princeton University Press, 2001), *Home, Exile, Homeland: Film, Media, and the Politics of Place* (edited, Routledge, 1999), *The Making of Exile Cultures: Iranian Television in Los Angeles* (University of Minnesota Press, 1993), *Otherness and the Media: the Ethnography of the Imagined and the Imaged* (co-edited, Harwood Academic, 1993) and *Iran Media Index* (Greenwood Press, 1984). He has also published many studies in Persian, including a two-volume book on documentary cinema, *Film-e Mostanad* (Free University of Iran Press, 1978–9). His forthcoming book is *Cinema and National Identity: A Social History of the Iranian Cinema* (University of Texas Press).

NASRIN RAHIMIEH is Professor of Comparative Literature and Associate Dean (Humanities) of Arts at the University of Alberta in Edmonton, Canada. Her research and teaching are focused on intercultural encounters between Iran and the West, immigrant and exile literature and women's writing. Her book *Oriental Responses to the West: Comparative Essays on Muslim Writers from the Middle East* was published in 1990 by E. J. Brill. Her second book, *Missing Persians: Discovering Voices in Iranian Cultural History*, was published by Syracuse University Press in 2002.

HAMID REZA SADR is a film writer working in Tehran. He has a BA from the Faculty of Economics, Tehran University and an MA in town planning from the Faculty of Arts. He was editor of the Iranian and world cinema section in *Zan-e Ruz* (1984–8), editor of the Iranian cinema section in *Sorush* (1988–90) and editor of the Iranian and world cinema section in *Film* (1990–8). He has worked with the National Film Theatre (London) and the London, Chicago and New York Film Festivals in the selection of Iranian films. He has published over 500 articles on Iranian cinema in *Zan-e Ruz*, *Sorush* and *Film*, and his books include *Sinema-ye Komedi* (*Comedy Cinema*, 1987), a translation of Molly Haskell's *From Reverence to Rape: Treatment of Women in the Movies* and most recently *Siyasat va Sinema dar Iran* (*Politics and Cinema in Iran*, 2001).

MEHRNAZ SAEED-VAFA is an independent filmmaker living in Chicago. Her documentary, *A Tajik Woman*, won the first prize at the Sony/BFI Video contest in Los Angeles 1994 and won the special Jury Prize from the Illinois Film and Video Artist in 1994. Her other films (*Ruins Within, The Silent Majority* and *Saless, Far From Home*) have been shown in different festivals. She has been teaching filmmaking at the department of Film and Video, Columbia College, Chicago since 1988; since 1989 she has worked with the Film Center, Art Institute of Chicago as artistic consultant for the Iranian Film Festival. Her book on Abbas Kiarostami (co-written with Jonathan Rosenbaum) will be published by the University of Illinois Press in 2002.

RICHARD TAPPER is Professor of Anthropology with reference to the Middle East at SOAS, University of London. He has done field research in Iran, Afghanistan and Turkey. Between 1999 and 2001 he convened three conferences on Iranian cinema at SOAS, where he also teaches a course on the subject as part of the MA in Anthropology of Media, and where he convenes the Media Research Programme. His books include *Pasture and Politics* (1979), *Frontier Nomads of Iran* (1997) and the edited volumes *The Conflict of Tribe and State in Iran and Afghanistan* (1983), *Islam in Modern Turkey* (1991), *Culinary Cultures of the Middle East* (with Sami Zubaida, 1994), *Technology, Tradition and Survival* (with Keith McLachlan, 2002) and *The Nomadic Peoples of Iran* (with Jon Thompson, 2002).

ROXANNE VARZI is a Fellow at Columbia University where she is completing her PhD in Social/Cultural Anthropology. Varzi holds the first Fulbright Fellowship to be awarded for research in post-revolutionary Iran. Her research concentrated on the construction and consumption of public space and popular culture in Tehran with an emphasis on the Iran–Iraq war and youth culture. She has published both scholarly articles and creative short stories which include 'Iran Gardi' in *Public Culture*, 'Mercury Rising: Tajik Refugees in Kyrgystan' in *Silk Road*, 'The Caravan' in *The New York Press*, January 2000, 'The Pelican' in *A World Between: Fiction, Poetry and Essays by Iranian-Americans* (New York, George Braziller, 1999) and 'Refugee' in *The American Magazine*.

A Note on Transliteration and Style

For transliteration from Persian, the full range of vowels is used: a (but no macron for alef), e, i, o, u; and the diphthongs 'ow' (as in Nowruz), 'ey' (as in Hoseyn), 'ay' (as in Baysikel). 'Ain (except initially) and hamzeh have been retained and distinguished. Proper and personal names, wherever possible, are given in conventional forms.

Film titles are always given in English in the text, and (in cases where there are alternative English versions) have been standardized. A filmography at the end lists separately both Persian and English film titles. In the text, for the first mention of a film in each chapter, the name of the director and the date of first screening are also given. Although there are sometimes considerable ambiguities in dating (completion, first screening etc.), the editor has, perhaps rashly, again attempted standardization, usually relying on the three-volume (so far) compilation by Jamal Omid (*Farhang-e Film-ha-ye Sinema-ye Iran*, Tehran, Negah, 1377–79/1998–2000).

1

Introduction[1]

Richard Tapper

In the early 1970s, a number of films by Iranian directors attracted considerable international attention, as Roy Armes notes in his seminal work *Third World Film Making and the West*:

> 1970 [saw] the appearance of a New Iranian Cinema...created by a fairly heterogeneous group of young intellectuals, many of them foreign-educated, and receiving some support from the Ministry of Culture and the state television service.[2]

A few years later, the 1978–9 Iranian Revolution, and the inauguration of what many saw as an oppressively puritanical and totalitarian Islamic Republic, seemed to threaten the end of the 'New Iranian Cinema' (also known as the 'New Wave'). As Devictor describes this process below:

> When the Revolution broke out in 1979, observers and professionals of the film industry were worried about the future of cinema in Iran. Cinema theatres were burned down in the name of morality and cultural independence, the chain of production was completely disrupted by the exile of numerous directors, actors and producers, creativity was jeopardized by the uncertainty of what would be allowed or forbidden. Nevertheless, far from dying, Iranian cinema has become more active and lively than ever before.

1. Mohsen Makhmalbaf's *Gabbeh*.

By the late 1990s, indeed, cinema in Iran appeared to be flourishing, its remarkable transformation paralleling wider changes in Iranian culture and society. It is widely recognized not merely as a distinctive 'national cinema' but as one of the most innovative and exciting in the world: films from Iranian directors are screened to increasing acclaim in international festivals.

The new international stature of Iranian cinema is often presented as a paradox, given, as Naficy puts it below, the 'Western perception that Shi'i Islam as practised in Iran today is anti-modern and backward. The Islamic Republic's widely reported curtailment of Western-style performing arts and entertainment and its maltreatment of entertainers, have certainly reinforced such impressions.' This apparent paradox at least partly explains the recent international fascination with Iranian cinema.

But hostile domestic conditions in the late 1970s had already drastically reduced the output of the New Wave. Iranian cinema has re-emerged not just in spite of government restrictions in the Islamic Republic. It has firm roots both before the Revolution, and in richer and more profound Iranian cultural traditions of drama, poetry and the visual arts that have survived many centuries of political and social change. The contributors to this book share a perception of the need for deeper – but accessible – analysis of the recent international success of Iranian cinema. They approach the topic from a range of perspectives: media studies and film criticism, literature, anthropology, sociology, politics and economics. Many have already published books on aspects of Iranian cinema. One interesting consequence of the Revolution has been that the field of Iranian studies in the West is now dominated by Iranians, not Westerners. Most of our contributors are Iranian: some live and work in Iran, others in the US and the UK.

The chapters below collectively consider how cinema has developed in Iran in the years since the 1978–9 Revolution, the place of cinema in Iranian culture and society, and how Iranian cinema has become a true 'world cinema'. All address important relevant issues, some in a general way, others by focusing on specific films or directors. This Introduction suggests how the chapters – as the editor reads them – relate to each other and to the wider contexts of Iranian society, culture and politics.

The focus of the book is Iranian cinema since the Revolution. Pre-revolutionary cinema is the subject of several published studies, and is referred to when necessary in several chapters; a short discussion will set the scene here.

Iranian Cinema up to the 1978–9 Revolution

Opinions differ as to whether Iranian cinema began in 1900 with the introduction of the first cine-camera by Mozafferoddin Shah's photographer Mirza Ebrahim Khan Akkas-bashi, or in 1930 with the first Iranian fiction film, Ovanes Oganians's *Abi and Rabi* (1930). Other films from the first half of the century, such as the first 'talkie', Ardeshir Irani's *The Lor Girl* (1933), had a major public impact – in the cities at least – and have achieved a mythical status.[3] But interesting though the history of the early years is, it must be said that nothing of distinction – nothing worthy of being called 'national cinema' – was produced until after the Second World War. For many years, the films shown publicly were mostly dubbed imports; local productions were imitations of Indian, Egyptian and other foreign films, the most popular being what became known as the *film farsi* genre.[4]

Unlike in some other countries, elements which constrain Iranian cinema today – such as its connection with politics, religion and national culture

– have always been present. Both government and religious authorities sought to control the images to be shown publicly.[5] Religious leaders condemned cinema from the start as morally offensive and ethically corrupting. As Farahmand notes below, formal censorship began in the 1920s, in the face of increasing imports of films depicting women, the family, sex and dancing, while political criticism or social realism in locally produced films was unthinkable. By the 1950s and 1960s, commercial enterprise determined film style. While political censorship if anything increased, greater freedom was allowed in the area of sex, leading Ayatollah Khomeini and other religious figures to condemn cinema in the 1970s.[6]

There were interesting developments in the 1950s and 1960s, particularly in documentary-making, by writers and filmmakers such as Farrokh Gaffary, Forugh Farrokhzad and Ebrahim Golestan; but the year 1969 is generally agreed to mark the birth of the Iranian art cinema, called the New Wave, with Daryush Mehrju'i's prize-winning *The Cow* and Massoud Kimia'i's *Qeysar*. For a brief period between 1969 and 1974, Iranian cinema became known internationally for the first time.[7] Domestically, art cinema was increasingly part of new Iranian movements in literature and politics, with the involvement of intellectuals and literary figures such as Kimia'i, Mehrju'i, Golestan, Farrokhzad, Bahram Beyza'i and Gholam-Hoseyn Sa'edi. The new films introduced the notion of director as *auteur* and the idea of cinema as an art like literature, poetry and theatre. Writers now wrote for cinema.[8]

The treatment of *The Cow* at festivals prefigured the reception of some post-revolutionary films. But it was not yet a 'world cinema'. And, as Armes notes, 'The films of the young directors had given Iran an international reputation, but they failed to reach a mass audience within their own country.'[9] From the mid-1970s, local audiences for Iranian films decreased, in the face of invasions from India and Hollywood. Local production declined through lack of financial support; only *film farsi* continued to draw popular audiences and make money.

Indeed, there is much agreement that pre-revolutionary Iranian cinema was nearly dead before the Revolution, killed by the wholesale import of foreign films. But politics was still an important factor. A combination of filming styles and the choice and treatment of topics and locations – rural and tribal societies and the urban poor – brought an association of the new cinema with anti-government politics. *The Cow* in particular started a genre of allegorical 'protest' film. However, such films were appreciated only by a small elite local audience and foreign critics, and the Pahlavi regime stifled the protest more effectively by appropriation than by censorship. As Dabashi puts it below:

> It is sad but nevertheless undeniable that much of the secular culture of 1960s and 1970s Iran, as expressed not just in the Tehran Film Festival but even more offensively in the Shiraz Art Festival, was sponsored by, and gave cultural credence to, the Pahlavi monarchy…the unfortunate state of the pre-revolutionary art was such that, in order to see the work of even Amir Naderi or Daryush Mehrju'i, two of the most progressive filmmakers at the time, one had to sit next to the Pahlavi ruling elite.

Like many twentieth-century nation-states, Pahlavi Iran sought legitimacy in early history. The Shahs looked to pre-Islamic times, reviving and glorifying Iran's earlier cultural and political heritage at the expense of Islam. Whatever was Islamic the state depicted as backward; 'tradition' was rejected to pave the way for 'modernization'. The Pahlavis' aggrandizement of their pre-Islamic precursors and of pre-Islamic Iranian cultural traditions was not well received by the general public, few of whom shared the values that were being promoted; in particular, they aggravated the antagonism of the religious classes towards the regime. The 1978–9 Revolution was a rejection of the Pahlavis and all they stood for. It was a populist revolution with many different elements, but the clerics had the deepest popular roots, were best organized and led, and emerged victorious as the rulers of an Islamic Republic.[10]

After the Islamic Revolution, an Islamic Cinema?

Before the Revolution, the *ulema* had either rejected cinema or ignored it; as a new art form, scholars had little to say about it, apart from applying to the depiction of images their juristic (*feqh*) rules of what was forbidden and what was allowed (*haram* and *halal*). Generally, the religious classes disapproved: for some pious families, going to the cinema was tantamount to committing a sin: it was *haram*. But the Islamists recognized the usefulness of the media, and when the state became Islamic and subject to the rulings of the jurists, they had to deal with the issue of cinema. They had two options: they could either forbid it (as the Taliban did in Afghanistan 15 years later) or Islamicize it. Realizing its power, they could no longer ignore it, but decided to bring it under proper control and use it for proper political purposes. Armes starts a chapter on "The

Middle East and Africa' with the following quotation from Ayatollah Khomeini: 'Cinema is one of the manifestations of culture and it must be put to the service of man and his education.'[11] For Khomeini, the adoption of cinema became an ideological tool to combat Pahlavi culture.

Early revolutionary discourse defined itself in opposition to the *ancien régime*, and aimed to undo and to rectify what were portrayed as non-Islamic elements; not only to establish a new Islamic political and economic base, and popular legitimacy through a new Constitution, but to reinvent culture, society, intellectual life, education and learning, 'Islamicized' and cleansed of the pollution of Western and Pahlavi elements.

In the 1980s, the new cultural policy brought the growth of regulation: all forms of communications media and arts were forced into the ideological straitjacket of *feqh* rules of *halal* and *haram*. The most powerful media, TV and radio, were brought firmly under state control. The arts – including music, theatre, cinema – and press and publishing were made subject to the new Ministry of Culture and Islamic Guidance (MCIG).

There was much debate on what an 'Islamic' art and cinema might mean. Naficy and Dabashi discuss this below. What would a new Islamic aesthetics be? Of course it was easier to focus on the negative (banning *haram* images and subjects, such as the portrayal of the body – especially women's – as part of the *hejab* system), but positive steps to promote Islamic subjects and images were suggested by the Revolution itself and then the war with Iraq (1980–88), which became subjects for major genres of art and cinema.

Naficy tells the story of the 'Islamization' of cinema, after the initial destruction of the film theatres themselves, a key symbolic act against the 'poison' of Pahlavi culture. He lists the elements of post-revolutionary 'Islamic culture', and the new regulations for cinema and video, and tells how an Islamic cinema was negotiated. His thesis is

> that the revolution led to the emergence of a new, vital cinema, with its own special industrial and financial structure, and unique ideological, thematic and production values. This is, of course, part of a more general transformation in the political culture of Iran.

He gives a detailed account and a chronology of events in the immediate post-revolutionary cinema, 1978–82. This was a period of uncertainty for Iranian filmmakers. Problems included:

financial damage that the industry suffered during the revolution, lack of government interest in cinema during the transitional period, a vacuum of centralized authority, antagonistic competition between various factions over cinema, lack of an appropriate cinematic model, heavy competition from imports, a drastic deterioration in the public image of the industry as a whole, the haphazard application of censorship, and the flight of many film professionals into exile.

No quality film was produced in those early years. Amir Naderi's *The Runner* (1986) was an isolated exception, which came about because of the director's perseverance.[12] After 1982,

> Political consolidation entailed direct control of the mass media and the film industry. However, the transformation of cinema from the Pahlavi to the Islamic involved a major cultural and ideological shift, which could not take place unidirectionally, monolithically or rapidly.

A number of new institutions assisted in the process: the Farabi Foundation was created in 1983, while the Mostazafan Foundation and the Jehad (later Ministry) of Reconstruction had important roles in film production and exhibition and in the use of media generally. By 1984, film production was being encouraged once more. Naficy examines in detail the dominant themes of the films being made, such as promotion of anti-Pahlavi, Islamic values, war subjects and a restricted women's cinema.

How much did the Revolution mark a break from pre-revolutionary cinema? Naficy focuses on differences, although some other writers stress the continuity, pointing to the many accomplished directors who made films both before and after the Revolution, to the abiding connection of cinema with politics, and to the continuation of censorship in various forms.[13] The main break was the public's reduced exposure to Hollywood films, which by the late 1970s had ruined Iranian local cinema and – Islamists would say – public morals.

Back to the Festivals

By the mid-1980s, the failure to establish an Islamic ideological cinema was evident. What happened in the world of Iranian cinema parallels other developments in Iranian society: a gradual stretching of the limits imposed by the jurists, and of the way social realities – facts on the ground – respond to ideology and law, and a further redefining and reinventing of culture. As far as the arts were concerned, some Muslim militants and radicals who had won the earlier battle with the secularists became moderates and liberals themselves. They were the so-called 'left', who formulated cultural policies in the 1980s. Among the key players was Mohammad Khatami, who began as Minister of Culture and Islamic Guidance in 1982 in the government of Mir Hoseyn Musavi, and with a team of Muslim intellectuals laid the foundation for an independent press and a new, national cinema.

In the first decade following the Revolution, art, including cinema, freed itself from the domination of ideology. The Farabi Cinema Foundation (FCF) realized that art cannot be dictated and that it was best to allow filmmakers to choose their own themes. Pre-revolutionary directors such as Mehrju'i, Beyza'i, Kimia'i and Abbas Kiarostami resumed their interrupted careers. Prominent newcomers included women directors. Gradually, the period of recovery and qualitative growth started, and with films like Mehrju'i's *The Tenants* (1986) and Beyza'i's *Bashu, the Little Stranger* (1988), Iranian films started to attract international attention again. Official attitudes and conditions changed. Morality codes were relaxed in 1988. From 1989 to 1993, scripts no longer needed approval. As Naficy says, 'Cinema, rejected in the past as part of the frivolous *superstructure*, [was] adopted as part of the necessary *infrastructure* of Islamic culture.' Strict censorship continued, but a process of cultural negotiation and accommodation resulted in a lively cinema and cinema culture.

With the end of the war in 1988, and Khomeini's death a year later, cinema became a focus for ideological and political dispute. The political skirmishes reached a peak at the Fajr Festival of 1991. Naficy describes the debates in summer 1991, leading to the resignations of Khatami and others, and the start of a new period of uncertainty. Rafsanjani's 'rightist' government banned many high-quality films, and adopted the habit of accusing internal opponents of supporting 'Western cultural invasion'.

But the change of policy was too late, and it backfired. It politicized the filmmakers and forced them to take positions, as became evident in the 1997 presidential elections: Khatami was a surprise candidate, and the artistic community – including prominent filmmakers – came out and took sides, the first time they had taken an active role in politics. Those producing art and progressive cinema openly supported Khatami. His campaign 'commercial' was made by Seyfollah Dad, who later became Deputy for Cinema Affairs under Ataollah Mohajerani, the new Minister of Culture and Islamic Guidance. Mohsen Makhmalbaf's interviews played an important role in Khatami's campaign.[14] With Khatami's election, a new phase in Iranian cinema began. Many long-suppressed films were now screened, and issues that had been taboo in the 1980s were now addressed in films such as Rakhshan Bani-Etemad's *The May Lady* (1998) and Tahmineh Milani's *Two Women* (1999).

With the phenomenal success – and festival exposure – in the late 1990s of new films by established masters like Kiarostami, Mehrju'i, and Mohsen Makhmalbaf, as well as newcomers such as Majid Majidi, Abolfazl Jalili, Samira Makhmalbaf, Ja'far Panahi and Bahman Qobadi, the international progress of Iranian cinema seemed unstoppable. Iranian cinema became the rage. No respectable film festival was without at least one example. Festivals devoted to Iranian films multiplied. In summer 1999, the National Film Theatre staged the largest season so far (and the third in London that year) with some 60 Iranian films, both pre- and post-revolutionary, screened over two months. In the same year Chicago held its tenth annual festival, and there were seasons devoted to Iranian films – or particular directors – elsewhere in the US, France, Canada and other countries.

International Success: Politics or Economics?

How much has Iranian cinema's international success been achieved despite, or because of, Iranian government intervention? Why does government intervene, whether to promote or to censor? How has censorship affected filmmaking styles and strategies? What has attracted international critics and festival organizers to Iranian films? What are the expectations and attitudes of audiences at home and abroad? How much have Iranian films succeeded despite, or because of, their limited range of themes and focus? Because of Iranian culture or in spite of it? The following chapters address these and other central questions.

Many have suggested that Iranian cinema could not survive without its international market. Not surprisingly, French cinéastes, traditionally hostile to Hollywood, have been foremost in welcoming Iranian cinema, as Mojdeh Famili notes; she adds that this was also a smart attitude economically,[15] a point developed by Farahmand below.

In their chapters Devictor and Ghazian both note the high rate of film production reached during the 1990s, and ask how far Iranian cinema's international success and high output are due to government policy towards cinema. Devictor suggests that Iranian government policy has been mainly ideological, rather than economic or artistic, but that it has used classical tools of intervention, and it is not unlike the policies of some Western democratic regimes. Like Naficy, she recounts the problems of cinema early in the Islamic Republic, being resolved only in 1982 in a coherent intervention policy with Khatami as Minister. She surveys the state institutions founded to deal with cinema production, such as Farabi; and the regulations – which the professionals demanded. She shows how the regime actually operated an ideological cinema, which was not peculiar to Iran: in the USSR, the US (under the Hays Code) and France too, cinema has been part of political debate. She draws parallels with state cinema policies in France – especially the tools used – then shows the limits of such a comparison, largely at the levels of political structure, ideology and motivation.

Ghazian takes an economic perspective, noting that the artistic success of Iranian cinema has not been matched by financial success. Many reputed films have failed in the domestic market. As before the Revolution, the public does not go to see Iranian films, but continues to prefer foreign films, despite the restrictions. The film industry is in severe financial crisis, and produces ever fewer films per head of population. Ghazian considers the role of government in alleviating this crisis, and suggests that state aid disrupts the supply–demand relationship. 'Ironically, this aid itself has aggravated the crisis, since it has come accompanied by ideological and political interference and a failure to appreciate the changes in the social structure of Iran over the past two decades.' The government supports films that the public does not want to see. He concludes that, if the government fails to recognize public demand by relaxing its controls, 'the eventual collapse of the Iranian film industry is a serious possibility'.

Political or Social Critique?

Farahmand and Haghighi examine, from different perspectives, the absence of political criticism in Iranian films. Farahmand looks sceptically at the international success of Iranian cinema, stressing its economic and political – rather than its artistic – basis. 'The recent recognition gained by Iranian cinema has overshadowed the remarkable Iranian film tradition of the past, and ignores the current crisis facing the industry.' Like

Ghazian, she highlights this financial crisis and suggests that government promotion of Iranian films abroad was strongly motivated by the promise of new external investment, especially by French production companies. It was also 'a promising means through which to renegotiate the imagery of the nation, and gradually to reclaim a place for the country within the global economy in the name of art', to foster a new (peaceful, artistic, childlike) image of Iran after the end of the war with Iraq.

Farahmand argues that Iranian films' 'entrance in and accolades at international festivals both reflect and produce a set of concerns that gradually and retroactively affect the film production and distribution process'. She is concerned about the internal consequences of censorship: how it interacts with film festivals to encourage and promote particular film styles, subjects and directors, and to exclude others:

> many filmmakers choose to avoid controversial themes entirely. In other words, filmmakers have been led to refrain from making confrontational and socially critical films for fear of being held accountable for making anti-system or anti-establishment statements through their work.

However,

> I am not suggesting that creative activity and critical expression are only possible in the absence of (self-)censorship, nor do I hold it the duty of filmmakers to be politically conscious and openly critical of society in their work... This, however, does not mean that censorship is good because it makes artists more creative.

Farahmand looks at the work of Kiarostami in particular, aiming 'to historicize and problematize aesthetic values and to subject them to a critical consideration...to situate Kiarostami's highly regarded works within a broader context'. He chooses 'village themes and location shooting in rural landscapes [which] reinforce the exotic look of Iranian films – and increase their marketability abroad'. She suggests that Kiarostami's 'political escapism...caters to the film festival taste for "high art" and restrained politics', and questions the politics of the festivals, drawing parallels with US–China 'ping-pong diplomacy' in the 1970s. Like Devictor, Farahmand refers to the politics apparently involved in Kiarostami's Palme d'Or and the last-minute screening of his *The Taste of Cherry* at Cannes 1997, just before Khatami's election as president.

While political cinema for Farahmand would involve open criticism of the Islamic Republic, for Haghighi, 'the basic essence of a political film is an engagement with the most important political issues of the time,' which in Iran today would concern the competing factions in government, representing opposed 'ideological, charismatic, populist and authoritarian' views of the nature of political power. He maintains that there never has been such a political cinema in Iran. The 'intellectual cinema' of the 1970s attracted attention for its resistance to Pahlavi culture, but its critique was social, not political. Before the Revolution, there was no political cinema for three reasons: strict political censorship, the consequent obscurity and complexity of the critical films that were made, and the absence among filmmakers of political activists – of any colour. Islamic intellectuals used other media and art forms – such as literature – but not cinema. Cinema was religiously disapproved, and remained strongly associated with Pahlavi dominance, consequently in the post-revolutionary years, in an atmosphere where politics were expressed through religion, cinema was neglected. Only with the war did we see the birth of a new engaged cinema, but in the form of war films, without 'political' significance. Cinema, Haghighi feels, has continued to offer a social, not a political critique. With censorship, filmmakers commonly express political opinions indirectly through symbolism; but this has not been common in Iran, and viewers often see symbolism where none is intended. Iranian cinema, he maintains, has avoided not only politics, but also the thriving ideological and intellectual debates that have engaged the press and literature in the 1990s, such as new formulations of arguments concerning religion, development and modernity.[16]

Modernity and Realism: The War and After

'Modernity' is a guiding theme of Dabashi's chapter, which offers a complex and lyrical interpretation of Mohsen Makhmalbaf's passage through revolutionary experience into Islamic cinema, and then into art. Inspired by Heidegger's philosophical critique of technological modernity as essentially colonial and as 'the categorical reduction of things, including the human, to their use-value', Dabashi finds Islamic art, and the Islamic cinema to which Makhmalbaf aspired, to be 'nothing but a further Islamization of ideological resistance to colonialism as the extended arm of Technological Modernity'. However, 'a fundamental feature of such resistance has been [the] categorical failure to recognize the formation of the so-called "native" or "traditional" mode as something in and of itself deeply colonial'.

In 1982, after an eventful early career as guerrilla, prisoner and revolutionary ideologue, Makhmalbaf started 'on a wild goose chase after an "Islamic Cinema", a figment of his own perturbed ideological imagination which even he himself cannot quite identify'. In his early films, 'his target is correct, but his political awareness is extraordinarily childish and idealistic, with no historical consciousness..."Cinema" for Makhmalbaf is...a classic case of a forbidden pleasure, both feared and yearned for.' Dabashi shows, in the contexts both of events in Iran at the time and of Makhmalbaf's personal trajectory, the formative effect of these early films in exorcizing 'the political demons inhabiting his still agitated imagination'. Then, after a near-fatal affliction by 'cine-mysticism', the artist emerges. 'Makhmalbaf's case is a spectacular example of a relentless honesty with the real literally pulling the artist out of the mystifying misery of casting a metaphysical gaze on an already brutalized world.'

Dabashi identifies the crucial change, the rebirth of Makhmalbaf into supreme cinema artist, in his short novel *The Crystal Garden*. Makhmalbaf starts to take his art seriously.

> [We] read an artist in the making, with no sign of Makhmalbaf the religious and revolutionary ideologue...Politics is almost absent from *The Crystal Garden*. But the consequences of politics are not...a far more serious intelligence is at work here, probing and discovering realities beyond the bland, tedious and insipid emptiness of all ideologies, Islamic or otherwise...Neither here nor later in his best films does Makhmalbaf attempt a logical narration of interrelated events. He has always pursued the virtual veracity of the real more than its actual or factual. Many of the characteristic features of his later films are anticipated in *The Crystal Garden*, where narrative movement is always virtual...the earliest moments of Makhmalbaf's later cinematic penchant for virtual realism, one of the characteristics which has led to the global celebration of Makhmalbaf as a filmmaker.

Makhmalbaf was trained as a war-film director, and *The Crystal Garden* is, among other things, a war story: the main characters are families of martyrs, and issues of death and identity are central to the plot.

Sacred Defence war films are the theme of Varzi's chapter. Like *The Crystal Garden*, the story of Rasul Mollaqolipour's *The Horizon* (1989), an action film of the war period, raises the main problem of post-war films – and society: the need for a body, the visible proof of death, before a 'martyr' can be properly mourned. In Ebrahim Hatamikia's later *The Scent of Yusef's Shirt* (1996), we see how 'the task of post-war Iranian cinema becomes the task of mourning itself.' In post-war films, the 'world of lost souls replaces earlier cinema by moving the battleground, from the Iraqi border and the body, to Tehran and the soul…battle and trance are incorporated in the search for bodies, for POWs and for meaning after the war.' The dead are kept alive by waiting and by faith – and by pictures and video film, which both identify those in the POW camps and (as in Yusef's case) ensure his return; though return is a mark of failed martyrdom. 'Hatamikia's films', Varzi concludes,

> deal brilliantly with the very different and unexpected types of return: the videotapes recovered from the front, dogtags, ghosts and, most interestingly, exiles from abroad…What cinema does is to re-appropriate possibly critical images and memories and place them in a space of controlled mourning, where the correct effect and proper ghostly nuances are at hand.

Representation and Reality: Documentary or Fiction?

Iran war films began, as Varzi notes, as TV documentaries. Many Iranian directors of the 1980s and 1990s cut their teeth on documentary: many notable examples were produced well before the Revolution by Golestan, Mehrju'i, Naser Taqva'i, Kamran Sherdel, Ebrahim Mokhtari and others, though their work was often banned. At the same time, questioning of what the camera reveals, and fuzzy boundaries between 'reality' and fiction – prominent features of much recent Iranian cinema – were prefigured in several pre-revolutionary films, such as Shirdel's *The Night it Rained* (1967).

This makes the problems encountered by Mir-Hosseini and Longinotto in persuading the Iranian authorities to let them shoot the documentary *Divorce Iranian Style* (1998) the more instructive. In the first of the final group of chapters, which address issues of representation, Mir-Hosseini narrates these problems, describing them as a series of negotiations of meaning, identity, purpose and reality. Her narrative gives insight into the *modus operandi* of the MCIG, both before and after Mohajerani's installation in 1997. And we get a clear picture of radically different expectations – among Iranian authorities, filmmakers and audiences – of what documentary films can and should do, whose 'reality' should be represented, and how.

Two related issues emerge: the nature and purpose of documentary, and the picture presented to the world by films of Iran, whether documentary or 'fiction'. A young documentary-maker articulated the common view to Mir-Hosseini: 'the main problem with Iranian films that get to festivals abroad is that they are all about people's misery, about poverty and backwardness.' Many others encountered by Mir-Hosseini and Longinotto held a view of documentary as justified only by either pedagogic or political aims, probably scripted in advance, with 'objective' pretensions, but with an authoritative commentary. Filmmakers and authorities did not seem able to accept *cinéma vérité*, the unscripted 'observational' and 'participatory' style of documentary which 'allows stories to present themselves to the camera, and to develop while filming', and reveals the engagement of people behind and in front of camera.[17]

What is scripted and filmed in a fiction film is also real; many Iranian directors play with this poetically, by filming the making of the film (*Salam Sinema*, Mohsen Makhmalbaf, 1995; *The Taste of Cherry*, Kiarostami, 1997), by filming real stories (*Close-Up*, Kiarostami, 1989; *Moment of Innocence*, Mohsen Makhmalbaf, 1996; *The Apple*, Samira Makhmalbaf, 1998) and by using documentary conventions and cinematic styles, minimal scripting, real people (not actors) and real locations.

Divorce Iranian Style, located almost entirely in a single small courtroom, contrasts strongly with most Iranian films, with their often colourful natural locations. In her chapter, Saeed-Vafa directs the focus to locations and their meanings for Iranian filmmakers and audiences. The very same issue of representation – of 'positive' and 'negative' images – arises with non-documentary films, particularly with reference to locations, why they are chosen and how they are viewed by Iranians at home and abroad. As she notes,

> there has been much debate among Iranian audiences abroad about what constitutes a true, authentic, undistorted representation or image of the 'homeland', Iran, and what should be shown in films…in order to avoid a 'negative image' of Iranian culture.

She argues that 'location manifests itself, often at an unconscious level, as an aspect of the filmmaker's psyche and identification with a particular culture at a given time.' Different audiences look for, and see, different images in the locations. Foreigners see the exotic (mystery and misery); Iranians abroad look for the familiar, the colourful homeland (that they have constructed).

Choice of film locations is constrained by numerous factors, among which are budget and filming styles, international demand for certain 'documentary' depictions of real locations in Iran (urban backstreets and beautiful rural scenery, but exotic images in particular), Iranian notions of privacy, the demands of the plot, and a filmmaker's own relationship to a place, which may become the 'star' of the film. Locations outside Iran have distinct meanings in terms of story, distance, division. Saeed-Vafa carefully analyses several films in their treatment of locations, real and imaginary (metaphorical), to show how they tell stories and give meaning. Dislocation (journeys, searches, homelessness, exile) is a major theme in Iranian films.

Women and Children: Dolls and Surrogates?

The treatment of women and children in Iranian films has drawn special attention, for good, but different reasons, both related to censorship. Women – veiled, restricted in their behaviour, and commonly exoticized – have suffered restrictions both in front of and behind the camera, while children – both boys and girls – have emerged both as surrogate adults and in remarkably realistic roles of their own.

In the next chapter, Lahiji demands more 'realistic portrayal' of women in Iranian feature films, that is the promotion of women heroines. She points to the Iranian tradition of powerful and independent women, in history, art and literature.[18] However, 'from its infancy, our cinema has treated women with great injustice and has been responsible, more than any other medium, for distorting the image of the Iranian woman, for creating a caricature of her real self.' Cinema in Iran missed the opportunity to add its massive potential weight 'to bring women out onto the social scene as women, and…to participate in social and economic processes as real persons'. The pre-revolutionary *film farsi* genre, where song and dance and semi-naked female stars ('unchaste dolls') appealed to the fantasies of sexually deprived young men, profited from 'neglecting, even damaging the social status of women…"Unchaste dolls" came to dominate the silver screen as the sole cinematic representation of Iranian women. The screen lacked real women and real men.'

But the intellectual and progressive filmmakers of the time were no better. In films like *Qeysar*, 'by an insidious piece of cultural fraud, [they] threw women off the cabaret stage and into the attic.' The increasing

numbers of women who had come out into society, in education, employment and politics, were nowhere to be seen in these pre-revolutionary
films, which allowed women only 'traditional' domestic roles as 'chaste
dolls' – 'as a sign of opposition to values promoted by the ruling regime'.
Commercial cinema of this time portrayed the 'new woman' who had
come out into society, as a 'creature of corruption and immorality...
unintelligent and unreliable'. Exceptions originating in the world of theatre
included films by Beyza'i, who portrayed women as real human beings.

Post-revolutionary cinema and TV initially only brought an institutionalization of the 'chaste doll' image: no real women were depicted,
working in offices or factories, thinking, deciding or opposing their
husbands' will.

> In the film sector, as in many other areas, all the sins committed by the fallen
> regime, as well as the output of vulgar filmmakers, were put on women's
> shoulders, ignoring the fact that women themselves had been the main
> victims. Women were now to pay the penalty by being banished altogether to
> the kitchen.

War films polarized women as goodies or baddies: they glorified the
ecstatic mothers of martyrs and denigrated a number of treacherous or
'difficult' types; the former of course had perfect *hejab*, the latter were
loose. After the war, some better films appeared: for example, Beyza'i's
Bashu, The Little Stranger and *Maybe Another Time* (1988). At the same
time, women, who had suffered and contributed much on the home
front, made their voices heard: 'they managed to open the gates of the
seemingly closed and male-dominated citadel of the film industry... The
way women filmmakers chose to object to the unrealistic image of
women in Iranian cinema was by making films themselves.' Male
directors had to follow.

> Today, Iranian films have risen to the level of international acceptance and
> adopted a different approach, with an attitude to women that is far more
> progressive than attitudes before the Revolution...The Iranian film industry,
> having ignored women's lives for almost 50 years, is purging itself of the
> notions of chaste and unchaste dolls in order to paint a real and realistic
> portrait of women and their presence.

The cinematic treatment of women in Iran has been an index of social
and political constructions of gender from the beginning, but especially
since 1979. Children – a somewhat different index – have had a special
place in Iranian cinema since the 1960s, when directors such as
Kiarostami and Beyza'i learned their trade with children's films. In his

chapter, Sadr comments on the prominence of children in post-revolutionary Iranian films. They have been burdened with portraying to outsiders a different, more poetic image of demonized Iranians; at the same time, for domestic audiences, they allow directors to show banned song and dance routines, to portray unshowable adult behaviour and emotions, and to allegorize. The new Iranian cinema 'on the one hand can be seen as a complete divergence from real life, and on the other it can and must be seen as a true reflection of the bizarre reality which actually characterizes contemporary Iran'. The charm of the classic prize-winning films is that they are 'concerned with realism or social problems and based on children's dilemmas'. And, one might add, the actors are both engaging as individuals, and non-professional: as in European New Wave and Neo-realist films, there are no Hollywood-style child stars. 'Because children have an existence in the world independent of their film appearances, we can believe that they are more real than other characters. This reality guaranteed the reality of the values they embodied.'

Iranian films about children are often films about parents – or their absence: 'the alienation of children and youth, unemployment, violence, broken families'. The central characters are the poor, orphaned, deprived, lonely, lost – not the wealthy middle class, with loving families and easy lives. 'The absence of family in these children's films suggests a comment on dominant social values.'

Poetic realism, Sadr observes, was

> built around the central image of childhood and was inescapably social commentary, yet it must not offend the audience... The continuing interest of poetic realism in Iranian cinema lies precisely in that it was neither a straightforwardly homogeneous nor a unitary phenomenon, but successfully crossed the boundaries between high-brow and low-brow, tradition and modernity, engagement and pleasure.

There is no sex – children are sexually innocent. The central characters earlier were boys (*Bashu, The Little Stranger; The Runner*), but increasingly in the 1990s they have been girls.[19]

Gender, Language and National Identity

Beyza'i's *Bashu, The Little Stranger* has been much quoted in different contexts. Lahiji picks it out as an exception to her dismal story of 'unreal' depictions of women. It is a war film, too, with strong social comment. As Rahimieh shows in the next chapter, it is about representations of national identity, gender and ethnic difference. The central characters are Bashu, a young boy, an Arab-speaker from the south, and – equally prominent – his adoptive mother, Na'i, a Gilaki-speaker from the north. In a complex and subtle analysis, Rahimieh shows the film as a conjoint critique of Persian ethnocentrism and patriarchy. On the one hand, 'it raises questions about the assumption that Iranian identity is inextricably bound to the dominant language of the nation, Persian.' On the other, 'the contradictory and ambivalent discourse of nationalism laid bare in *Bashu* also brings to light the problematic position occupied by women in the "imagined community" that makes up Iran.'

> Through the difficulties Na'i and Bashu encounter in communicating with each other and overcoming their mutual anxieties about linguistic and ethnic differences, the film exposes the manner in which the construction of Iranian national identity has insisted upon the erasure and elision of gender, language and ethnicity... What Na'i and Bashu have in common is their status as peripheral to the existing linguistic, social and cultural systems of signification, which isolate and vilify difference... In the course of their encounter, they are forced to confront their own ethnocentric blindspots and to re-examine their naturalized modes of interaction. If they do not radically change a symbolic system intolerant of difference, be it in gender, linguistic or ethnic identities, together they pose an ethical challenge to it.

Na'i and Bashu both start ethnocentrically; but she engineers his acceptance into her family; and he then demonstrates his own authority by using Persian with her husband; Na'i, without Persian, compromises her authority to the two males. In an ironic ending, '*Bashu* succeeds in its critique of Persian nationalism through the agency of a woman whose final resubmission to patriarchal family replicates the patterns of sub-ordination the film lays bare in the discourse of nationalism.'

Rahimieh concludes that what the film communicates to Iranian audiences is

> a need to rethink the space assigned to the marginalized and the minorities. The film points out that the comfortable and easily identifiable expressions and idioms that situate us within language also have the power to define and limit us. The Iranian viewer is subjected to the very linguistic alienation from which Bashu and Na'i suffer.[20]

National Identity at Stake

Lively late-twentieth-century debates have probed the main elements of *iraniyat* (Iranian national identity) and analysed the dialectic between them: Iran as homeland and Persian as dominant language and culture; modernity, western or otherwise; and Shi'a Islam. The question is complicated now by the massive Iranian diaspora in numerous countries of the world, interacting with different host cultures and different versions of modernity, now into second and third generations, with hybrid/ hyphenated identities, often further compounded by ancestral, linguistic and religious differences in Iran.[21] In the twentieth century, extreme versions of all three original elements of *iraniyat* have been tried and have failed: Iranian nationalism/Persian chauvinism; westernization/top-down modernization; Islamic fundamentalism. There is now a widely perceived imperative to negotiate an acceptable balance for the new millennium, together with a strong movement, massively supported by the youth and women in Iran, to reject the traditional politics of monopolization of power, control, secrecy and violence, in favour of democracy, transparency and political, religious and ethnic pluralism.

Cinema has become a major focus and arena for these discussions and debates, whose root concern is the nature of Iranian culture and identity. The distinctive forms and achievements of Iranian cinema, owing little or nothing to Hollywood or Western models (other than the medium itself, and the rewards of international acclaim) have shown that, culturally at least, the fear of 'Western invasion' can be dismissed as a chimera. Cultures have always borrowed from each other then appropriated what is borrowed and transformed it into their own style. Iranian cinema has much to teach the world about poetry, children, emotion and class. But what do audiences see – and what do they want to see?

Audiences and critics tend to have a series of (often contradictory) expectations of international cinema: an appealing aesthetic, fitting current trends in filmic style, with professional and expert filming and cutting; a focus on universal human themes such as family relationships, loss and search, survival; 'documentary' portrayal of a little-visited country; images which contradict standard media stereotypes of a given people and culture, for example of Iran, generally demonized as anti-Western, irrational, terrorist. Alternatively, they expect a lively, country-specific, social and political critique, confirming stereotypes created in

Hollywood productions such as *Not Without My Daughter* (Brian Gilbert, 1991) and *Midnight Express* (Alan Parker, 1978) or any number of films involving 'Ay-rabs' and Muslims.

In terms of style and content, Iranian films have drawn international attention by their neo-realism and reflexivity, their focus on children and difficulties with the portrayal of women. In the age of ever-escalating Hollywood blockbusters, part of their attraction (like much 'third-world' cinema), comes from shoestring budgets and use of amateur actors. Many successful films have had strikingly simple, local, small-scale themes, which have been variously read as totally apolitical or as highly ambiguous and open to interpretation as politically and socially critical.

Given such contradictory expectations and interpretations, evident in film reviews in both popular and intellectual presses, it is not surprising if Iranians abroad themselves show confused reactions and understandings of foreign audiences' responses to the images of their country displayed in the films, as described in many of the chapters below. The political opposition abroad ranges from wealthy middle-class exiles, such as monarchists who fled early on, to different groups of leftists who feel 'cheated' of the Revolution. The mixed – often heated – responses of Iranians abroad to the new Iranian cinema, and to other aspects of Iranian culture and politics, as viewed in the West, reflect not only their different politics, but also different assumptions about what foreign viewers look for, and see, in these films. They often claim that films shown abroad distort the 'reality' of Iranian society, and hide the strict censorship.[22] They expect that films about Iran, even if 'fictional', should be politically and socially critical: that they should give information about Iranian culture and society. They expect positive representations of Iranian society, that is propaganda for a particular construction of Iranian culture and social reality. They question the motivation of the censors in allowing films to be made and released. It may be argued that such reactions misread foreigners' readings of Iranian cinema, misunderstand the aims and objectives of the filmmakers, and betray a distorted view of Iranian culture and society. The filmmakers can't win: if they show prosperous middle-class life, they are criticized as too optimistic; if they depict poor, rural people, they are ignoring the great civilization of Iran; if they film idealized peasants, they are hiding the realities of oppression.

Meanwhile, the Iranian government, while avoiding the issue of censorship, claims that the films they allow to be made and exported are realistic. Unfortunately for governments, international audiences are uninterested in officially promoted culture. Naficy says, with much justification, that the Iranian government has not benefited politically from the renewed international success of Iranian cinema:

> Iranian exiles, international audiences and film-reviewing establishments abroad were sophisticated enough to understand the constricted political contexts in which the films were produced. Unlike some exiles who focused on the political issues and on governmental machinations and manipulations, these viewers and reviewers tended to highlight the initiative and skilfulness of the filmmakers.

Indeed, the wealth of interviews that have been published with well-known filmmakers such as Kiarostami, Mohsen and Samira Makhmalbaf, Majidi and others, throw considerable light on their motivations and the conditions in which they work. Kiarostami's films, for example, are widely interpreted both as social critique and as comment on universal human problems. There is a contradiction here, but a (re)solution may be found by listening to what Kiarostami says himself about his films. He has claimed that without 'restrictions' (his word for censorship) he would probably have made the same films; while he has been much quoted to the effect that the 'restrictions' have actually encouraged creativity in cinema; like Makhmalbaf, he particularly pointed to the banning of Hollywood films as a spur.[23]

We may conclude that not least of the achievements of the new Iranian cinema has been that it provides both a social critique and a forum for discussion between Iranians inside and outside the country. The international success of Iranian cinema has been for many in the diaspora a source of renewed pride in their culture and heritage, as well as a channel for reconciliation between Iranians of different persuasions inside Iran and in the diaspora.[24] Through viewing and debate, cinema has become an important medium for the renegotiation of Iranian cultural identity. The causes of these achievements have of course been much debated – as they are here – particularly by Iranian intellectuals, who are as sceptical as ever of uniformity or conformity of ideas and opinions.

Notes on Chapter 1

1.   I am grateful to Ziba Mir-Hosseini, Hamid Naficy and Lloyd Ridgeon for their comments on an earlier draft of this chapter.
2.   *Third World Film Making and the West* (Berkeley, University of California Press, 1987), p. 191.
3.   One of the all-time cinema classics, the documentary *Grass*, made by the US team Merian C. Cooper, Ernest B. Schoedsack and Marguerite Harrison in 1924, was shot in Iran. See Elizabeth Fagg Olds, *Women of the Four Winds* (Boston, Houghton Mifflin, 1985), pp. 155–230.
4.   For shorter accounts of early Iranian cinema, see notably the articles under 'Cinema' in *Encyclopædia Iranica 5* (1991), pp. 567–90; Farrokh Gaffary, 'Coup d'oeil sur les 35 premières années du cinéma en Iran', in Yann Richard (ed.), *Entre l'Iran et l'Occident* (Paris, Maisons des Sciences de l'Homme, 1989), pp. 225–34; Houshang Golmakani, 'Pre-revolution years of Iranian cinema' (http://www.CinemaIran.com/); Hamid Naficy, 'Iranian cinema', in Geoffrey Nowell-Smith (ed.), *Oxford Dictionary of World Cinema* (Oxford, Oxford University Press, 1996; reprinted in Rose Issa and Sheila Whitaker, *Life and Art*, British Film Institute, London, 1999, pp. 13–25); Shahin Parhami, 'Iranian cinema: before the revolution' (http://www.horschamp.qc.ca/new_offscreen/preiran.html) (1999). For longer accounts, see Shahrokh Golestan, *Fanus-e Khiyal* (series of 16 programmes, BBC Persian Service, 1994); Mohammad Ali Issari, *Cinema in Iran 1900–1979* (Metuchen/London, Scarecrow, 1989); Bahman Maghsoudlou, *Iranian Cinema* (New York, Kevorkian Centre for NE Studies, 1987); Massoud Mehrabi, 'The history of Iranian cinema', 5 parts, in *Film International*, 1995–6.
5.   On early censorship, see Jamsheed Akrami, 'Cinema. iv. Film censorship', *Encyclopædia Iranica 5* (1991), pp. 585–6; Houshang Golmakani, 'New times, same problems', *Index on Censorship* (3), 1992, pp. 20–21.
6.   Naficy, below, notes the different metaphors used in pre-revolutionary religious condemnations of cinema (p. 27).
7.   Armes notes: 'Among the 1970s films noted in the west were Dariush Mehrjui's *The Cow/Gav* (1970), *The Postman/Postchi* (1972) and *Mina Cycle/Dayera-e-Mina* (1974) and works by Parviz Kimiavi, Sohrab Shahid-Saless, and Bahram Beyzai…', *Third World Film Making*, p. 191.
8.   See Hamid Naficy, 'Iranian writers, the Iranian cinema, and the case of *Dash Akol*', *Iranian Studies* 28/2–4, 1985, pp. 231–51.
9.   Armes, *Third World Film Making*, p. 192.
10.   There is an extensive literature on the Revolution: see particularly Shaul Bakhash, *The Reign of the Ayatollahs* (London, I.B. Tauris, 1985); Said Amir Arjomand, *The Turban for the Crown* (Oxford, Oxford University Press, 1988).
11.   Armes, *Third World Film Making*, p. 189.

12. Houshang Golmakani, 'A history of the post-revolutionary Iranian cinema', in *Chicago Film Center's 10th Annual Festival of Films from Iran* (1999) (http://www.webmemo.com/iran/articleview_2.cfm). *The Runner* appears to have been shot in 1982, although it was not distributed until 1986.

13. See, for example, Gaffary, 'Cinema. i. History of cinema in Persia'; Parhami, 'Iranian Cinema: before the Revolution'.

14. See Babak Dad, *Sad Ruz ba Khatami*, (Tehran, MCIG, 1377/1998), pp. 54–5. Khatami's supporters deliberately delayed resorting to these interviews in order to increase their impact in the last days of the campaign. Khatami had sided with Makhmalbaf in the controversy at Fajr 1991 over the latter's film, *A Time to Love*.

15. See Mojdeh Famili, 'The Iranian cinema in France', *Iran Nameh* 14/3, 1996.

16. For an analysis of Mohsen Makhmalbaf's political cinema, see Lloyd Ridgeon, *Makhmalbaf's Broken Mirror: the Socio-Political Significance of Modern Iranian Cinema* (Durham Middle East Paper no 64, 2000).

17. *Cinéma vérité* has a long pedigree in documentary and fiction, beginning in 1960 with Drew and Leacock's *Primary* and Rouch and Morin's *Chronicle of a Summer* – see analyses in William Rothman, *Documentary Film Classics* (Cambridge, Cambridge University Press, 1997). Many different strands have developed, but in the 'pure' form such films are structured in the camera or in the cutting room using dramatic events that 'happen', not by reconstruction or by scripting. The camera does not 'lie', though the editor can 'persuade' through selecting the 'truths' to be shown. And by filming, the camera can also create 'truth' in the form of action.

18. See also M. Habibian, 'Under wraps on the stage: women in the performing arts in post-revolutionary Iran', paper given at the Fourth Nordic Conference on Middle Eastern Studies, The Middle East in Globalizing World, Oslo 13–16 August 1998 (http://www.hf-fak.uib.no/Institutter/smi/pao/habibian.html) (http://www.hf.uib.no/smi/pao/habibian.html).

19. Even in pre-revolutionary films, love between children was portrayed as distant and impossible. See also Jamsheed Akrami, 'The childhood of the dispossessed: images of children in Iranian films', in *Chicago Film Center's 9th Annual Festival of Films from Iran* (1998), pp. 9–12 (http://www.webmemo.com/iran/articleview_1.cfm); Hamid Dabashi, 'Neither a simple story, nor a secret message: children in Iranian cinema', in *ibid.*, pp. 13–17.

20. See also Nasrin Rahimieh, 'Framing Iran: a contrapuntal analysis of two cinematic representations of postrevolutionary Iran', *Edebiyat* 9, 1998, pp. 249–75.

21. See especially Hamid Naficy, *The Making of Exile Cultures: Iranian Television in Los Angeles* (Minneapolis, University of Minnesota Press, 1993); Ron Kelley *et al.* (eds), *Irangeles: Iranians in Los Angeles* (Berkeley, University of California Press, 1993).

22. Some prominent filmmakers have also criticized foreign audiences' disregard of the censorship issue: see Beyza'i's and Sayyad's articles in *Irannameh*, 14(3), 1996.

23. Interviews with Kiarostami include: David Walsh, '"Human beings and their problems are the most important raw material for any film"', *World Socialist Web Site*, October 1994 (www.wsws.org/arts/1994/oct1994/kiar.shtml); Walsh, 'The compassionate gaze: Iranian filmmaker Abbas Kiarostami at the San Francisco Film Festival', *World Socialist Web Site*: Arts Review: Film Festivals: 2000 San Francisco International Film Festival—Part 8, 12 June (www.wsws.org); Patrick Z. McGavin, 'Kiarostami will carry us; the Iranian master gives hope', *indieWIRE* 1 August 2000 (http://www.indiewire.com/film/interviews/int_Kiarostam_Abbas_000801.html); Ali Akbar Mahdi, 'In dialogue with Kiarostami', *The Iranian*, August 25 1998 (www.iranian.com/Arts/Aug98/Kiarostami/index.html). In spring 2000, however, Kiarostami did come out against the silencing of the reformist press.

24. See Hamid Naficy, 'Mediating the other: American pop culture representation of postrevolutionary Iran', in Yahya Kamalipour (ed.), *The US Media and the Middle East: Image and Perception* (Westport, Greenwood, 1995), pp. 73–90.

2

Islamizing Film Culture in Iran: A Post-Khatami Update[1]

Hamid Naficy

On 10 August 1978, a hot summer's day during the last year of the reign of Mohammad Reza Shah Pahlavi, Hoseyn Takab-'Alizadeh and his two friends, Farajollah and Hayat, walked into the Rex Theatre in Abadan, the site of one of the largest oil refineries in the world. They were each carrying a brown paper bag containing a bottle of high-octane aircraft fuel and matches. They joined the audience, which was engrossed in Massoud Kimia'i's *The Deer* (1975), a film about an anti-government smuggler. Half way through, Hoseyn and Farajollah left the hall, doused the three closed exit doors with fuel, set the doors on fire and fled from the scene. The fire quickly spread, engulfing the entire building. Unable to escape or quell the flames, Hayat burned to death in the inferno, along with over 300 others trapped inside.[2]

Anti-Shah revolutionary fervour found its rallying point, and the city of Abadan, which up to that time had remained relatively calm, was galvanized into action and joined the protest movement. Although government sources attempted to place the blame for the incident on religious factions, overwhelming public consensus held the by now discredited government responsible. Testimonies and documents compiled after the fall of the Shah, however, established a clear link between the arsonists and anti-Shah clerical leaders.[3]

From then on, the destruction of cinemas became a key symbolic act against the government of the Shah, during whose time cinema was considered – especially by clerics and religious folk – to be filled with Western mores of sex and violence, and part of the imperialist strategy to 'spray poison' and corrupt people's thoughts and ethics.[4] Although some among the opposition accused the Shah's government of setting cinemas on fire, the leaflets and samizdats they themselves issued clearly show that they either urged the destruction of cinemas and banks as symbols of the Pahlavi cultural and economic system, or reported such actions in glowing terms.[5]

Anti-cinema feelings run deep in Iran. Since the introduction of films into Iran in 1900, religious attitudes, intensified by activist clerical leaders, have consistently condemned cinema as a morally offensive and ethically corrupting Western influence. This influence was thought to be direct and unidirectional. In fact, the clerical elite seem to have subscribed to a 'hypodermic theory' of ideology whereby, similar to Althusser's formulation, the mere injection of ideology transforms an autonomous and ethical 'individual' into a dependent, corrupt 'subject'.[6] Cinema as a Western import is condemned consistently in religious literature on account of its hegemonic and interpellative power, which is seen to be irreversible and total. For instance, there is a report that in 1904 a major clerical figure, Sheykh Fazlollah Nuri, attended Iran's first public cinema in Tehran and proscribed it, causing it to shut down after only one month of operation.[7] We do not know for certain his reasons for this, but this action fits his general paradigm of westernization as either a drug ('sleeping potion')[8] that puts believers in a stupor or a 'fatal, killer disease'[9] that annihilates its victims.

Mojtaba Navab-Safavi, one of the leaders of Fedayan-e Eslam, a fundamentalist group operating in Iran in the 1940s, selects a different but equally powerful and graphic metaphor to describe cinema and its supposedly direct effect on society. Along with other Western imports (romantic novels and music), he calls cinema a 'smelting furnace', which melts away all the wholesome values and virtues of a Muslim society.[10]

In two of his important pre-revolutionary works, Ayatollah Khomeini too links cinema directly with the onset of corruption, licentiousness, prostitution, moral cowardice and cultural dependence. While Nuri employs a medical metaphor, Navab-Safavi's is industrial, and that of Khomeini in *Kashf ol-Asrar* is sexual. According to Khomeini, cinema and other manifestations of westernization (theatre, dancing and mixed-sex swimming) 'rape the youth of our country and stifle in them the spirit of virtue and bravery'.[11] In *Velayat-e Faqih*, written years later, Khomeini reiterates this theme of cinema and entertainment as the direct cause of prostitution, corruption and political dependence. Indeed, he is a proponent of the hypodermic theory of ideology, using the term *tazriq* (injection) to describe the ill effects of westernization. For example, he posits that Reza Shah's policy of removing women's veils and making men wear hats and Western clothing 'injects' immorality, vice and dishonesty,[12] while religious education 'injects self-sacrifice and service to the country and to the people'.[13]

It is significant to note that, despite the hypodermic and unmediated formulation of the effect of motion pictures, these leaders seem to have considered cinema's ideological 'work' only in the context of overdetermination of westernization in Iran. Cinema is seen as part of the ideological apparatus imported from the West by a despotic regime, which in tandem with other media and leisure activities such as theatre, radio, popular music, dancing, mixed swimming pools and gambling, is said to produce its ideological work of interpellation. This formulation is significant in that it considers, however crudely and unself-reflectively, the intertextuality and cross-fertilization of the signifying institutions of the society, such as mass media. The drawbacks to this formulation, however, are that, unlike Michel Foucault's polysemic cultural analysis,[14] that of Khomeini elides the possibility of resistance, ignores the local conditions and the contradictions existing among the media, and effaces the specificity of their unique ideological work, all of which can undermine and *mediate* the effects of the 'injection' of westernization. Without taking into consideration these contradictory structurations, we can discuss neither what Horkheimer and Adorno have pessimistically called the 'ruthless unity' of the culture,[15] nor what Khomeini and others have called the 'society of idolatry' or the 'culture of idolatry'.[16]

It is also significant to note that both Navab-Safavi and Khomeini are willing to entertain the idea of adopting cinema only if it is done 'properly' and 'ethically'. They talk about this in rare passages. Here is what Navab-Safavi says:

> Cinemas, theatres, novels and popular songs must be completely removed and their middleman punished according to the holy Islamic law. And if the use of motion picture industry is deemed necessary for society, [then] the history of Islam and Iran and useful material such as medical, agricultural, and industrial lessons should be produced under the supervision of chaste professors and Islamic scholars observing the principles and criteria of the holy religion of Islam and then shown [to the public] for education, reform, and socially wholesome entertainment.[17]

Khomeini spelled out a similar theme, years later, on his triumphant return to Iran after the fall of the Shah. In Behesht-e Zahra cemetery, he announced:

> We are not opposed to cinema, to radio or to television…The cinema is a modern invention that ought to be used for the sake of educating the people, but as you know, it was used instead to corrupt our youth. It is the misuse of cinema that we are opposed to, a misuse caused by the treacherous policies of our rulers.[18]

These clerical leaders are not proposing the removal and proscription of cinema; instead, they are advocating its adoption as an ideological tool to combat Pahlavi culture and usher in an Islamic culture.

The major concepts frequently pronounced by authorities when speaking of 'Islamic culture' can be classified under the following categories: nativism (return to traditional values and mores), populism (justice, defence of *mostaz'afan*, the disinherited), monotheism (*towhid*), anti-idolatry (anti-*taqut*), theocracy (*velayat-e faqih*, rule of the supreme jurisprudent), ethicalism and puritanism *(amr-e be-ma'ruf va nahy az monkar)*; political and economic independence (*esteqlal*), and the combating of arrogant world imperialism (*estekbar-e jahani*), a concept often condensed in the slogan 'neither East nor West'.

In order to appreciate the process of its development, a more or less chronological history of cinema since the Revolution of 1978–9 will now be presented, making reference to these cultural categories when warranted.

Over the two decades after the establishment of the Islamic Republic, a new cinema has emerged which is markedly different from the one that existed previously. Periods of transition and social turmoil seem to produce some of the most innovative cinéastes and cinematic movements.[19] Thus, there is good cause to expect the Iranian Revolution and its preconditions to have helped create a new cinema. This expectation is marred, however, by the perception, almost universal in the West, that Shi'i Islam as practised in Iran today is anti-modern and backward. The Islamic Republic's widely reported curtailment of Western-style performing arts and entertainment and its maltreatment of entertainers have certainly reinforced such impressions.

Nevertheless, it is the thesis of this chapter that the Revolution led to the emergence of a new, vital cinema, with its own special industrial and financial structure and unique ideological, thematic and production values. This is, of course, part of a more general transformation in the political culture of Iran. However, Iranian post-revolutionary cinema is not Islamic in the sense that it is not by any means a monolithic, propagandistic cinema in support of a ruling ideology. In fact, at least two cinemas have developed side by side. The 'populist cinema' affirms post-revolutionary Islamic values more fully at the level of plot, theme, characterization, portrayal of women and mise-en-scène. The 'art cinema', on the other hand, engages with those values and tends to critique social conditions under the Islamic government. There are many variations and cracks in the hegemony of the post-revolutionary cinema, which in this overview cannot be fully considered, so passing references must suffice.

From '*Taqut* Cinema' to 'Islamic Cinema' (1978–82): The Purification Process

The Film Theatre

The first stage in transforming Pahlavi cinema – dubbed 'cinema of *taqut* (idols)' by Islamists – into an Islamic cinema was the cleansing of the Pahlavi film theatres by means of what in retrospect turned out to be a literal baptism by fire. By the time the Islamic government was established, less than a year after the Rex Theatre fire, up to 180 cinemas nationwide (32 in Tehran alone) had been burned, demolished or shut down, leaving only a total of 256 cinemas extant.[20] Fortunately, with the exception of the Rex, no casualties were reported, since most of the theatres had been empty at the time of attack.[21]

The theatres that remained had their names changed, usually from Western names popular during the Pahlavi period to Islamic, third world ones. For example, in Tehran, Atlantic was changed to Efriqa (Africa), Empire to Esteqlal (Independence), Royal to Enqelab (Revolution), Panorama to Azadi (Freedom), Taj (Crown) to Shahr-e Honar (City of Art), Golden City to Felestin (Palestine), Polidor to Qods (Jerusalem) and Ciné Monde to Qiyam (Uprising).[22]

The Imports

Immediately after the Revolution, the volatile and uncertain economic and political conditions discouraged investment in the production of new films, but encouraged the exhibition of old films and the importation of new ones. Thus, foreign-made films flooded the market. Comedies and 'spaghetti' westerns came from Italy, and karate films from Japan. American imports covered a broad range, from comedy to political and from classical to current, such films as *It's a Mad, Mad, Mad, Mad World, Modern Times, Three Days of the Condor, The Cassandra Crossing, The Great Escape, Cinderella, The Jungle Book*, and *Papillon*.

Russian and Eastern-bloc films – inexpensive to import – also flourished to the point of overtaking American, Italian and Japanese films. For example, 74 – more than a third – of the 213 foreign films licensed by the Ministry of Culture and Islamic Guidance (MCIG) in 1981 came from the Soviet bloc. Sixty-nine of these were produced in the Soviet Union alone. Italy ranked second with 38 films and, surprisingly, the US was in third place with 27 films.[23] Of the new imports, those that catered to the revolutionary spirit of the time clearly dominated. The best known of these, banned during the Shah's era, were such films as Costa-Gavras's *Z* and *State of Siege*, Guzman's *Battle of Chile*, Akad's *Mohammad, Messenger of God*, and Pontecorvo's *Battle of Algiers*. The latter was so popular that it was shown simultaneously in 12 cinemas in Tehran and 10 in the provinces.[24]

The clerical establishment was concerned but divided on the issue of film imports. Some praised these so-called 'revolutionary films' because, they felt, such films show 'the struggle of people oppressed by colonialism and imperialism'.[25] Others condemned them as made-in-Hollywood films with only a 'revolutionary mask'.[26] Likewise, Hojjat-ol-Eslam Ahmad Sadeqi Ardestani, a leading cleric in charge of supervising the film industry in 1981, invoked the Islamic values mentioned earlier when writing that Iran had 'continued its cultural dependence on imperialists' by importing American (Western) and Russian (Eastern) films into the country, where 'millions of people are mentally and culturally nourished by cinema'. Updating the language of Navab-Safavi and Khomeini, he predicted that continued 'acceptance of Western and Eastern films will lead us to cultural colonization and economic exploitation'.[27]

Secular intellectuals, too, worried about the influx of so-called revolutionary foreign films, but for different reasons. For example, Gholam-Hoseyn Sa'edi, a leading dissident writer and editor of the literary monthly *Alefba*, would later – from exile – define the 'revolutionary' films shown in Iran as 'full of cannons, tanks, rifles, weapons and corpses, without regard to quality or artistic merit'.[28]

As early as July 1979, efforts were begun to purify the imports, by restricting their inflow. First, the importation of B-grade Turkish, Indian and Japanese films was curtailed, followed closely by a ban on all 'imperialist' and 'anti-revolutionary' films.[29] American films were the next group to be excluded, as the political relationship between the two countries deteriorated. A larger percentage of Western films were denied exhibition permit than films from any other region, corroborating the link made between films produced in the West and the moral corruption of the indigenous population. In the first three years of post-revolutionary government, a total of 898 foreign films were reviewed, 513 of which were rejected, the bulk of them Western imports.[30] The curb, however, was not hermetic, in that American films imported prior to the cut-off, such as *Airport 79* and *High Noon*, continued to appear on the screens even during the 'hostage crisis'.

Locally Produced Films

To purify the existing stock of films, many pre-Revolution films were re-edited to conform to Islamic standards. Some films were cut, re-cut and re-titled. In this process, film producers engaged with the government in a cat-and-mouse game of resistance/submission. The most interesting result of these cinematic negotiations was the exhibition of films little changed apart from their titles. When the producers of these films were caught, they merely re-titled them. For example, the title of Amir Shervan's film *Freeze, Don't Move* (*Bi Harekat, Tekun Nakhor*), was changed in 1978 to *The Thug and the Student* (*Jahel va Mohassel*); after the Revolution it was changed again to *Heroin*. This apparently did not help the sale of the film. In general, changed elements in basically unchanged films created such contradictions that these films failed badly at the box office.[31]

Sensing the inevitability of the Islamization of cinema, film exhibitors attempted to contain the damage by voluntarily keeping sex off the screens, claiming that 'our contribution to the Islamic Revolution would be made best by replacing dirty films with entertainment of an educational caliber.'[32] One way to accomplish this was the 'magic marker' method of censorship, which involved painting over naked legs and other exposed body parts. When this failed, more drastic methods were used. As the manager of the Rex Theatre in Tehran stated, 'We have to show films in keeping with Islamic standards. When the Magic Marker doesn't work, we cut.'[33]

Dissatisfied with the limited changes made by producers and exhibitors, the government threatened to close down the cinemas and made exhibition permits compulsory for all films.[34] The procedures for acquiring permits meant a review of all films made, with the result that many indigenous films produced before the establishment of the Islamic Republic were banned outright. Table 2.1 shows the outcome of the official review of Iranian features produced both before and immediately after the Revolution. Since post-Revolution films were few in number, these figures can be construed as a decisive condemnation of Pahlavi-era films, and an effective end to the post-revolutionary *laissez-faire* atmosphere.

Table 2.1: Iranian Films Granted or Denied Exhibition Permits, 1979–82[35]

Year	Films Reviewed	Permit Granted	Permit Denied
1979	2000	200	1800
1980	99	27	72
1981	83	18	65
1982	26	/	19
Total	2208	252	1956

As well as cheaply produced exploitation films, many films produced by progressive New Wave directors were banned, among them *The Divine One* (Khosrow Haritash, 1976), *The Chess of the Wind* (Mohammad Reza, Aslani, 1976), *OK Mister* (Parviz Kimiavi, 1979) *Tara's Ballad* (Bahram Beyza'i, 1978), *The Yard Behind Adl-e Afaq School* (Daryush Mehrju'i, 1980), *Mr Hieroglyphic* (Gholam Ali Erfan, 1980) and *Yazdgerd's Death* (Beyza'i, 1980).[36]

While most filmmakers applauded the curbing of sleazy imports, they did not condone their banning, as Beyza'i, a noted New Wave filmmaker (whose films *Tara's Ballad* and *Yazdgerd's Death* had been banned) observed, 'It is enhanced public awareness which should be driving these trite films off the screens, not government force.' What is more, he said, the vacuum created by the absence of imports must be filled with local productions, but the regulations, mechanisms and structures conducive to the flourishing of local films are non-existent.[37]

Entertainers, Filmmakers

Many entertainers and filmmakers were regarded as too closely associated either with the westernized excesses of the Shah or with SAVAK, his national security agency. As a result, they were not immune to purification measures, which included the bringing of legal charges, incarceration, the banning of activities, the censoring of products, and, on rare occasions, execution.[38] Mehdi Misaqiyeh, a famous producer, was jailed for five years and his properties and theatres confiscated.[39] He was released apparently some time after he publicly renounced his Baha'i faith.[40] In March 1983, when New Wave filmmaker Bahman Farmanara returned to Iran after an absence of four years, he was prevented from leaving the country again. His powerfully allegorical film, *Tall Shadows of the Wind* (1978), had been banned by the Forbidden Acts Bureau, and he was accused of making anti-Islamic films. Farmanara commented, 'Ironically both the Shah's and the Islamic regime interpreted the scarecrow, which in the film terrorizes a village, as symbolizing their own rule and tried to ban it.'[41] Some theatre owners were arrested and charged with crimes such as smuggling narcotics, peddling pornographic material and prostitution.[42]

The aforementioned purification measures and persecutions, however, are only one set of reasons for the slow revival of cinema during the transitional period. Islamization was by no means a given, as many other factors contributed to the creation of a fluid and contentious atmosphere within the film industry. These included the financial damage that the industry suffered during the Revolution, a lack of government interest in cinema during the transitional period (for example, the first five-year budget plan in 1983 ignored cinema altogether),[43] the absence of centralized authority and thus antagonistic competition over cinema between various factions (for example, MCIG, the Foundation of the Disinherited, and the Revolutionary Committees),[44] a lack of an appropriate cinematic model (there was no 'Islamic' film genre),[45] heavy competition from imports, a drastic deterioration in the public image of the industry as a whole, the haphazard application of censorship, and the flight of many film professionals into exile.

In January 1980, in a letter addressed to the Minister of Culture and Higher Education, the Society of Cinema Owners justifiably chided the government for its neglect of cinema. It declared that, if the government 'approved the necessity of the existence of cinema', then, with government assistance, the private sector could align the film industry with 'the revolution and the people' within five years. The letter concluded by reminding the Minister that unplanned, 'spontaneous reform' in cinema is not possible.[46]

Filmmakers, too, shared the concerns of theatre owners, and in 1981 in an open letter to the 'people and government' they took the government to task. They charged that two years after the 'holy and anti-dependence revolution of Iranian people' the Revolution had failed to take root in the film industry and 'fostered a kind of dependency', akin to that existing before the Revolution. The writers urged the government to apply the new Constitution 'organically and comprehensively'; Iranian cinema would otherwise become a caricature of Eastern-bloc solutions to cinema, and the 'solution to the problem will result in the elimination of the problem'.[47]

Negotiating an Islamic Cinema (1982–9)

In this period, the Islamic hardliners gradually took charge of all major institutions, and, with the continuation of the Iran–Iraq war, the resolution of the American 'hostage crisis' and the defeat of major organized opposition, they consolidated their grip on the country. Political consolidation entailed direct control of the mass media and the film industry. However, the transformation of cinema from the Pahlavi to the Islamic involved a major cultural and ideological shift, which could not take place unidirectionally, monolithically or rapidly. Mohammad Beheshti, director of the Farabi Cinema Foundation (FCF) observed that 'transformation in the context of cinema occurs with a "dissolve" not a "cut".'[48]

The new structure of the entertainment and broadcasting industries under the Islamic Republic partly resembles that which existed during the Shah's time, but there are major differences, which have helped to shape an Islamized cinema.

Emergence of Committed Islamic Filmmakers

One factor in the Islamization of cinema seems to have been cronyism based on shared Islamic ideology and values. A case in point is that of a production company named Ayat Film, which was formed prior to the Revolution, apparently in response to a call by Ali Shari'ati urging the youth to turn to the arts to express their Islamic beliefs and their anti-Pahlavi politics. In 1979, immediately after the Revolution, Ayat Film produced two films: *Athar's War* (Mohammad Ali Najafi), a work of fiction, and *The Night of Power* (Ali Najafi), a documentary about the Revolution.

The impact of Ayat Film, however, far exceeded its limited production output because of the way in which its committed (*mota'ahhed*) and religious (*motadayyen*) members fanned out soon after the Revolution to take key positions in government, the motion picture industry and allied institutions. Mir Hoseyn Musavi became Prime Minister; Fakhreddin Anvar took up a number of high posts within both the MCIG and the

Voice and Vision of the Islamic Republic TV networks; Mohammad Ali Najafi obtained high policy positions within the MCIG and continued to direct films; Mostafa Hashemi was appointed to a high position in Khomeini's propaganda office; Mohammad Beheshti became the director of the powerful FCF. Immediately after the Revolution, these and other members and affiliated members of Ayat Film were among those few whom the government could trust on account of both their artistic abilities and their 'correct' Islamic values. As a result, they became ensconced in positions that allowed them, from early on, to influence the direction of the Islamization of cinema. Their impact was augmented by their longevity in office, since by and large they retained their influential positions throughout the first decade of the Islamic regime.

Regulations Governing Exhibition of Films and Videos

The MCIG has overall responsibility for supervising the motion picture industry. The concentration at the Ministry of the power to set, regulate and enforce policy has helped both to reduce the confusion of the previous period and to enhance government control, thereby setting the stage for the emergence of Islamic unity out of revolutionary destruction and post-revolutionary uncertainty.

In June 1982, the cabinet approved a set of landmark regulations governing the exhibition of films and videos, charging the MCIG with their enforcement.[49] These regulations, codifying many of the Islamic values noted earlier, were instrumental in facilitating the shift from Pahlavi to Islamic cinema. They stipulate that all films and videos shown publicly must have an exhibition permit. Further, they ban all films and videos which:

weaken the principle of monotheism and other Islamic principles or insult them in any manner;

insult, directly or indirectly, the Prophets, Imams, the guardianship of the Supreme Jurisprudent (*velayat faqih*), the ruling Council or the jurisprudents (*mojtaheds*);

blaspheme against the values and personalities held sacred by Islam and other religions mentioned in the Constitution;

encourage wickedness, corruption and prostitution;

encourage or teach dangerous addictions and earning a living from unsavoury means such as smuggling;

negate the equality of all people regardless of colour, race, language, ethnicity and belief;

encourage foreign cultural, economic and political influence contrary
to the 'neither West nor East' policy of the government;

express or disclose anything that is against the interests and policies of
the country which might be exploited by foreigners;

show details of scenes of violence and torture in such a way as to
disturb or mislead the viewer;

misrepresent historical and geographical facts;

lower the taste of the audience by means of low production and
artistic values;

negate the values of self-sufficiency and economic and social
independence.

The first three regulations are the most telling; these establish the
Islamic character of present-day Iranian cinema. According to these, films
that question, alter or negate any of the following are forbidden:

monotheism and submission to God and to his laws;

the role of Revelation in expressing laws;

resurrection and its role in the evolution of man towards God;

the justness of God in creation and in law;

the continuity of religious leadership (*Emamat*);

the role of the Islamic Republic of Iran under the leadership of
Ayatollah Khomeini in ridding Muslims and the downtrodden
from world imperialism.

Clearly these regulations codify the Islamic values hinted at at the
beginning of this chapter, which during the transition period remained
largely undefined and subject to local and expedient interpretations. Of
course, the above regulations themselves contain many ambiguities, which
the cabinet dictated must be resolved by appropriate committees.

Cinemas and Audience Demography

Despite being incomplete and inconsistent, statistics show that the
number of theatres and filmgoers increased in the first decade after the
Revolution.[50] However, numbers did not reach the peaks of the Shah's era
– even though the curtailment of previously allowed activities made
cinema one of the few permissible forms of mass entertainment. In 1983,
in an audience survey of 1800 Tehran high school students, 78 per cent of
the boys and 59 per cent of the girls said that they went to the cinema.[51]
This figure is not high, considering that this age group comprised a major
share of audiences. Apparent audience disinterest may be explained by

a post-Revolution decrease in the number of theatres nationwide, the undesirability of theatre locations, the bad conditions of halls and projection systems, the low quality of many of the films exhibited and the demographics of spectators, who were predominantly young, unmarried and unemployed men who sometimes heckled women. These factors were compounded by the highly aggressive and male-oriented genres and themes of many of the films.[52]

Film Imports

The regulations governing film production and exhibition, together with the centralization of the industry, gave the authorities a firmer grip on imports. After some deliberation, the government took control of all film imports. The non-profit FCF was created in 1983, attached to the MCIG and given, among other responsibilities, a complete monopoly over the selection and importation of ideologically suitable films.[53] Table 2.2 shows the numbers and origins of films imported in 1983–4.

Table 2.2: Films Imported in 1983–4[54]

Exporting Country	1983	1984
USSR	28	29
US	12	24
Italy	16	20
UK	9	15
France	6	5
Yugoslavia	6	1
Japan	4	5
North Korea	2	2
People's Republic of China	1	3
Australia	1	2
Total	85	106

In the mid-1980s, the Soviet-bloc countries dominated the import scene, but films from the US and its Western allies increased their share considerably. The anti-Western, especially anti-American, rhetoric of official mass media might have led an observer to conclude that a limitation on US and Western imports was – or should be – in effect. This was not so, demonstrating both the tensions in cultural policy within the Islamic

Republic and the pragmatism of the policy-makers. Exhibition permits were issued to any film, regardless of source, as long as it lived up to the aforementioned Islamic values. For example, in 1983 the following American films were publicly screened: *Star Wars, Close Encounters of the Third Kind, The Ten Commandments* and *A Bridge Too Far*, and in 1984 *War Hunt, Law and Disorder, Black Sunday* and *The Chase* were shown.

Indigenous Productions

All film ideas had to go through a five-stage process at the MCIG before being made and shown to the public. It was during this process that the regulations codifying 'Islamic values' were implemented. The MCIG reviewed a film's synopsis, evaluated and approved the screenplay, issued a production permit (approving the cast and crew by name), reviewed the completed film and, finally, issued an exhibition permit that specified the cinemas in which it would be shown. Until mid-1989, all film ideas were subject to this process, during which they underwent many changes before final release.[55] Statistics bear out the effectiveness of the review process – and perhaps the low quality of the scripts submitted: of the 202 screen-plays reviewed between 1980 and 1982, only 25 per cent were approved.[56]

Despite the rigour of the review process, a large number of films that were made were not released.[57] In April 1989, however, the government loosened its grip and began allowing previously censored films to be screened.[58] Barely a month later, for the first time in Iranian cinema the requirement for screenplays to be approved was removed. There were two chief reasons for this liberalization policy: the authorities were confident that Islamic values had been sufficiently inculcated (that is, interpellation or 'injection' had had the desired effect), so that less supervision was now required; secondly, the government, being more self-assured, wished to open up cultural discourse and to reduce criticism of its iron-clad control, thereby boosting morale and film quality. Whatever the reason, it seemed likely that the black market in screenplays would disappear and that film subjects would diversify.[59] At the same time, the removal of the script approval stage may have had a negative effect: concerned for their heavy investments, producers may have become more cautious and prone to self-censorship.

These measures were not isolated. From 1984, the government introduced new regulations demanded by filmmakers to encourage local production. In the first six months of 1984, for example, the municipal tax was reduced from 20 per cent to 5 per cent on Iranian films, and was increased from 20 per cent to 25 per cent on imports. Ticket prices were increased by 25 per cent. The FCF was exempted from paying any customs duty on its imports. Furthermore, representatives of producers and exhibitors were allowed to participate in the process of assigning films to film theatres.[60]

To generate funds for health, social security and injury insurance of entertainers and filmmakers, the Majles passed a resolution in late 1985, which imposed a 2 per cent tax on the box-office receipts of all theatres in the country.[61] To bolster local production further, the 1987 national budget passed by the Majles included a provision for banks to offer long-term loans for film production.[62] A year later, in June 1988, the MCIG instituted a system of rating films, according to which producers of highly rated films would earn increased revenues by exhibiting their films in higher-class theatres. In addition, they would be entitled to extensive publicity and advertising on TV.[63] In May 1989, the MCIG announced further measures to encourage local filmmaking: foreign exchange funds were allocated for importing technical equipment and supplies, of which there was a chronic scarcity; interest-free credits and long-term loans were made available; local films were sponsored in international film festivals; and the inauguration of a social-security system for film workers was approved by parliament.[64]

Political consolidation, the centralization of imports and the passing of regulations concerning production and exhibition enhanced co-ordination and cohesiveness within the industry, brought cinema into line with Islamic values and criteria and improved overall film quality. Yet the government had not entirely monopolized the industry. Indeed, there seemed to be more production centres in Islamic Iran than in Pahlavi Iran, and they were not all concentrated in Tehran. These production centres were dispersed among three sectors: public, semi-public and private. Table 2.3 lists production centres in the late 1980s under each sector, a number of which had branches in the provinces.

In 1987 the public sector produced one-third of all films but, given the government's financial contribution through loans and credits, its actual impact on film production exceeded the statistics.[65] At any rate, multiplicity of production centres and sectors bolstered competition among both production companies and sectors, leading to increased diversity and enhanced quality.

The figures for films produced during this period (Table 2.4) show an initial downward spiral followed by a definite pattern of increase, coinciding with the aforementioned reforms.

Table 2.3: Motion Picture Production Sectors[66]

Public (governmental) sector
 Office of Film, Photo and Slide Production (MCIG)
 Farabi Cinema Foundation (MCIG)
 Centre for Developing Experimental and Semi-amateur Films (MCIG)
 Islamic Centre for Film Instruction (MCIG)
 Young Cinema Society (MCIG)
 Foundation of the Disinherited
 Centre for Intellectual Development of Children and Adolescents
 Voice and Vision of the Islamic Republic (TV networks)
 Ministry of Reconstruction Jehad
 University Jehad
 War Propaganda Command
 Revolutionary Guard's Cultural Unit
 Revolutionary Committees' Film Section
 Traffic Organization
 Iran Air
Semi-public (semi-governmental) sector
 Islamic Propaganda Organization
 Islamic Culture and Art Group
Private (commercial) sector
 film co-operatives
 independent producers
 commercial production companies
 film studios

Table 2.4: Feature Fiction Films Produced, 1979–88[67]

Year	Films Produced
1979–80	14
1980–1	16
1981–2	12
1982–3	11
1983–4	22
1984–5	56
1985–6	57
1986–7	49
1987–8	46

In addition to FCF and MCIG, other post-Revolution institutions, such as the Foundation of the Disinherited and the Ministry of Reconstruction Jehad, helped Islamize the motion-picture industry during the first decade of the Islamic Republic. Considered one of the largest economic conglomerates, controlling 15 per cent of all the industry in the country and owning an estimated US$10 billion worth of land,[68] the Foundation of the Disinherited was by mid-1983 operating some 137 cinemas in 16 provinces, approximately half of all cinemas in the country.[69]

Because of the large number of cinemas it was operating, the Foundation had a profound effect on the production and exhibition of films. But it was not economically successful, since attendance in its theatres dropped by 300,000 in just one year, 1981 to 1982,[70] and the number of theatres it owned declined to 80 by mid-1987.[71] The manager of the Foundation's cultural department attributed this to a shortage of foreign imports with appropriate Islamic values. To offset the situation, the Foundation began to assist 'Islamically committed' local filmmakers to make trend-setting 'model' films inspired by the Revolution and by Islamic values. One such film, *The Dossier* (Mehdi Sabbaghzadeh, 1983), deals with the revenge of a worker unjustly accused of the death of a feudal landlord and jailed for 15 years. *The Monster Within* (Khosrow Sina'i, 1984) focuses on an ex-SAVAK torturer's struggle with his own sense of guilt immediately after the Revolution, and *The Bus* (Yadollah Samadi, 1985) portrays a typical Heydari–Ne'mati family feud in a village. To adjust to the financial realities of production and exhibition and to increase the reach of its films, the Foundation announced in May 1988 that it would sell 40 more of its theatres in order to obtain sufficient funds to build new theatres in poorer areas of cities, and that it would subtitle and export Islamic films for exhibition to Iranian expatriates.

The Jehad for Reconstruction, which later became the Ministry of Reconstruction Jehad, also contributed to the emergence of an Islamized cinema. The Jehad was established on 17 June 1979 by an edict from Ayatollah Khomeini, its aim being to 'repair the ruins' caused by the Shah's government and to help reconstruction and self-sufficiency of rural Iran.[72] The Ministry is in charge of rural development and the propagation of Islamic ideology, a mission it accomplishes by distributing appropriate films, slides, videotapes, posters and audio cassettes through its vast nationwide network. In 1983, for instance, it held 31,024 theatre, film and video shows, distributed 74,789 audio cassettes and 2,912,062 posters and photographs nationwide.[73] The Ministry's reach is actually wider than these statistics indicate, since many of its films are shown on national TV, in mosques and in theatres operated by the Foundation of the Disinherited. Such use of audiovisual media is not new in Iran, and is clearly influenced by the model of the mobile film unit programme started by the US Information Agency (Point 4 programme) in Iran in the 1950s.[74] The basic difference is not operational but ideological: while the Point 4 film programme emphasized Western-style modernization, technology transfer and monarchy, the Ministry's film effort relies on indigenous, nativistic and Islamic solutions.

Genres and Themes of Indigenous Features

The application of Islamic regulations and the political exigencies of the time resulted in the domination of action-adventure, war, comedy and family drama genres. But these genres embody varying themes, which taken together can throw light on the tensions the society is experiencing and the way Islamic values are played out on the screen. These themes can be seen in Table 2.5, taken from Mas'ud Purmohammad's study of the screenplays of films made in 1987.

Table 2.5: Themes of Films Made in 1987[75]

Themes	Number of Films
Amnesia as a result of shock	5
Psychological disorders	9
Emigration or escape from the country	11
Family problems and disputes	14
War as a principal and ancillary theme	12
Wealth does not bring happiness (Islamic values)	20
Exposing the Pahlavi regime	11
Exposing anti-government groups (goruhak-ha)	4

In what follows, the major themes identified in Table 2.5 are examined.

Exposing the Pahlavi Regime

Given the anti-Pahlavi character of the Revolution, it is understandable that populist cinema was concerned with exposing that regime's moral corruption, economic dependence, subservience to the West and political suppression. The rather large number of films in this category shown seven years after the fall of the Shah indicates that this topic had not been exhausted. Also, unsurprisingly, early favourite themes included the operations of SAVAK, torture and armed struggle against the Shah. Although some of these 'SAVAK films' deal with social and political ills under the Shah, the majority are amateurish, superficial tracts. An exception is Khosrow Sina'i's *Long Live* (1980). It portrays political repression by depicting the way in which a professional, affluent engineer inadvertently becomes involved with anti-Shah forces. Corruption, too, is shown effectively in *The Senator* (Mehdi Sabbaghzadeh, 1984), which focuses on graft and heroin smuggling: this film was the box-office record holder for 1984, with sales of nearly one million dollars.

Islamic Values

Emphasis on Islamic ethical values and on spiritual – not material – rewards are also clearly indicated in Table 2.5. Post-revolutionary cinema can be characterized as a 'moralist cinema', whose films are imbued with a generalized sense of morality and dispense moral advice to the point that even bad guys participate in it. Traditional values and conventions characteristic of rural folk are compared favourably with the consumerist ideology of urban areas. However, the populist, moralist cinema, instead of concentrating on deeper Iranian and Islamic mystic values, catered chiefly to a superficial morality, characterized by easy hopes, cheap emotions and inexpensive good deeds.[76] The art cinema films are also moralistic, as exemplified by Abbas Kiarostami's *Where is the Friend's House?* (1987). This film, dubbed 'agonizingly slow' but ultimately rewarding,[77] depicts the relentless efforts of an honest boy to find a friend's house in order to return a copybook he had taken by mistake.

Leading clerics, including Hojjatoleslam Mohammad Khatami, Minister of Culture and Islamic Guidance, urged filmmakers to propagate the notions of 'self-sacrifice, martyrdom and revolutionary patience'.[78] Accordingly, such themes inundate the moralist cinema and find their most natural expression in films about the war with Iraq.

War Films

Soon after Iraq invaded Iran, Ayatollah Khomeini ordered the mobilization of all sectors. However, it took the MCIG and the private sector some time to solve the twin problems of the shortage of raw stock and the lack of funds. Many films were awaiting screening, and thus could not produce income to invest in war films.[79] Although the first film about this war, *The Border* (Jamshid Heydari, 1981), was made by the private sector, the lion's share of war films were produced by the public sector, hence forming an official cinema.

During the war period, a total of 56 feature films about the war were made, two-thirds of which focused primarily on fighting and military operations, the rest concerning themselves with war's social and psychological impact.[80] Apparently, many of the warfront films emphasized action and violence over sensitivity and psychological depth. But in the mid-1980s private-sector producers began to pay more attention to the specificity of the conflict by exploring both psychological and ideological dimensions of the war. Hasan Karbakhsh's *The Domain of Lovers* (1983) examines the psychology of a young reserve soldier and the meaning of self-sacrifice and duty. Manuchehr Asgarinasab's *A House Waiting*, broadcast on TV in 1987, is a technically polished film that portrays a wartime society without showing trench warfare. Throughout the 1980s, Seyyed Morteza Avini's Jehad TV Unit produced a massive series of films for national broadcast, collectively called *Narrative of Victory* (*Ravayat-e Fath*). Finally, Islamically committed filmmaker Ebrahim Hatamikia, in his early war films *The Sentry* (1988) and *The Emigrant* (1990), explored the psychological and sociological impact of the war on the home front.

Although war led to an increase in the quantity of films emphasizing the Islamic values of martyrdom and self-sacrifice, it had a negative effect on the quality of films, which by and large were limited to circulating clichés and slogans.[81] Issues relating to the causes, conduct and consequences of the war were foregrounded in the post-war cinema, so war remained a viable topic. As early as 1985, New Wave filmmaker Beyza'i made *Bashu, The Little Stranger*, a deeply pacifist and humanist film, which suffered from censorship. Mohsen Makhmalbaf, the most promising 'Islamist' filmmaker, made *Wedding of the Blessed* (1989), which used the war to critique government and society. In this film, the protagonist, a shell-shocked photographer, is used to explore the social symptomatology of the war, its causes and many of its unresolved consequences.

Women's Cinema

The themes of shock and psychological disorder, split families, dislocation and exile are explored particularly in family melodramas which, because they involve women, bear particular scrutiny, for it is in the portrayal and treatment of women that the tensions surrounding the Islamization of cinema crystallize.

The film and video regulations mentioned above set out rules concerning the portrayal of women. According to these rules, Muslim women must be shown to be chaste and to have an important role in society as well as in raising God-fearing and responsible children. In addition, women were not to be treated like commodities or used to arouse sexual desires.[82] These general and ambiguous guidelines had a profound effect on the use and portrayal of women in cinema. Filmmakers could evade entanglement with the censors by self-censorship and the avoidance altogether of stories involving women. As the star of *Report of a Death* (Muhammad Ali Najafi, 1987) stated, filmmakers were 'afraid to turn to women … even when authorities have invited [them] to consider women'.[83] Statistics compiled by Purmohammad point to the very low presence of women as heroes in films made in 1987: of the 37 films he reviewed, the chief protagonists in 25 films were men, in three films they were women, and in seven films, men and women shared equal billing.[84]

If women appeared at all, they were given limited parts: reflecting the role spelled out for them in MCIG regulations, they were usually portrayed as housewives or as mothers. To use women, a new grammar of film evolved, which included the following features: women actors being given static parts or filmed in such a way as to avoid showing their bodies. A post-Revolution film director underlined these practices by saying that women in Islamic performing arts should be shown seated at all times so as to avoid drawing attention to their 'provocative walk', thereby allowing the audience to concentrate on the 'ideologies' inherent in the work.[85] In addition, eye contact, especially when expressing 'desire', and touching between men and women were discouraged.[86] All this meant that until recently women were often filmed in long-shot, with few close-ups or facial expressions.

The processes of filming and acting were also affected, especially in the first few years after the Revolution. Government agents appeared during filming to ensure that no 'unethical' conduct occurred on set. In at least one case, the male and female actors playing the parts of husband and wife were reported to have had to marry each other for the duration of the filming in order to stay within Islamic interpretations.[87]

Since women in films have to don the *chador* or other Islamic cover, their portrayal is unrealistic, as they are shown covering themselves from close kin, which in real life they would not do. Such intrusions into the realm of acting and filming undermine the actors' art, distort the portrayal of family life and love relationships, and relegate women, in the words of an official, to a marginal position in the patriarchal system of Iranian cinema.[88] Another side-effect is that depictions of the Pahlavi period and of the western world have been excluded from Iranian cinema altogether. Naser Taqva'i, director of *Captain Khorshid* (1987), corroborates these points when he says,

> This very same problem about the character of woman has made it impossible [for us] to make a film about the Pahlavi era. You cannot show with ease the relationship of a husband and a wife, a sister and a brother, in the streets or at home, let alone portray other relations of blood or marriage.[89]

Such constraints, which have gradually lessened, affect the relationships of men on screen as well, resulting in fascinating gender reconfigurations and re-inscription.[90] A few exceptional directors, such as Beyza'i in *Bashu, The Little Stranger* and *Maybe Another Time* (1988), did continue to explore women, gender roles and women's issues seriously.

If women had problems appearing in front of cameras, they had less difficulty attending film schools and working behind the camera in both the motion picture and TV industries – provided they observed the evolving 'Islamic' codes of conduct, dress, acting and the gaze. There are more women feature-film directors currently working in Iran than there were in all the preceding eight decades combined. They include the following: Tahmineh Ardekani, Rakhshan Bani-Etemad, Faryal Behzad, Marziyeh Borumand, Puran Derakhshandeh, Tahmineh Milani and Kobra Sa'idi. Their films deal with a range of topics – from family and housing problems to physical and mental disability – and genres – from social comedies to psychological dramas.[91]

The Ideological Repositioning of Cinema

A major criticism of films made in the Islamic Republic, especially the populist variety, is their low quality and ideological earnestness and superficiality. Even when ideas and screenplays are approved and made into films, quality is not guaranteed. In 1985, the authoritative journal *Mahnameh-ye Sinema'i-ye Film* assessed post-Revolution films and found them utterly wanting. It rated 35 films 'sleazy' (*mobtazal*), 57 'bad', 22 'mediocre', one 'good', and none 'excellent'.[92] The general quality of films has improved because of measures taken since then, as borne out by a series of awards received in recent international film festivals.

The generally poor quality of the films and the overall lack of variety on TV and in the cinema helped to nurture a new medium, as VCRs provided a popular way of spending one's leisure time. In 1983, 74 per cent of Tehran's households had a black-and-white TV, 16 per cent a colour TV, and 2 per cent a VCR. The figures for the nation as a whole were much lower: 67 per cent, 6 per cent and 0.5 per cent respectively.[93] These figures, however, belie the actual size of the audience, since video-watching is a communal activity, during or after dinner. This development, like other aspects of society, was the subject of cultural negotiation. Over the years, government and public played a cat-and-mouse game, with government alternately banning and permitting importation of film videos, and the public purchasing, renting and circulating bootleg copies of videos on the black market. At any rate, the latest feature films from the West (including some pornographic material) are now easily available to those who want them.[94]

The ideological earnestness and superficiality of films are related to such issues as post-revolutionary conditions, the pall of the war with Iraq, the bureaucratization of filmmakers, the timidity of filmmakers unfamiliar with Islamic precepts, self-censorship, governmental censorship and the uneven application or varied interpretations of Islamic codes and regulations. For instance, the changing interpretations of codes, often based on political expediency, puts certain topics suddenly off-limits. This in turn tends to make filmmakers shy away from tackling controversial, social or political issues, encouraging them instead to seek safe topics. Barbod Taheri's feature documentary about the Revolution, *The Fall of '57* (1980), is a good case in point. Once popular, in 1984 it was banned because it dealt with topics that the authorities no longer wanted discussed. Taheri was told, 'There are moments in a nation's life when people no longer need to know what has actually happened.' If he were to apply for a new exhibition permit, he would have to remove documentary footage of actual events, showing wide participation by secular and leftist groups in the Revolution, armed forces attacking demonstrators, and even Khomeini's first speech delivered in a Tehran cemetery, in which he condemned the Shah for making cemeteries prosperous.[95]

As documented above, after the mid-1980s there was a steady move towards the rationalization of the film industry and the encouragement of local production. Concurrently, and equally significantly, major shifts in attitudes and perceptions towards both cinema and working in the motion picture business have taken place. Cinema, rejected in the past as part of the frivolous superstructure, has been adopted as part of the necessary infrastructure of Islamic culture. Fakhreddin Anvar, Undersecretary of Culture and Islamic Guidance in charge of the Film Affairs Department, describes this process: 'Believing culture to be the structure undergirding all aspects of running a society…the Department has directed all its efforts towards ensuring that cinematic activities and filmmaking are included in all legislation, laws, systems, and regulations.'[96] Working in film, once despised and disparaged, has become acceptable and respectable. Hojjatoleslam Ali Akbar Hashemi Rafsanjani, speaker of the Majles, publicly endorsed this shift when he declared in March 1987, 'Our entertainers, male or female, did not enjoy the same esteem that they enjoy today from lay and religious people…This is a real revolution.'[97]

Films, judged immediately after the Revolution solely on their ideological purity and instructional values, began to be assessed for their ability to entertain and enlighten. In 1985, Rafsanjani acknowledged the necessity for a lighter treatment of themes in cinema, stating, 'It is true that a film must have a message, but this does not mean that we must deny its entertaining aspects. Society needs entertainment; lack of joy reduces one's effectiveness and involvement.'[98] Khatami, too, declared this shift in perception and repositioning of cinema in no uncertain terms:

> I believe that cinema is not the mosque…If we remove cinema from its natural place, we will no longer have cinema…If we transform cinema to such an extent that when one enters a moviehouse one feels imposed upon or senses that leisure time has changed to become homework time, then we have deformed society.[99]

The morality codes that had become a straitjacket for cinema, limiting the portrayal of women and the use of music, were eased considerably after December 1987 when Khomeini issued an edict to this effect.[100]

Mehrju'i's social satire *The Tenants* (1986) was immensely popular, and generated the highest revenues in the history of Iranian cinema. This was testimony that the public, too, wanted films to be well made and entertaining as well as enlightening. In fact, as Mohammad Beheshti observed, 'a new and unprecedented situation has developed in post-revolutionary Iran, whereby the best quality films are also the most popular films'.[101] While this was not true of populist films, it was generally true of an increasing number of art cinema films.

Conclusion

Throughout its existence, the Islamist regime has shown a surprising degree of flexibility and a great capacity for learning from its own mistakes. After 1983 it steadfastly sought to rationalize the film industry and to provide it with support and leadership. Filmmakers and audiences too demonstrated both resolve and ingenuity in the face of incredible constraints. In fact, it was through a process of cultural negotiation and haggling – not just through acclaim (interpellation) – that a new cinema emerged, embodying many of the aforementioned Islamic values. Gradually, a new crop of 'Islamically committed' filmmakers was trained, at the same time that experienced New Wave filmmakers of the Shah's era were resurrected and allowed to work. In fact, the latter group led the charge in transforming post-revolutionary art cinema, though neither type of filmmaker was forced into a rigid position. In the same way that pre-revolutionary filmmakers such as Beyza'i, Mehrju'i, Kiarostami, Taqva'i, Kimia'i, Hatami and Sina'i adapted to new post-revolutionary realities, the new generation of Islamist filmmakers, such as Makhmalbaf, Hatamikia and Bani-Etemad also evolved and matured. The price of adaptation and evolution, however, was accommodation and the charge that the filmmakers had sold out. For example, the endings of Mehrju'i's films *The Tenants* and *Hamoon* (1990), which seem to contradict the body of the films, have been criticized because of the perception that the director had caved in to the authorities and changed his original endings. Such textual contradictions reveal the process of cultural negotiation in Iran, and indicate the degree to which filmmakers must compromise or appear to compromise their own ideals if they want their socially critical films to be released. Refusal to compromise may relegate their controversial films, such as Makhmalbaf's *A Time to Love* (1991), to archival shelves, underground circuits and foreign markets.

These and similar cultural contradictions have found expression not only in the film texts themselves but also in the development of a lively film culture in general. A number of annual film festivals show a mixture of local and foreign-made products, film archives regularly offer screenings, a number of institutions offer academic degrees and training in film and TV, serious film and theatre journals are being published, and film reviews appear in a range of periodicals.[102] Since the late 1980s, Iranian cinema has gone beyond its national borders. After a period of mutual hostility, post-revolutionary films began to appear in international film festivals in increasing numbers, garnering high praise and recognition. In 1986 only two post-revolutionary films were shown in foreign festivals, while in 1990 a total of 230 films were screened in some 78 international film festivals, winning 11 prizes.[103]

Post-Khomeini, Post-Khatami Cinema – a Postscript (1990–9)

Since the early 1990s, Iran's politics, economy and culture have undergone a number of significant developments affecting the film industry and cinema. One of these was a debate that surfaced during the summer of 1991 over what one faction of the government called an organized, multifaceted 'cultural invasion' of the country by 'Western imperialism'. Many high-ranking political figures, including the nation's religious leader Ayatollah Khamene'i, President Rafsanjani and Minister Khatami, as well as most of the mainstream and specialist press, participated in this debate. Surprisingly, the relatively new literary journal *Gardun*, whose cover (nos 15–16, Mordad 1370/1991) had originally sparked the cultural invasion debate, and had come under strong attack, continued publication. It was shut down a few months later, however, and its editor prosecuted. Subsequently other editors were also harassed and prosecuted. The debate took its toll among high-ranking officials too: Khatami, who as Minister of Culture and Islamic Guidance had been one of the most enduring public leaders in the country, presiding over the flourishing of the arts and cinema since the Revolution, resigned in mid-1992. In February 1994, Rafsanjani's brother, Mohammad, who had headed the broadcasting networks for many years, was ousted. Soon after, Mohammad Beheshti, who as director of the FCF had built it into a formidable film institution, was also removed. These changes followed the earlier dismissal of prime minister Mir Hoseyn Musavi, during whose reign these and other officials had created the nucleus of 'Islamically committed' cinema, culture and broadcasting. With their removal, a new, post-Khomeini era began. The immediate impact on the film industry was to set in motion a period of anxious uncertainty, from which it emerged relatively unscathed. The reasons for the industry's resilience may be found partly in the institutionalization of cinema and the film industry, with the result that it now appears both less subject to direct ideological manipulation and less dependent on the presence of sympathetic officials – although ideology and influence continue to be important factors.

The Rafsanjani government's attempt to privatize major industries led to the re-evaluation and partial removal of the subsidies provided to the film industry. This move prompted dire predictions of the industry's imminent collapse; this did not happen. Apart from censorship, factors that threatened the industry during Rafsanjani's term were high rates of inflation (30–50 per cent) and unemployment (12–20 per cent), low investment in non-oil industries, and the slow rationalization of foreign-exchange policies (three different rates competed).[104] Measures taken in this period that helped the industry included a progressive rating system, which encouraged the production of quality films. Grade 'A' films were awarded the best exhibition sites and opening dates, and longer runs; the makers of such films were granted higher budgets and lower interest loans. Grade 'A' filmmakers were also exempted from having to submit their screenplays for approval before production.[105] These measures created the unusual situation in which higher-quality films were sometimes the most popular. Censorship and intimidation of filmmakers, artists and intellectuals, however, continued. A number of films were banned, even those of grade 'A' filmmakers. Beyza'i's *Tara's Ballad* and *Yazdgerd's Death* continued to be banned, as were Makhmalbaf's *A Time to Love* and *Zayandehrud Nights* (1991). In mid-1995, a group of 214 film workers wrote an open letter to the MCIG demanding a thorough re-evaluation of the complex rules and procedures governing film production and exhibition. Noting that both state-subsidized and strictly commercial cinemas are likely to undermine the 'national film industry', the signatories demanded a reduction of the stifling rules and a strengthening of truly independent professional guilds, which could replace government agencies in supervising and controlling the industry.[106] In essence, they were demanding that the industry be allowed to move out of the political and into the professional sphere – a demand that may take years and a paradigmatic ideological reorientation to materialize. In the meantime, despite the 'cultural invasion' debates fanned by hardliners, the high cost of newsprint and stringent censorship, film journalism thrived, with a diverse menu of daily, weekly, monthly, and quarterly periodicals about cinema.[107]

The exhibition of art cinema films in international film festivals continued apace, garnering increasingly positive evaluations for both Iranian cinema and individual filmmakers. In 1992, the director of the New York Film Festival was quoted as saying that Iranian cinema is 'one of the most exciting in the world today'.[108] Likewise, the Toronto International Film Festival called it 'one of the pre-eminent national cinemas in the world today'.[109] International acclaim for Iranian cinema did not translate into political prestige for the Islamist government, as the regime's opponents in exile had feared. Iranian exiles, international audiences and film-reviewing establishments abroad were sophisticated enough to understand the constricted political contexts in which the films were produced. Unlike some exiles who focused on the political issues and on governmental machinations and manipulations, these viewers and reviewers tended to highlight the initiative and skilfulness of the filmmakers. They credited these qualities, not government largesse or manipulative capacity, for the high quality of the films. Iranian films are being shown in series and in festival forums annually in many countries and in many US cities, from Los Angeles to Chicago and from Houston to New York.[110] A number of filmmakers have been praised repeatedly in US and European publications and festivals, among them Mehrju'i, Makhmalbaf, Kiarostami, Bani-Etemad, Majidi, Milani and Beyza'i. No one has received more critical as well as popular acclaim abroad than Kiarostami, whose picture appeared on the cover of the July–August 1995 issue of *Cahiers du cinéma* (no. 493) above the caption: 'Kiarostami le magnifique'. Inside, nearly 50 pages were devoted to discussions of his work.

Iranian participation in international film festivals is not just intended to gain prestige – for the film industry, individual filmmakers, and the government. However popular some current Iranian films might be inside Iran, the 65-million population of the country does not appear to be large enough (or economically robust enough) nor the exhibition circuit powerful enough to support fully an indigenous commercial film industry. Iranian cinema will not be able to flourish as a viable, non-governmental, commercial industry without foreign markets. Entering films in international festivals and airing them on European TV networks are the right steps towards creating such markets, but they are only a beginning. More effort is applied to breaking into global commercial and academic distribution networks. As a result, art cinema films are increasingly being screened by commercial exhibitors outside festival circuits. In summer 1995, for example, Makhmalbaf's *Salaam Cinema* (*Cinema, Cinema,* 1995) was screened not only at the Cannes International Film Festival but also simultaneously in three cinemas in Paris. At the same time, Ebrahim Foruzesh's *The Jar* (1992) was on the screen in a Paris commercial theatre. In the US, too, Iranian films are routinely shown across the country in commercial theatres, and several video mail-order outlets distribute them. This is highly significant, for the internationalization and commercialization of the art cinema has made possible the emergence of an inchoate, independent, auteurist cinema that is independent from Iranian tastes, commercial concerns and governmental control.

Although women continue to be the most regulated and officially controlled sector of Iranian society and cinema, their presence and influence both behind and in front of the cameras has steadily grown. As a legitimate profession, one that has been 'purified' of its previous ills of lax morality, sexuality and corruption, the film industry now attracts women to all its areas, including cinematography, which was until very recently dominated by men.

Video and satellite TV continue to pose particularly vexing problems for the regime, offering its opponents opportunities for cultural negotiation and resistance. From the beginning, the Islamist government had a love–hate relationship with video, fearing that it would undermine the 'Islamic culture' it was propagating. As a result, it frequently vacillated, alternately banning, curtailing, ignoring or grudgingly allowing video cassettes and VCRs. This in turn encouraged a burgeoning but fluctuating black market in major cities. However, the popularity of global satellite networks in Iran in the mid-1990s forced the government to act decisively by becoming itself a distributor of feature and TV films on video. It hoped by this means to combat the cultural invasion that the powerful global satellites were supposedly leading with their highly attractive programming. But the quantity, quality and variety of officially allowed videos fell short of expectation and of the competition. As a result, after much debate in parliament and the ruling circles, in 1994 Grand Ayatollah Mohammad Ali Araki issued a *fatwa* banning satellite TV, declaring: 'Installing satellite antennae, which open Islamic society to the inroads of decadent foreign culture and the spread of ruinous Western diseases to Muslims, is *haram* (forbidden).'[111] It is interesting to note that Araki's description of foreign TV and pop culture as 'disease' is entirely in line with Navab-Safavi's and

Khomeini's metaphors of decades earlier. The government urged owners of satellite equipment to remove their dishes 'voluntarily', and threatened to fine culprits up to US$750 and to confiscate their equipment. It also declared that those who were found to be importing, selling or installing dishes would be jailed and fined the huge sum of US$25,000.[112] Despite some arrests and fines, the ban was not entirely successful, as equipment owners found creative ways of camouflaging or miniaturizing their satellite dishes. This failure, together with regulation loopholes exempting government officials and foreign legations from the ban, created a fluid cultural space in which all kinds of slippage and transgressions, as well as countermeasures, are possible. The government responded to the fluidity of the situation not only by freeing video and banning satellite TV, but also by launching massive efforts to increase film production, to build new cinema complexes and to create new TV networks aimed at satisfying the needs and desires of two of the largest segments of the population: young adults and city-dwellers.[113]

Mohammad Khatami, former Minister of Culture and Islamic Guidance, who had been swept aside by the cultural invasion debate, was elected president in a landslide election in 1997, massively supported by young people and women. He introduced new secularist values of transparency, civil society, rule of law and pluralism. In terms of foreign relations, he replaced the previous 'neither East nor West' doctrine with the 'dialogue of civilizations'. These values were a marked departure from and modification of the previously articulated Islamic values. Economically, he promoted privatization and heightened relations of exchange with other national economies. He appointed two women to cabinet positions and nurtured a lively independent press, even though it was heavily persecuted by a legal system under the authority of Supreme Leader Ali Khamene'i. Everywhere there were signs of a deadly power struggle over culture, the most ominous of which were the assassinations of five intellectuals, writers and opposition figures, apparently by rogue elements within the state security apparatus. Incredibly enough, these elements were arrested. In a cat-and-mouse game with the hardline courts, some of the reformist newspapers resurfaced under different names as soon as they were shut down. When *Jame'eh* was banned, *Tous* came out, looking exactly like its predecessor in typeface, layout and editorial policy; when *Tous* was shut down, *Neshat* was launched, similarly echoing its predecessor.

Khatami took a more public role in cultural negotiations over cinema, defending quality films and openness. One example is Davud Mirbaqeri's *The Snowman* (1994/7), which had been banned for several years, and was released only after Khatami's election as president. The film immediately became highly controversial, however, as Islamist hardliners, including the militant Supporters of the Party of God (*Ansar-e Hezbollah*), attacked the theatres that showed it in major cities, including Tehran and Isfahan.[114] Significantly, government officials, including Khatami, voiced support for the film and audiences, too, endorsed it by flocking to the theatres. The film became so popular that the Isfahan theatre, which had been attacked, continued to show it for over a month afterwards.

Ostensibly, the reason for the attack was the film's theme of transvestism. Its protagonist (played by Ali Abdi) dreams of going to the US, but as there is no American embassy in Iran, he travels to Turkey to obtain a visa. After his various disguises fail to get him a visa there, he gets involved in a scheme, hatched by expatriate Iranian tough guys, to disguise himself as a woman and to marry a willing American, for US$6000. Abdi dons women's clothes, hair and makeup; thus dressed, he appears unveiled in public (which is unlawful in Iran) and he skillfully adopts a camp gay masquerade (also unlawful). The reasons for the hardliners' protests, therefore, may have been not just transvestism but also the film's treatment of such important taboo subjects as unveiled women, homosexuality and the celebration of tough-guy lifestyles – including drinking alcohol and singing – all of which are severely punished in Islamist Iran, where the boundaries segregating genders, inside and outside, self and other, and religiously lawful and unlawful are so strictly patrolled and enforced.

Khatami intensified the privatization of the country's shattered economy, and in 1999 offered a five-year plan to turn over the communications, post, railway and tobacco industries to the private sector in a 'total restructuring of the Islamic Republic's economy'.[115] Privatization meant the reduction of government involvement in film financing, production and exhibition. For example, to deal with the unauthorized use of videos and satellite TV, the government formulated a plan to relinquish its monopoly on video distribution to the private sector by licensing local film producers and video distributors to import foreign films on video. Up to this point, the government had protected the local film industry from competition by essentially banning foreign imports. This plan is likely to change things drastically. To prevent unfair competition, it has tied the importing of foreign films on video to the production of local films. Accordingly, local film producers can import four foreign films for every feature film they produce in Iran.[116] This is designed to encourage both production and importation of film, raising the level and choice of films available. However, the long-term effects of privatization on the film industry, particularly on art-cinema films, is hard to predict, for under both the Pahlavi regime and the Islamic Republic this cinema benefited from government support, which shielded it to a great extent from the vagaries of the markets. Fortuitously, a new factor has emerged this time: the foreign film markets. If managed properly, income from these markets may be sufficient both to offset government withdrawal and to protect art-cinema films from low public taste at home and high competition from abroad.

As demonstrated, the post-revolutionary cinema is not monolithic or univocal, although the state has dominated the private sector so far. This cinema cannot be regarded as one imposed by a 'ruthlessly united' ideological apparatus controlled by the state; rather, it is one that has grown out of considerable ideological work and negotiation.

No discussion of the Iranian cinema is complete without considering the output of Iranians filmmakers in exile since the Revolution. In one study I conducted, they had made over 300 fiction, non-fiction, animated and avant-garde films in two decades of displacement in nearly a dozen European and North American countries. This made them by far the most prolific filmmaking group among the Middle Eastern exiles in the West. Although these filmmakers are diverse politically and religiously, the majority of them are united in their opposition to the Islamist regime. And while they work in different countries, making films in various languages, their films share certain features that place them as films of exile and of the diaspora. Theirs is part of an emerging global cinema, what I have called an "accented cinema," which is centrally concerned with expressing the pains and pleasures of displacement and the problematics of multiple locations and identities. This is a cinema that is produced in the interstices of dominant cultures and film industries, using an artisanal mode of production.[117]

The most accomplished feature narrative films made in exile include the following: Sohrab Shahid-Saless's *Utopia* (1982) and *Roses for Africa* (1991), Parviz Sayyad's *The Mission* (1983), Marva Nabili's *Nightsongs* (1984), Ghasem Ebrahimian's *The Suitors* (1989), Reza Allamehzadeh's *The Guests of the Hotel Astoria* (1989), Jalal Fatemi's *The Nuclear Baby* (1990), Caveh Zahedi's *A Little Stiff* (1992, with Greg Watkins) and *I Don't Hate Las Vegas Anymore* (1994), Amir Naderi's *Manhattan by Numbers* (1993) and *Avenue A.B.C...Manhattan* (1997), Shirin Etessam and Erica Jordan's *Walls of Sand* (1994) and Houshang Allahyari's *Fear of Heights* (1994).

This Iranian accented cinema evolved in several phases, from disavowing dislocation to seriously engaging with the problematics of multiple locations. Its form also evolved, from feature fiction to documentary to avant garde. Women are a rising force among non-narrative filmmakers, including Mehrnaz Saeed-Vafa, Shirin Neshat, Shirin Bazleh, Persheng Sadeq Vaziri and Shirin Etessam. Of interest also is the emergence of the 'music video' genre in the US, particularly in Los Angeles. The videos are aired frequently on Iranian exile TV in Europe and North America, and they are also available in ethnic music and grocery stores – and in bootleg form in Iran. These videos offer the exiles a new form of both self-expression and collective identity formation, and they provide researchers of trans-national media with fascinating textual materials.[118]

Notes on Chapter 2

1.   This chapter updates two earlier versions: 'Islamizing film culture in Iran', in Samih K. Farsoun and Mehrdad Mashayekhi (eds), *Iran: Political Culture in the Islamic Republic* (London, Routledge, 1992), pp. 173–208, and 'Islamicizing film culture in Iran – an update', in *CEMOTI (Cahiers d'Études sur la Méditerranée Orientale et le Monde Turco–Iranien)* 20 (juillet –décembre 1995), pp. 145–85. It is reprinted with permission. Minor alterations and corrections have been made throughout and the section on 'Post-Khomeini and post-Khatami cinema' has been completely rewritten for this publication.

2.   Mostafa Abkashak, *Mosabbebin-e Vaqe'i-ye Faje'eh-ye Howlnak-e Sinema Rex-e Abadan Cheh Kasani Hastand?* (Los Angeles, n.pub., 1985). After the Revolution, this incident was a hot topic in the Iranian press, where the proceedings of the trial of Takab-'Alizadeh and others accused of setting the theatre on fire were extensively reported. More details on the incident are available in mass-circulation newspapers such as *Kayhan, Ettela'at* and *Enqelab-e Eslami*, and opposition publications such as *Mojahed*, especially 1/93, 31 Khordad 1359/1980, p. 7 and *Peykar* 17, 29 Khordad 1358/1979, p. 12.

3.   Homa Nateq, 'Yaran-e motahhed dar kudeta va enqelab', *Zaman-e Now* [Paris] 8 (Ordibehesht 1366/1987), pp. 17–19; 'Iran's film biz nipped in the bud by Islamic belief', *Variety*, 9 May 1979, p. 91.

4.   Ruhollah Khomeini, *Velayat-e Faqih: Hokumat-e Eslami* (Tehran, Amir Kabir, 1360/1981), p. 188.

5.   *Asnad va Tasaviri az Mobarezat-e Khalq-e Mosalman-e Iran*, vol. 1, part 3 (Tehran, Abuzar, 1357/1978).

6.   Louis Althusser and Etienne Balibar, 'Ideology and ideological state apparatuses (notes toward an investigation)', in Ben Brewster (trans.),

Lenin and Philosophy and Other Essays (New York, Monthly Review Press, 1971), pp. 127–89.

7. Hamid Naficy, 'Iranian writers, the Iranian cinema, and the case of *Dash Akol*', *Iranian Studies* 28/2–4, Spring–Autumn 1985, p. 237.

8. Fazlollah Nuri, *Lavayeh-e Aqa Sheykh Fazlollah Nuri* (Tehran, Nashr-e Tarikh-e Iran, 1362/1983), p. 49.

9. *Ibid.*, p. 27.

10. Navab-Safavi, *Jame'eh va Hokumat-e Eslami* (Qom, Entesharat-e Hejrat, 1357/1978), p. 4.

11. Ruhollah Khomeini, *Kashf ol-Asrar* (n.pub, n.d.), p. 194.

12. *Ibid.*, p. 292.

13. *Ibid.*, p. 276.

14. Alan Sheridan (trans.), *Discipline and Punish: the Birth of the Prison* (New York, Vantage, 1979), pp. 209–22.

15. Max Horkheimer and Theodore Adorno, *Dialectic of Enlightenment*, John Cumming (trans.) (New York, Herder & Herder, 1972), p. 123.

16. Khomeini's concept of the 'culture of idolatry' is reminiscent of Debord's formulation of 'the society of the spectacle'. See Guy Debord, *Society of the Spectacle* (Detroit, Black and White, 1983).

17. Navab-Safavi, *Jame'eh va Hokumat-e Eslami*, p. 11.

18. Ruhollah Khomeini, *Islam and Revolution: Writings and Declarations of Imam Khomeini*, Hamid Algar (trans.) (Berkeley, Mizan Press, 1981), p. 258.

19. For example, the Soviet formalist films of Eisenstein and Vertov followed the Russian Revolution, the British realist documentaries immediately preceded and followed the Second World War, the Italian neo-realists emerged immediately after the Second World War and the Polish 'black films' were made possible during the 'spring thaw' of de-Stalinization in the mid-50s. Several innovative film movements emerged alongside the worldwide social turmoil of the 1960s and the 1970s: *cinema novo* in Brazil, New Wave in Iran, *cinéma vérité* in the US, France and Canada, 'new German cinema' in West Germany, and 'militant' and 'liberationist' cinema in many parts of the third world.

20. See 'Iran's film biz nipped in the bud', *art. cit.*; 'Sadha sinema dar barabar-e atash bi-defa'-and', *Kayhan*, 15 Shahrivar 1357/1978, p. 12; 'Iran theatres to ban sex on their own', *Variety*, 23 May 1979, p. 7; '300 sinema-ye keshvar fa'aliat-e khod-ra az sar gereftand', *Kayhan*, 23 Tir 1358/1979, p. 12. In 'Lots of mullah in Iran's show biz', *Variety*, 13 June 1979, p. 1, Hazel Guild estimates that 40 per cent of cinemas were burned down. The figures quoted in *Kayhan* are official figures issued by the Society of Theatre Owners.

21. After the Revolution, many film theatres were used for other purposes. For example, the sole cinema in Ferdows was turned into storage for hay, and one of the film theatres in Gorgan was converted into a prison. See 'Tabdil-e sinema be kahdani', *Iran Times*, 26 April 1985, p. 15; *Mojahed*, 13 Day 1363/1985, p. 4.

22.   When renaming was deemed insufficient, revolutionary zeal produced bizarre syncretic rituals. Rudaki Hall, a major cultural centre with a revolving stage, on which many performances had taken place during the Shah's era, was made literally to undergo ceremonial ablution (*ghosl*) in order to be fully cleansed, causing the stage mechanism to rust. See Gholam-Hoseyn Sa'edi, 'Namayesh dar hokumat-e namayeshi', *Alefba* [Paris] 5, new edition, Winter 1363/1984, p 7.

23.   'Moscow gets Tehran's Oscar', *Iran Times*, 2 April 1361/1982, p. 16.

24.   'Salshomar-e sinema-ye pas az enqelab 2', *Mahnameh-ye Sinema'i-ye Film* (henceforth *Mahnameh*) 6, Mehr 1362/1983, p. 43.

25.   'Sokhani kutah dar bareh-ye namayesh-e filmha-ye khareji', *Enqelab-e Eslami*, 13 Khordad 1359/1980, p. 6.

26.   'Yaddasht-ha'i bar mas'aleh-ye sinema-ha-ye darbasteh dar Iran', *Enqelab-e Eslami*, 10 Tir 1359/1980, p. 5.

27.   'Barrasi va rahyabi-ye moshgelat-e film va sinema', *Ettela'at*, 27 Farvardin 1360/1981, p. 10.

28.   'Farhang-koshi va farhang-zade'i dar Jomhuri-ye Eslami', *Alefba*, new edition, Winter 1361/1982, p. 7. For a translation of this piece see, 'Iran under the Party of God', *Index on Censorship* (1/1984), pp. 16–20.

29.   See, 'Az vorud va kharid-e film-ha-ye khareji jelowgiri mishavad', *Ayandegan*, 17 Tir 1358/1979; 'Vorud va kharid-e filmha-ye khareji mamnu' shod', *Kayhan*, 18 Tir 1358/1979, p. 14; 'Iran's Islamic regime kicks out Bruce Lee & "imperialist" films', *Variety*, 18 July 1979, p. 2; 'Sinema-ye Iran dar rah-e tazeh', *Ettela'at*, 28 Esfand 1358/1980, p. 10; 'Dowlat varedat-e film-ha-ye khareji ra beh ohdeh migirad', *Ettela'at*, 20 Farvardin 1360/1981.

30.   Unpublished internal document obtained by the author: *Marahel-e Mokhtalef-e Nezarat bar Sakht va Namayesh-e Film* (Tehran, Ministry of Culture and Islamic Guidance), pp. 38–9.

31.   'Salshomar-e sinema-ye pas az enqelab 2', *art. cit.*, p. 42.

32.   'Iran theatres to ban sex on their own', *art. cit.*

33.   'Magic Marker cinema censor', *Iran Times*, 29 June 1979, p. 16.

34.   'Namayesh-e film-e bedun-e parvaneh dar sinemaha mamnu' shod', *Ettela'at*, 9 Esfand 1358/1980, p. 3.

35.   Sources: *Marahel-e Mokhtalef*, pp. 38–9; 'Namayesh-e film-ha-ye Hendi va Torki mamnu' shod', *Ettela'at*, 27 Esfand 1358/1980, p. 10.

36.   'Salshomar-e sinema-ye pas az enqelab 2', *art. cit.*, p. 42; also, 'Salshomar-e sinema-ye pas az enqelab 5, 1359', *Mahnameh* 17, Mehr 1363/1984, p. 28. For films banned in 1979 see Mas'ud Mehrabi, *Tarikh-e Sinema-ye Iran az Aghaz ta 1357* (Tehran, *Mahnameh-ye Sinema'i-ye Film*, 1357/1978), p. 184. In 1989, Daryush Mehrju'i's *The Yard Behind Adl-e Afaq School (Hayat-e Poshti-ye Madraseh-ye Adl-e Afaq)* was re-titled *The School We Went to (Madrase'i keh Miraftim)* and released.

37.   'Sinema-ye Iran dar rah-e tazeh', *art. cit.*

38. For details of the maltreatment of entertainers and filmmakers under the Islamic Republic, see Hamid Naficy, 'The development of an Islamic cinema in Iran', in *Third World Affairs*, 1987, pp. 447–63.

39. 'Iran's film biz nipped in the bud', *art. cit.*

40. Author's interview with film producer Ali Mortazavi, August 1985, Los Angeles, CA.

41. Author's telephone interview with Bahman Farmanara in Toronto, Canada, July 1985. For an extended review of this film, see Hamid Naficy, 'Tall Shadows of the Wind', in *Magill's Survey of Cinema: Foreign Language Films* (Los Angeles, Salem Press, 1985), pp. 3016–20.

42. 'Yek modir-e sinema beh etteham-e dayer kardan-e eshratkadeh bazdasht shod', *Kayhan*, 10 Khordad 1358/1979, p. 5.

43. 'Ja-ye sinema dar "Barnameh-ye Panj Sal-e Avval" kojast?' *Mahnameh* 6, Mehr 1362/1983, pp. 4–5.

44. 'Dah sinema-ye Tehran ta'til shod', *Ettela'at*, 29 Bahman 1358/1980, p. 1; *Iranshahr*, 20 June 1980, p. 1; *Iranshahr*, 4 July 1980, p. 2; 'Sinemaha-ye sarasar-e keshvar ta'til shod', *Kayhan-e Hava'i*, 2 July 1980, p. 8.

45. 'Karnameh-ye dowlat-e Jomhuri-ye Eslami dar zamineh-ye siasat-ha-ye kolli-ye keshvar va arzesh-ha-ye hakem bar an', *Sorush* 252, 3 Shahrivar 1363/1984, p. 22.

46. *Ettela'at*, 10 Bahman 1358/1980, p. 20.

47. 'Nameh-ye sargoshadeh-ye sinemagaran-e Iran beh mellat va dowlat', included as a flier inside *Daftarha-ye Sinema* 4, Ordibehesht 1360/1981.

48. 'Degarguni dar zamineh-ye sinema, ba "dizolv" ettefaq mi'oftad nah ba "kat"', *Mahnameh* 46, 1366/1987, p. 4.

49. All the regulations listed and discussed here are taken from *Marahel-e Mokhtalef*, pp. 40–9.

50. For example, the number of theatres nationwide grew from 198 in 1979 to 277 in 1984; seating capacity in the same period increased from 141,399 to 170,265. Likewise, attendance at theatres in Tehran rose from 24 million in 1984 to nearly 28 million in 1986. For sources, see *Salnameh-ye Amari-ye Sal-e 1360* (Tehran, Esfand, Markaz-e Amar-e Iran, 1361/1983), p. 203; *Iran dar A'ineh-ye Amar* (Tehran, Mordad, Markaz-e Amar-e Iran, 1364/1985), p. 46; *A Selection of Iranian Films* (Tehran, FCF, 1987), p. 8. The attendance figure nationwide for 1984 topped 48 million. For sources, see Gholam Heydari, 'Javanan va sinema', *Mahnameh* 44, Dey 1365/1986, p. 6. Theatres were classified into four distinct categories: for example, in 1984, the 78 theatres in Tehran were rated as follows: 14 were distinguished, 30 were first class, 17 were second class and 17 were third class. See Edareh-ye Koll-e Tahqiqat va Ravabet-e Sinema'i, *Sinema-ye Iran 1358–1363* (Tehran, MCIG, 1984), pp. 37, 295.

51. Heydari, 'Javanan va sinema', p. 7.

52. Heydari's survey of students in Tehran in 1983 shows an audience preference for action and war films: 45 per cent favoured 'revolutionary' films, 39 per

cent comedies, 32 per cent religious films, 32 per cent crime films and 10 per cent socially relevant films.

53.   'Iranian film biz revisited: lotsa U.S. cassettes, picture backlog', *Variety*, 4 June 1984, p. 2.
54.   From the author's correspondence with the MCIG, 15 Tir 1364/1985.
55.   'Doshvari-ha-ye filmsazi dar sali keh gozasht', *Mahnameh* 23, Farvardin 1364/1985, pp. 5–7.
56.   *Marahel-e Mokhtalef,* pp. 35–6.
57.   For a list of these films, see Jamal Omid, *Farhang-e Film-ha-ye Sinema'i-ye Iran, Az 1351 ta 1366,* vol. 2 (Tehran, Entesharat-e Negah, 1366/1987), pp. 696–713.
58.   'Sansur az do negah', *Mahnameh* 76, Ordibehesht 1368/1989, pp. 10–11.
59.   'Green light to screenwriters', *Mahnameh* 66, Mordad 1367/1988, p. 1, English section.
60.   'Sinema-ye Iran 1358–1363', *Mahnameh* 18, Aban 1363/1984, pp. 293–4.
61.   'Poshtvaneh-ye ta'min-e ejtema'i va herfe'i-ye dast andarkaran-e sinema', *Mahnameh* 35, Farvardin 1365/1986, pp. 6–8.
62.   'Vam-e banki bara-ye filmsazan', *Mahnameh* 52, Mordad 1366/1987, p. 18; also 'Rahi besu-ye esteqlal-e eqtesadi-ye filmsazan', *Mahnameh* 60, Bahman 1366/1988, pp. 5–8.
63.   'Goruhbandi-ye film-ha-ye Irani va sinema-ha dar sal-e jari', *Mahnameh* 63, Ordibehesht 1367/1988, pp. 12–13; also 'Iranian films rated according to merit', *Mahnameh* 49, Ordibehesht 1366/1987, p. 1, English section.
64.   'New policies for a year of challenge', *Mahnameh* 77, Khordad 1368/1989, p. 1, English section.
65.   'Moruri bar vizhegi-ha-ye moshtarak-e film-ha-ye Irani-ye emsal', *Mahnameh* 79, Mordad 1368/1989, pp. 12–13.
66.   From Ahmad Talebi-Nezhad, 'Raval-e kar dar nahad-ha-ye filmsazi-ye Iran', *Mahnameh* 53, Shahrivar 1366/1987, pp. 6–11.
67.   Statistics for all years except 1986–8 are from 'Iranian cinema: a turning point', *Mahnameh* 41, Mehr 1367/1988, English section, pp. 1–2. Statistics for 1986–8 are from Omid, *Farhang-e Filmha.*
68.   'Bonyad-e Mostaz'afan miliard-ha dolar beh bank-ha bedehkar ast', *Iran Times*, 9 December 1983; 'Bonyad-e Mostaz'afan 45 miliard rial bedehi darad', *Iran Times*, 24 February 1984, p. 5.
69.   'Az ravayat va qesas-e Qor'an film-e sinema'i sakhteh mishavad', *Iran Times*, 29 July 1983, p. 5.
70.   'Zarar-e Mostaz'afan az kar-e sinema-ha', *Iran Times*, 18 May 1984, p. 13.
71.   'Videotapes of Iranian films for export', *Mahnameh* 49, Ordibehesht 1366/1987, p. 1, English section.
72.   From a leaflet entitled 'Reconstruction Jehad – 1', put out in the early 1980s by the Moslem Student Association in the US and Canada. For more information on the ideology and operations of the Jehad, see the periodical *Jehad*, published in Tehran by the Jehad.

73. Markaz-e Amar-e Iran, *Salnameh-ye Amari-ye 1362* (Tehran, Vezarat-e Barnameh va Budjeh, 1363/1984), p. 723.
74. Hamid Naficy, *Iran Media Index* (Westport, Greenwood Press, 1984), pp. 190–220.
75. From Mas'ud Purmohammad, 'Ebteda sang-ha-ye kuchek', *Mahnameh* 64, Khordad 1367/1988, p. 8.
76. Iraj Karimi, 'In Nakoja-Abad kojast?' *Mahnameh* 72, Dey 1367/1988, pp. 52–4.
77. *Variety*, 16 August 1989.
78. 'Sarmaqaleh', *Faslnameh-ye Honar* 3, Spring–Summer 1362/1983, p. 16.
79. 'Basij-e emkanat-e jang dar khedmat-e jang', *Mahnameh* 37, Khordad 1365/1986, pp. 6–7.
80. 'How the war was reflected on screen', *Mahnameh* 72, Dey 1367/1988, p. 1, English section.
81. 'Sinema-ye Iran va Hafteh-ye Jang', *Mahnameh* 5, Shahrivar 1362/1983, pp. 4–5. For a similar analysis three years later, see 'Durbin dar jebheh va posht-e jebheh', *Mahnameh* 41, Mehr 1365/1986, pp. 6–7.
82. *Marahel-e Mokhtalef*, pp. 40–9.
83. 'Goftogu ba Homa Rusta, bazigar-e film', *Mahnameh* 58, Dey 1366/1987, p. 59.
84. Purmohammad, 'Ebteda sang-ha-ye kuchek', p. 8.
85. 'Honarpishegan-e zan az film hazf shodeh-and', *Kayhan* [London], 26 September 1985, p. 11.
86. Based on lengthy interviews with a prominent Iranian actress who wishes to remain anonymous.
87. 'Andar ahvalat-e filmi keh mojavvez-e shar'i nadasht', *Fowgholadeh* [Los Angeles], Mehr 1364/1985, p. 16.
88. 'Zan dar donya-ye honar hashiyeh-neshin ast', *Zan-e Ruz*, 18 Esfand 1362/1983, p. 33.
89. 'Aramesh dar hozur-e Hemingway', *Mahnameh* 60, Bahman 1366/1988, p. 59.
90. For example, in *The Weak Point* (Mohammad Reza Alami, 1983), the relationship between a political activist and the security agent who captures him displays strong but deeply ambiguous and incommensurate sexual undercurrents: the captive is treated as though he were a woman. The two engage in activities that are typical of the boy-meets-girl-falls-in-love formula films. They go to a park and play soccer with the kids, kicking the ball back and forth to each other like two lovers; at the beach they sit side by side and gaze at the horizon as a wild horse gallops by and an extradiegetic romantic music seals the scene in its romantic moment. During the course of the film the roles are reversed, with the captive assuming the masculine position.
91. For detailed historical, critical and theoretical analysis of the representation of women in post-revolutionary cinema and their aesthetics and politics, see my articles, 'Zan va "mas'aleh-ye zan" dar sinema-ye Iran ba'd az

enqelab', *Nimeye Digar* 14, Spring 1991, pp. 123–69; 'Zan va neshanehshenasi-ye hejab va negah dar sinema-ye Iran', *Iran Nameh* 9/3 , Summer 1991, pp. 411–26; 'Veiled visions/powerful presences: women in postrevolutionary Iranian cinema', in Mahnaz Afkhami and Erika Friedl (eds), *In the Eye of the Storm: Women in Postrevolutionary Iran* (London, I.B. Tauris, and New York, Syracuse University Press, 1994) pp. 131–50.

92.   The figures are for the first nine months of 1985. See 'Movafaqiyat-ha-ye eqtesadi va natayej-e keyfi'.

93.   *Natayej-e Amargiri az Hazineh va Daramad-e Khanevar-ha-ye Shahri Sal-e 1362* (Tehran, Markaz-e Amar-e Iran, 1363/1984), chart 3.7.

94.   Naficy, 'The development of an Islamic cinema', pp. 461–2.

95.   Author's interview with Barbod Taheri, September 1985, Los Angeles, CA.

96.   'Sinema-ye pas az enqelab, dar aghaz-e dahe-ye dovvom', *Mahnameh* 75, Nowruz 1368/1989, p. 73.

97.   'Sinema jozv-e zendegi-ye mardom shodeh-ast', *Mahnameh* 48, Nowruz 1366/1987, p. 73.

98.   'Khamene'i ba sinema mokhalef ast va Rafsanjani ba an movafeq', *Kayhan* [London], 30 May 1985, p. 2.

99.   'Ma agar sinema-ra az ja-ye khodesh kharej konim digar sinema nakhahim dasht', *Kayhan Hava'i*, 24 October 1984, p. 15.

100. 'Nazar-e Emam Khomeini dar bareh-ye film-ha, serial-ha, ahang-ha, va pakhsh-e barnameh-ha-ye varzeshi e'lam shod', *Kayhan Hava'i*, 30 December 1987, p. 3.

101. Interview with the author, Tehran, August 1991.

102. Hamid Naficy, 'Cultural dynamics of Iranian post-revolutionary film periodicals', *Iranian Studies* 25/3–4, 1992, pp. 67–73.

103. Jalal Khosrowshahi (ed.), *Baztab-e Sinema-ye Novin-e Iran dar Jahan* (Tehran, Entesharat-e Ghazal, 1370/1991), pp. 28–31.

104. The Statistics are from Robin Wright, 'Losing faith', *Los Angeles Times Magazine*, 25 April 1993.

105. *Mahnameh* 172, April 1995, p. 15.

106. *Mahnameh* 174, June 1995, pp. 24–25.

107. In the late 1990s, these periodicals included: *Asr-e Honar, Donya-ye Tasvir, Farhang va Sinema, Faslnameh-ye Sinema'i-ye Farabi, Film International, Film va Sinema, Gozaresh-e Film, Mahnameh-ye Sinema'i-ye Film, Setareh-ha, Sinema, Sinema va Video* and *Tasvir-e Ruz*. Almost all other general-purpose periodicals, even specialized journals such as those devoted to sports and women's issues, carry regular articles about cinema.

108. Judith Miller, 'Movies of Iran struggle for acceptance', *The New York Times*, 19 July 1992, p. H9.

109. *Toronto International Festival of Festivals Catalog* (4 September 1992), p. 8.

110. The largest festival of Iranian films was 'Life and Art: the New Iranian Cinema', at London's National Film Theatre, which screened over 50 films from 20 directors during June and July, 1999.

111. *Iran Times*, 25 May 1994, p. 1.
112. *Kayhan Hava'i*, 26 April 1995, p. 23.
113. *Kayhan Hava'i*, 19 July 1995, p. 15; *Kayhan Hava'i*, 26 July 1995, p. 15.
114. Scott Peterson, 'Reluctant nod to cultural shift: Iran eases ban on its own films', *Christian Science Monitor*, 23 December 1997.
115. 'Iran's President would privatize big industries', *The New York Times*, 16 September 1999, p. A13.
116. 'Sakht-e sad sinema ta payan-e emsal', *Mahnameh* 239, Shahrivar 1378/August 1999, p. 27.
117. 'Between rocks and hard places: the interstitial mode of production in exilic cinema', in Hamid Naficy (ed.), *Home, Exile, Homeland: Film, Media, and the Politics of Place* (London and New York, Routledge, 1999), pp. 125–47.
118. Hamid Naficy, 'Identity politics and Iranian exile music videos', *Iranian Studies* 31/1, Winter 1998, pp. 52–64.

3

Classic Tools, Original Goals: Cinema and Public Policy in the Islamic Republic of Iran (1979–97)

Agnès Devictor

Studying public intervention in cinema in the Islamic Republic of Iran (IRI) means looking at cinema from a certain angle, taking into consideration the production process and the regulations applied to the film industry, rather than the aesthetics of the films. This opens up a rich and significant perspective on how the Islamic regime actually operates.

To begin with, the mere existence of a state policy on cinema is not at all obvious; most countries do not have a comprehensive system for organizing their national cinema. In those countries where this does occur, the development of a state policy for cinema is supposedly intended to reinforce this sector, both as an industry and as an art. In these respects, Iranian policy might be regarded as an undisputed success. The proliferation of awards at international festivals and the wide critical and public acclaim for Iranian films – which were almost never distributed abroad under the previous regime – testify to the progress of the art of cinema in Iran. And the fact that Iran regularly ranks among the 12 major film producing countries[1] is evidence of the success of its economic support. As it happens, however, the main goal of the IRI's policy on cinema has been neither artistic nor economic, but rather the achievement of an ideological project.

In this chapter, I do not attempt a comprehensive overview of the IRI's public policy towards cinema – its rules, its operation and its evolution – but rather to summarize this state intervention, before pointing to similarities with public policies in other states. Predictably, some comparisons can be made with other revolutionary regimes, but within the limited frame of this chapter it seemed of greater interest to stress the more unexpected similarities with Western democratic regimes. Finally, I shall show the limits of such comparisons, due to the political structures and the ideology inherent in Iranian state interventions.

This comparative analysis – seldom attempted with reference to Iran – shows that the Islamic regime has managed to adapt to its specific needs certain classical tools of public cultural intervention.

State Intervention in the Film Industry in the IRI

When the Revolution broke out in 1979, observers and professionals of the film industry were worried about the future of cinema in Iran. Cinema theatres were burned down in the name of morality and cultural independence, the chain of production was completely disrupted by the exile of numerous directors, actors and producers, creativity was jeopardized by the uncertainty of what would be allowed or forbidden. Nevertheless, far from dying, Iranian cinema has become more active and lively than ever before.

The Aims of State Policy

As soon as Ayatollah Khomeini returned to Iran, he declared that the Islamic government was not against cinema itself, but against moral corruption (*fahsha*), which must be eliminated. According to him, only 'pure' cinema had a place in society.[2] Soon, the idea of an 'islamized cinema' was proposed, though without a precise definition of its form and content.

The goal of the cultural leaders was to create a new national style: a purified cinema from which 'immorality' would be erased, both in the making of the films and in the films themselves. Islamic morality must be respected in front of as well as behind the camera.

In order to fulfil these aims, the state had to intervene in two different but related fields: moral control and economic support. Indeed, purifying cinema meant, first of all, abandoning *film farsi*, a popular genre based on comedy, action and titillation which used to be the mainstay of the film industry.[3] The proscription of *film farsi* and the severe restrictions placed on the importation of foreign films led the cinema sector into a critical financial situation.

Even though some directors – such as Kimia'i – managed to continue working on their projects during the revolutionary era, they were in fact subject to unclear and unpredictable censorship, which had not yet been defined. This nebulous situation inhibited producers from investing in new and expensive projects.

In these disorganized circumstances, public intervention was necessary if the cultural rulers wanted to keep national film production within their own Islamic criteria. In fact it was only in 1982–4 that the first coherent measures were implemented, with the nomination of Mohammad Khatami to head the Ministry of Culture and Islamic Guidance (MCIG).

Institutions

In order to reorganize the film industry and to fulfil its targets, the state created a number of institutions, the main one being the Farabi Cinema Foundation (FCF), founded in 1983. This institution was not at first intended to produce films, but later, because of the weaknesses of the national industry, it involved itself in producing and co-producing films shaped by the ideology. Its first task was to take care of equipment, to support projects, and (until 1996) to deal with the monopoly of import and export of films. With Mohammad Beheshti as Director, FCF undeniably contributed to saving the national film industry. Another institution, Experimental Cinema (*sinema-ye tajrobeh*), was created in the same year as FCF to promote the young generation of the Revolution, and to give its members their first experience in cinema.

Religious foundations too began to deal with cinema, for example the Foundation of the Oppressed (*Bonyad-e Mostaz'afan*). Created by Khomeini in March 1979 as an independent institution, in practice this foundation has strong political and financial links with the state. Its initial task was to manage the equipment confiscated during the Revolution: it ran the largest number of cinemas in the country until the 1990s, when the cinemas were given to the Arts Centre of the Organization of Islamic Propaganda. It produced about seven feature films each year in the 1980s, including films with social backgrounds like *Talisman* (Daryush Farhang, 1986), *Out of Limits* (Rakhshan Bani-Etemad, 1988), *The Cyclist* (Mohsen Makhmalbaf, 1989) and *Wedding of the Blessed* (Makhmalbaf, 1989). Its production decreased during the 1990s.

Other public institutions were established during the Revolution, such as the Arts Centre (Howzeh-ye Honari) of the Islamic Propaganda Organization, which did not actually depend on the MCIG. The cinematographic department of the centre was particularly active in producing war films during the 1980s. Until the mid-80s, it tried also to produce a genre of propaganda films exalting the Islamic regime: among these were Makhmalbaf's first films: *Justification* (1981), *Nasuh's Repentance* (1982), *Two Sightless Eyes* (1983) and *Boycott* (1985). During the 1990s, the Arts Centre produced fewer war films and political films, preferring popular comedy and social dramas, which were sometimes far from expressing the ideology of the Revolution. Nevertheless, the Arts Centre played an active role in public film production.

As in many other countries, TV became an important film producer. The National Iranian TV (IRIB) produces films and TV series through a special production company, Sima Film. Apart from popular productions, TV also produces *auteur* films, such as those of Abolfazl Jalili, which were all forbidden until Khatami's election as president. IRIB represented an 'orthodox' institution, linked to the Supreme Leader. As for the Arts Centre, its films are not subject to MCIG censorship, but self-censorship imposes a high degree of control over all its production.

One pre-revolutionary public producer continues to work: the famous Centre for Intellectual Development of Children and Adolescents (*Kanun-e Parvaresh-e Fekri-ye Kudakan va Nowjavanan*). The Kanun was created by Queen Farah, and its Department of Cinema, opened in the late 1960s, was directed by Ebrahim Foruzesh and Abbas Kiarostami. It was a very active producer not only of films for children, but also of *auteur* films. Most famous Iranian directors worked with the Kanun between the 1970s and the 1990s, among them Bahram Beyza'i, Daryush Mehrju'i and Amir Naderi. It did not close during the Revolution, but its production declined in the 1990s.

This public institutionalization did not lead to the collapse of the private sector. Very few private companies were able to survive and continue to operate after the Revolution – as Pakhsh-e Iran Film did – but, little by little, a network of private producers has grown in the 1990s, to number around 60 companies by 1999.

The state could have nationalized the film industry completely, or left the responsibility for production to the private sector, while still remaining in charge of censorship. To achieve its aims, however, the state decided to involve itself in the cinema industry.

Regulations

After the Revolution, cinema became a highly regulated sector, in which the state strictly controlled the entire industry. Professionals have often asked their cultural masters to clarify their needs, their wishes and the limits not to be transgressed, and they have repeatedly protested at the vagueness and lack of clarity in the censorship rules, so as to avoid becoming their target.

Censorship regulations are of course the most explicit examples of coercive state interventionism. Censorship has always existed, though the authorities did not specify what was permitted and what was forbidden until 1984. Before that, professionals were conscious that censorship was concerned with the 'Islamic norm': male–female relationships, behaviour, and the image of women...but again, nothing was clarified. Then, almost every year between 1984 and 1997, a booklet of regulations concerning the production, distribution and screening of films was published. The 1996 booklet[4] is the most detailed as to what is forbidden: it is not allowed for women to be filmed in close-up, to use makeup, to wear tight-fitting or colourful clothes; men must not wear ties or short-sleeved shirts unless they are negative characters; no Western music is allowed, no intimate lighting; even the editing must correspond to the Islamic norm. These regulations have already been the subject of numerous articles.[5]

Before it can be completed, a film must go through several stages of control, which lead to long delays. The producer is responsible to the state for his project. First he must submit the project to preliminary censorship; if passed, it goes back and forth between the censorship office and the producer in order to get each single detail checked and agreed upon: names of production personnel and actors, costumes, makeup, different locations, etc. Until at least 1997, unofficial control was implemented during the shoot to ensure that the Islamic norm was strictly observed. Once finished, the film must of course be shown to a commission, for the final award of the censor's certificate. This process could last up to two years, and the regulations might change during this period, which might lead, in the end, to the banning of a film which was originally approved. Following Khatami's election as president in May 1997, censorship became less stringent.

Ownership of cinemas and screenings of films are highly regulated. Films and cinemas are classified under different categories, in order to determine in which theatres a film will be shown and for how long. Ticket prices are linked to this categorization. Every year the MCIG publishes a calendar announcing the release of films; a film can be disadvantaged by release in a bad period for film-going, such as the Islamic lunar month of Moharram. The theatre itself is highly controlled, from the colour of the attendants' clothes to the safety regulations to the temperature and lighting of the auditorium.

Even though it would often be much more profitable to turn a cinema into shops or restaurants, the owner in theory has no right to sell it, in the interest of preserving a place of culture.

Professional regulations have become more and more precise and detailed with the creation in 1993 of the House of Cinema (*Khaneh-ye Sinema*), a corporate body which organizes the profession according to the directives of the MCIG. For example, it issues the professional licences needed to work officially in the cinema sector, according to a number of conditions: a director's card is issued after two engagements as first assistant in Iran, and so on.

IRI Cinema Policy Compared to State Interventions Elsewhere

Although they were established in a very specific political and cultural frame, the post-revolutionary Iranian state's interventions in the cinema sector can be compared, to a certain extent, with cinema regulations observed in other places and at other times.

Puritan Censorship

The rules implemented by the IRI can be compared with the Hays Code implemented in the US in the 1930s by the studios, not by the state.[6] Of course, the US code sprang from an intensification of conservative power which was totally different from the context of post-revolutionary Iran, but as in Iran, the content of the Hays Code was the expression of a strict control of films. In the US, too, relationships between men and women, and what women wore, were strictly controlled; the depiction of a man and woman in the same bed was equally strictly forbidden. This led to comparable tricks in the script to bypass the effects of the regulations.

Subsidy: 'Advance on Profit' ('l'Avance sur Recette')

The subsidy system was created in 1959 in France in order to support national production.[7] Subsidies were awarded after an examination of the project or after completion of the film. The Islamic Republic implemented a similar financial intervention for a while. In Iran, as in France, this sum had to be reimbursed after a certain level of box-office success. Low-interest loans specially reserved for film production existed in Iran as well as in France.

The House of Cinema and the Centre National de la Cinématographie

The House of Cinema was created in 1993 to fill the task performed by the Centre National de la Cinématographie (CNC)[8] in France: organizing, regulating and sharing responsibility with Parliament and the Ministry of Culture for elaborating rules for the cinema sector. The House of Cinema assesses the needs of the profession, makes rules and regulations to a lesser extent, and protects the social and professional rights of people involved in cinema. It is the place where all the professional associations gather, an intermediate body between the state and the professionals. Like the CNC, the House of Cinema represents a corporate state organization, and it allows the state to have a certain control over the entire profession. Less successful and less efficient than the CNC, the House of Cinema has implemented rules and regulations very similar to those concerning the issue of professional licences mentioned above.

Protectionism: 'Cultural Exception' in Iranian Style

Iranian cinema executives sometimes use the example of the 'French cultural exception'[9] to justify protectionist or even isolationist measures. On an ideological level, the Iranian measures exist to confront the 'cultural invasion' and the 'Western imperialistic cinema which spreads corrupted values'. The MCIG strictly controls every single imported film and censors every scene considered 'sensual' (kisses, hugs, low-cut dresses etc.). On an economic level, the national market has to be similarly protected, in order to preserve a specific national creation.

With the opening of cinematic frontiers, Iranian producers will have to reconsider their production strategy, and the government, if it does not want to see the death of Iranian production, will have to consider a quota system.

Cinema and Political Debate

Since the 1930s, cinema has been an issue at stake in the political life of France,[10] as has been the case in Iran since the Revolution. These two countries are perhaps the only cases of such a mobilization of politicians on this issue, because of the importance of cinema in public life. Let us look at two cases from Iran: first that of Davud Mirbaqeri's *The Snowman* (1994/97), then the turmoil surrounding Kiarostami's 1997 Palme d'Or, both of which illustrates the stakes in the 1997 presidential campaign.

The Snowman crisis between 1995 and 1997 showed both the consequences of the dual power structure in the IRI and the activism in the public sector of an informal group, the Ansar-e Hezbollah. *The Snowman* was a feature film produced by a public institution, the Arts Centre. It tells the story of an Iranian man in Istanbul trying to get a visa for the US. After several rejections from the US embassy, he has no choice but to dress up as a woman and try to get married to an American. This popular comedy does not exactly correspond to Islamic standards, and includes taboo subjects such as an actor playing a female part and dressing as an attractive woman, the suicide of a Muslim woman and the presence of *film farsi* characters. Such a film was possible because Arts Centre productions do not need MCIG permits, and do not even go through pre-censorship. Nevertheless, in 1995, Mostafa Mir-Salim, the Minister of Culture and Islamic Guidance, refused to allow the distribution of *The Snowman* and threatened to close the Arts Centre film theatre if the film were shown. The Minister even threatened to resign over this incident. But Supreme Leader Khamene'i officially declared that he was not opposed to the film. The film became an issue in the struggle between public cultural institutions. The situation changed only after the political changes of May 1997: Ataollah Mohajerani, the new Minister of Culture, authorized the screening of the film. Then the Ansar-e Hezbollah protested against the screening,[11] condemning the film as counter-revolutionary; they organized demonstrations against it, causing violence and arrests. Finally, after the Ministry of Culture strongly supported the screening, *The Snowman* became a great popular success.

When Kiarostami's film *The Taste of Cherry* (1997) was selected for the Cannes Film Festival, the Iranian authorities refused to send a copy, on the pretext that it had not been screened during the Fajr Film Festival

2. Abbas Kiarostami's *The Taste of Cherry*.

in Tehran in February 1997. At the beginning of May, Ali Akbar Nateq-
Nuri, Speaker of the Islamic parliament and favourite candidate for the
presidential elections, criticized the sending of Iranian films to Western
festivals and accused some Iranian directors of working for Westerners.
Then, during the election, Kiarostami was awarded the Palme d'Or, the
highest honour in the film world. As he accepted the award, he was
kissed (on the cheek) by the famous French actress Catherine Deneuve.
This was enough for the director's opponents and cultural conservatives
in Iran to condemn Kiarostami and his film. For a while the affair
fuelled political debate in this highly volatile period. Some of Khatami's
supporters congratulated the director and asked for a national reception,
whereas some supporters of Nateq-Nuri demanded that the film be banned.

These are only two examples among others of the place occupied by
cinema in political life. As in France, it is not uncommon for cinema to be
part of political debate in parliament and in other political arenas.

Limits of the Comparison

Our aim in this chapter has been to underline common points between
the policy of the IRI and that of some other countries. Marked differences
concerning ideology and administrative and political structures delimit
the boundaries of this comparison.

The Structure of the Regime

The structure of government in the IRI calls for new analytical frames for studying policy towards cinema. The very existence of both a Supreme Guide of the Revolution and a President of the Republic, and their consequences for the entire administrative organization, defy classical analysis.[12] In the case of cinema policy, this structure leads to the existence of an institution such as the MCIG, which does not have authority over all cinematographic production in the country. MCIG censorship does not affect films produced by institutions such as the Arts Centre and the national TV network, which have their own censorship bodies. This is a unique situation internationally, because these two institutions depend on the Supreme Leader, while the MCIG depends on the President, so that there actually is no single body responsible for censorship. This same division of responsibilities and jurisdiction exists in other areas of cinema: import–export, choice of main themes, choice of directors and so on.

Similar Machinery but Different Ideology

Having pointed to similarities between the machinery of state intervention in Iran and that of countries such as France, we must bear in mind that the ideologies behind them are profoundly different. For example, to mention again the comparison of the advance on profits, the machinery for state funding in Iran differs sharply in its motivation from the French example. In Iran the 'moral' and political guarantees of the director, producer and technical staff matter more than a well-defined project or a good-quality script. The policy of the Iranian state towards cinema has been to promote a generation of directors who are products of the war and the Islamic Republic, a generation dedicated to projecting on the screen an image of the Islamic society that the Revolution should have brought. The goal is not to show a bright future, but to show a strict respect for Islamic behaviour and a society in which no moral corruption can exist. The machinery may be comparable, but the underlying ideology is completely different.

Notes on Chapter 3

1.   Iran, producing at least 60 feature films per year, now stands in an eminent position in the world of cinema. Between 1995 and 1997, annual production figures (excluding international co-productions) for the Middle East and Europe are as follows: Egypt produces fewer than 20 feature films, Syria around 2 films, Iraq none; Portugal – ranked highly for cinematic creativity – produces 12 films, Germany 52 and Great Britain 65.

2.   On the purification process, see Naficy's chapter in this volume.

3.   See Jamsheed Akrami, 'Feature films', *Encyclopædia Iranica* 5 (1991), p. 574; Farrokh Gaffary, 'History of cinema in Persia', *Encyclopædia Iranica* 5 (1991), pp. 567–72.

4.   *Siyasat-ha va Ravesh-ha-ye Ejra'i-ye Towlid, Towzi' va Namayesh-e Film-ha-ye Sinema'i 1375/1995* (Tehran, MCIG, 1374/1996).

5.   For example, in *Iran Nameh* 14/3, Summer 1996.

6.   Richard S. Randall, *Censorship of the Movies: The Social and Political Control of a Mass Medium* (Madison, University of Wisconsin Press, 1970); see also Anne-Marie Bidaud, *Hollywood et le Rêve Américain* (Paris, Masson, 1997).

7.   Jean-Michel Frodon, *L'age moderne du cinéma français* (Paris, Flammarion, 1995), pp. 135–50.

8.   *Textes du cinéma français* (Paris, CNC, 1996); see also René Bonnel, *La vingt-cinquième image* (Paris, Gallimard/FEMIS, 1994).

9.   Joëlle Farchy, *La fin de l'exception culturelle?* (Paris, Éditions du CNRS, 1999).

10.   Pierre Billard, *L'age classique du cinéma français* (Paris, Flammarion, 1995), pp. 177–95.

11.   *Shalamcheh* 22, Dey 1376/1998.

12.   Asghar Schirazi, *The Constitution of Iran: Politics and the State in the Islamic Republic* (London and New York, I.B. Tauris, 1997); see also Said Amir Arjomand (ed.), *Authority and Political Culture in Shi'ism* (Albany, State University of New York Press, 1988).

4

The Crisis in the Iranian Film Industry and the Role of Government[1]

Hossein Ghazian

The Problem

In the two decades following the Islamic Revolution, the Iranian film industry has been entangled in a continual economic crisis, despite its artistic achievements on the international scene. This crisis is caused by the Iranian public's poor reception of the films: most films have not broken even at home. The root of the crisis is inefficient marketing mechanisms, influenced by the state's ideological and economic interference, which increased during the 1990s, thus aggravating the crisis. As a result of this series of government interventions, the supply and demand equilibrium has been violated: production fails to match demand. This failure is not, however, limited to the film industry; the political arena in Iran suffers from the same weakness. The presidential elections of May 1997, and the coming to office of Seyyed Mohammad Khatami, reduced this deficiency – momentarily, at least – in the political arena. The cultural scene, however, and especially the film industry, has yet to undergo any fundamental change.

77

Background

Iranian cinema has achieved remarkable artistic success in the 1980s and 1990s, as measured by the numbers of awards at international film festivals; in 1997–8 alone, Iranian films won over 100 awards. However, by the important – and linked – standards of industry and media, Iranian cinema has not been successful.

The economic crisis in Iranian cinema is an obvious index of its failure by industrial and media standards that indicate little domestic interest. In fact, Iranian cinema has been experiencing a severe economic crisis for at least two decades. From the mid-1970s, when it was threatened by the influx of foreign films into the country, to the late 1990s, when the public's inclination towards foreign films continued despite an abundance of restrictions, the economic crisis has persisted.

As this crisis has persisted, so interpretations of it have proliferated; one of the few points on which most Iranian filmmakers and analysts are unanimously agreed is the prevalence of the crisis. The state's financial and monetary aid to the Iranian film industry has so far concealed the gravity and depth of the crisis and prevented an explosion. Ironically, this aid itself has aggravated the crisis, since it has been accompanied by ideological and political interference and a failure to appreciate the changes in the social structure of Iran over the past two decades. Consequently, it has brought about major disruptions in the marketing mechanisms of Iranian cinema.

What is the Crisis?

Simply put, the crisis in the Iranian film industry is that sales of most films are not even able to cover production and marketing costs. Even though between 40 and 50 feature films are produced in Iran every year, the number of filmgoers has fallen, to the extent that by the mid-1990s each Iranian went to the cinema on average 0.79 times a year.[2]

Then again, certain films produced in the same period managed to take over a million dollars at the box office.[3] Many others took over half a million dollars. In the second half of the 1990s the budget required to produce a film in Iran averaged US$90,000; half a million dollars in box-office receipts would indicate a warmly received financial success. This success has been, nevertheless, relative and sporadic, and has not continued. Moreover, it is limited to only a small number of Iranian films. As a result, most producers are caught in the economic crisis, as they have not managed to cover costs.[4] In actuality, the Iranian film industry is suffering severe economic hardship.

What is the Mechanism of the Crisis?

To explain the economic–media crisis of the industry, the adoption of a 'market model' can be useful. This model demonstrates how the relationship between the quality and quantity of demand and of supply has been disconnected, and how this disconnection has led to a disruption in the processes of 'pricing' and 'allocation'.

To understand the disruption and inefficiency of the film market inside Iran, it is necessary briefly to review the development of the demand and supply sides since the Revolution.

Developments within the Social Structure

Several developments of varying importance have taken place in the social structure which relate to demand.[5] Some of these developments have led to an increase in the rate and variety of demand for cultural products in general and for film in particular.

The population of Iran increased from 33.7 million in 1976 to over 60 million in 1996, a 78 per cent increase. Supposing that the potential demand rate for films remained the same, a 78 per cent increase in population should mean at least a 78 per cent increase in demand.

In the same period, the population of Iranian cities grew by 133 per cent, a higher rate than the population as a whole. In 1976 there was only one city in Iran with a population of over 4 million; 20 years later, there were five such cities, accounting for 32 per cent of the total urban population of the country. Considering that cinema-going is a feature of city life and that cities are sources of variety and plurality, one can guess to what extent these developments have brought about an increase and variety of demand for films.

From 1976 to 1996, the population in the 13–19 age group grew by 102 per cent, and that in the 15–25 group grew by 91 per cent – a faster rate than the population as a whole. Iranian youth are enthusiastic about cinema, consequently the increasing youth numbers should indicate a quantitative increase in demand for films.

Literacy has grown at an accelerated pace throughout the country. In the late 1970s, less than half the population were literate; 20 years later, 79 per cent were able to read and write. The growth of literacy among women and villagers has been faster than among men and city-dwellers: for women it has been 1.2 times faster than that of the population in general. Besides the expansion of literacy, the trend for higher education is also increasing. In 1996 there were 1.2 million students in Iran, a 790 per cent growth from 1976. The promotion and spread of education leads to both a quantitative increase in demand for cultural products and an increase in the variety of demand for such products, including films.

The trend in Iran is towards the establishment of nuclear families. In the last two decades, average household size has decreased from 5.0 to 4.8. More importantly, the numbers of small, three- and four-member families have increased by 224 per cent, compared to larger, six- and seven-member families, which have increased by only 69 and 54 per cent respectively. This structural change has brought changes in family activities. One such change, relevant to the topic of this chapter, is that some recreational and spare-time activities that previously took place within the family have been transferred outside the home to public places. This includes cinemas, which are institutions for responding to the public's cultural demands.

There have been extensive movements of population. Apart from a rise in the rate of rural–urban migration in Iran, and immigration from abroad, large numbers of Iranians emigrated after the Revolution. Accurate statistics concerning the numbers of Iranians resident abroad are not available; the important point is that many Iranian emigrants, especially those who left Iran on social grounds, are not completely disconnected from their homeland. Their temporary or permanent return to the country, and visits to and from their relatives, bring a transmission of needs, desires, models and ultimately different cultural demands. These changes have eventually led to a greater variety of demand for cultural products such as films.

The position of the 'new family' in relation to the fields of education, employment and politics is analogous to the position of the private arena in relation to the public. Accordingly, the increase in women's public participation in society in the last two decades has been considerable. The most significant index of this trend is the fall in the percentage of women housewives, from 69 per cent in 1976 to 55 per cent in 1996. This trend is, however, uneven: women's presence in education is very strong, but their rate of employment is very low, and falling. Not only have women acquired literacy faster than average, the number of female university students has increased 2.8 times as fast as the general growth in student numbers. The result of women's increasing public participation is not only a quantitative growth of demand for the cultural products that have recently entered the market, but also a growing variety of demand for these products.

These developments signify that the potential demand for films in the last two decades has increased in quantity, quality and variety. The prime element in the establishment of an industrial production line, the necessary demand, has thus grown in the 20-year period. Moreover, that demand has also increased in variety, so that a range of different products have had the opportunity to hit the market.

Developments in Film Production

On the supply side, developments in film production must be considered. Some conventional trends may be observed in this respect, although all elements put together demonstrate the existence of a crisis on this side of the Iranian film industry too.

Film production in the last two decades has fluctuated, but the average number of films produced per million people has generally decreased.

Table 4.1: Film Production Trends and Population[6]

Year	Population (millions)	Number of films produced	Number of films per million of population	Index
1976	34	56	1.7	100
1986	59	48	1.0	59
1991	59	47	0.8	47
1996	60	58*	1.0	59

(* based on 1995 record)

Table 4.1 shows that the index of film production per million people has fallen from a base of 100 in 1976 to 59 in 1996, a 41 per cent decrease. The actual number of films produced has actually increased, though unevenly – from a low of 40 in 1985 to 56 in 1993, as shown in Table 4.2. Ironically, the ratio of filmgoers to films produced has fallen in these years, from a base of 100 in 1985 to 72 in 1993.

Table 4.2: Film Production Related to Numbers of Filmgoers[7]

Year	Number of films produced	Index of films produced	Number of filmgoers (tickets sold)	Index of number of filmgoers	Index of filmgoers: films produced
1985	40	100	75,050,879	100	100
1986	48	120	78,259,135	104	87
1987	48	120	80,304,222	107	89
1988	42	105	76,868,546	103	97
1989	49	123	80,525,435	107	87
1990	42	105	81,131,958	108	103
1991	47	118	66,634,644	89	75
1992	46	115	54,030,745	72	63
1993	56	140	53,809,150	72	51

Despite the fall in the numbers of filmgoers and the consequent increasing financial losses – the costs of film production have risen constantly, sometimes dramatically – the number of films produced is increasing. Naturally, these losses are made up through resources other than the film industry itself, that is state support. As stated earlier, this support has of course been coupled with increasing control and monitoring of films, which leads to the accommodation of these films to the state's ideological policies, and hence to a distancing from the market's natural demands and requirements. The result of this gap between the natural demands of the market and the ideological obligations of the state is shown in the general public's decreasing interest in going to the cinema. This is why the index of the number of filmgoers compared to the number of films produced is falling faster (a decrease of 49 per cent) than the index of the number of filmgoers in the population (a decrease of 28 per cent).

State control and support are the key to understanding the aforementioned conflicting trends, and demonstrate that, on the supply side, the quantity of films produced has decreased per person and that what has been produced does not match existing market demand.

Why Does the Crisis Persist?

As stated earlier, the origin of the crisis is due to the disruption of the natural equilibrium between the demand and supply sides of the film market. The crisis has persisted as a result of this continuing disruption. This vicious cycle has been aggravated by the ever-increasing scope of state interference in the supply and demand market for films. The state has acted as a filter, 'purifying' the viewers' demands, distinguishing 'good' demands from 'bad' ones and allowing only the 'good' demands to reach the supply side. Obviously, this interference has distorted the natural demand in such a way that film production is not compatible with public demand. Accordingly, the films produced only reflect that part of society's demands which has been approved by the state.

The Islamic Republic of Iran has very openly displayed its strong will to control the market for cultural products. This controlling tendency is based on three different factors: the state's existential origins, which are considered a complete revolution, the state's ideology, which manifests more or less strong totalitarian roots, and the state's legal structure, which is represented in the Constitution.

It seems that the state's determination to control culture strengthened in the 1990s. This can be considered a reaction to the decline of the state's charismatic and traditional legitimacy during the decade. The consequence of these circumstances is the constant increase and expansion of supply control in the Iranian film industry. Following the Revolution, the state began its monitoring policies by controlling the import of foreign films into Iran, which resulted in almost no foreign films being screened in cinemas; meanwhile it extensively censored the films produced domestically. This censorship went well beyond the screening stage; screenplay, production and even marketing previews and trailers had to be approved. Furthermore, state censorship had both negative and positive aspects, in that the prevalence of censorship, which marked the state's determination to control films more seriously, totally disrupted the supply and demand balance and hence the natural process of pricing and allocation in the Iranian cinema market. Consequently, the only films produced were those that had survived the state screening procedures, that is those which comprised the 'good' demand category. It goes without saying that many demands did not enjoy a suitable supply in this market; the viewers' general lack of interest in films shown led to a fall in box-office receipts and continued financial losses. The state extended its economic support to this deteriorating cinema only on cultural grounds, thus postponing its financial death; this postponement allowed the crisis to linger.

Prospects for the Crisis

In the conflict between the supply and demand sides, the most important element is that the pressure of social reality has overcome the state's control, removing its efficiency in practice. This control mechanism has not only failed to monitor and organize the market, it has led to a strengthening of the market for foreign films. The events of 1997 to 1999 in Iran indicate that the pressure of reality on the political arena – represented symbolically in the presidential elections of May 1997 – eventually seriously weakened the state's interference in the political scene. Khatami's landslide victory was in reality a surrender of the polity to grassroots demands seeking policies, measures and persons that had not been available previously. In other words, the political arena surrendered to the logic of the demand market, hence diverting attention from the crisis, at least temporarily. Nevertheless, the cultural crisis – including that of the Iranian film industry – has not developed in accordance with the political scene. Following the establishment of the new government, the pressure of demand for cultural freedom, especially in cinema, has increased. The state's control policies, on the other hand, are being removed more slowly than people's growing expectations. The development and promotion of the Iranian film industry can only come about when the state's control policies have been seriously decreased. If the state does not reduce its control mechanism to match its decreasing economic power and growing public expectations of civil society, the eventual collapse of the Iranian film industry is a serious possibility.

Notes on Chapter 4

1.   Translated from Persian by Hamid Marashi.
2.   *Iran Statistics Almanac for March 21 1995 to March 20 1996* (Tehran, Iran Statistics Center, 1996).
3.   M. Mohseni *et al.*, *A Study of Sociopolitical Knowledge, Attitudes and Practice in Iran* (Tehran, Fundamental Research Center of the Ministry of Islamic Guidance and Culture, 1997). This figure was reported to be about 72 per cent in the mid-1970s; see A. Assadi *et al.*, *Cultural Trends and Social Attitudes in Iran* (Tehran, Faculty of Media Studies and Development of Iran, 1974).
4.   According to the regulations of a film's revenue distributor, almost 35 per cent of the box-office receipts of a film's first performance, excluding marketing and advertising costs, belong to the producer(s).

5.   These data are extracted from the censuses of 1976 and 1997

6.   Population figures are extracted from *Population Indices of Iran 1956–1996* (Tehran, Iran Statistics Center, 1998). Films produced in 1976 extracted from M. Zamaninia, *A Dictionary of Iranian Cinema and Six Articles on Cinema* (Tehran, Adineh, 1984). Films produced in 1986, extracted from G. Heydari, *Filmography of Iran (1979–1986)* (Tehran, Bureau of Cultural Research and Iran National Film Library, 1992). Films produced in 1992, extracted from *Iran Statistics Almanac for March 21, 1995 to March 20, 1996* (Tehran, Iran Statistics Center, 1996).

7.   Films produced in 1985 and 1986, extracted from G. Heydari, *op. cit.* Films produced between 1987 and 1990, extracted from G. Heydari, *Filmography of Iran (1987–1990)* (Tehran, Bureau of Cultural Research, 1992). Films produced between 1991 and 1993, extracted from *Iran Statistics Almanac for March 21, 1995 to March 20, 1996*. Numbers of film-goers extracted from H. Honarkar, 'The roots of the economic crisis in the Iranian film industry', *Naqd-e Sinema* 5 (1996), p. 22.

Perspectives on Recent (International Acclaim for) Iranian Cinema[1]

Azadeh Farahmand

Introduction

International film festivals, in their tradition of creating an alternative and contentious outlet for non-commercial cinemas, have a reputation for discovering and introducing non-American and non-European directors to the world. For example, the recognition gained by Akira Kurosawa and Satyajit Ray through the Cannes Film Festival in the 1950s brought both filmmakers national and international reputations which also helped invigorate the international attention paid to the cinemas of Japan and India. In the 1990s, the festival acclaim of a handful of Iranian filmmakers, most significantly Abbas Kiarostami's 1997 Palme d'Or at Cannes, helped put a stamp of approval on Iranian cinema. By virtue of the ensuing festival approbation in the last decade, Kiarostami has jumped in status from a moderately known director of short films and documentaries within Iran to an esteemed international celebrity, praised by the renowned French New Wave veteran Jean-Luc Godard, and compared to well-known figures of world cinema such as Kurosawa and Ray. This chapter offers perspectives on the complex mechanisms that have contributed to the increasing attention that Iranian films and filmmakers, Kiarostami in particular, have gained in recent years. Rather than focusing on such filmmakers as *auteurs*, however, I employ here a non-romantic approach that examines how socio-economic factors and institutional politics contribute to the elevation of films, filmmakers and national cinemas to the level of high art.

The international presence of Iranian cinema has increased during the 1990s. This phenomenon is related to the ongoing and escalating economic crisis that has led to the deterioration of local filmmaking in Iran. Amidst this crisis, international markets have become viable arenas for increasing film revenue and supplementing the likelihood of future production funding for just a small proportion of Iranian filmmakers. On the other hand, since the end of the Iran–Iraq war in 1988, which allowed cinema to become a priority for state consideration, Iranian cinema has been rediscovered as a promising means through which to renegotiate the imagery of the nation, and gradually to reclaim a place for the country within the global economy in the name of art.[2]

In this chapter, 'recent Iranian cinema' is defined as a sub-category of the post-revolutionary cinema of Iran. It refers to films that have gained exhibition, reception and special attention outside Iran since the late 1980s, and therefore reflect and refract international as well as national concerns.[3] In what follows, I sketch a brief history of film censorship in Iran, and discuss economic challenges to filmmakers exacerbated or eased through state interventions, in order to highlight the context which partially situates the fates of film and filmmaking in Iran. I suggest that this cinema is realized in a web of relations between international and Iranian national politics, and I explore the impact and implications of film festivals as venues for the commercial success and critical attention gained by films. I argue that Iranian films' entrance in and accolades at international festivals both reflect and produce a set of concerns that gradually and retroactively affect the film production and distribution process. I also explore and suggest historical reasons for the particular appeal of Kiarostami's films beyond Iran's national boundaries. My methodological scheme benefits from, but is not limited to, an industrial model, which considers the films in relation to different stages that interactively affect the cinematic product – namely financing, production, distribution and exhibition. In this case, the model is complicated, as the national perspective is linked to an international one.

Censorship: a Sustaining and Struggling Legacy

While Iranian cinema has undergone inevitable changes since the 1979 Revolution, it has inherited and maintained the legacy of state control. Film censorship has a long tradition in Iran. Jamshid Akrami states that the first attempts at censorship as early as the 1920s were aimed at film exhibition, with theatre owners succumbing to the pressure of religious groups worried about Iranians' exposure to Western morals and to the overt sexuality displayed in imported films.[4] Later there were efforts to institutionalize, professionalize and legitimize film censorship by delegating to municipalities and governmental agencies the task of establishing censorship rules and guidelines. In 1950, a committee was assigned to draft regulations for the revision and supervision of films that were either imported or locally produced. This committee was composed of the police chief and representatives from the Ministries of Internal Affairs and Culture as well as the Department of Publications and Broadcasting. When SAVAK was formed in the mid-1950s, some of its members were added to this committee. The committee issued and adopted a 15-part edict forbidding, among other things, themes that were subversive to Islam and Shi'ism, instigated opposition to monarchy and the royal family, depicted victorious revolts in prisons, or portrayed illicit affairs with married women, the seduction of girls or women in the nude.[5]

In 1968, the task of film supervision was relocated to the Ministry of Culture and Arts, which added a few measures to the 15-part edict, elaborating on forbidden themes that were critical of the monarchy.[6] These regulations resulted in the outright banning of certain imported 'revolutionary' films, such as Pontecorvo's *Battle of Algiers* (1965), Costa-Gavras's *Z* (1969) and Guzman's *Battle of Chile* (1976), and in the manipulation of other films through dubbing, cutting, and even re-editing to conform to 'acceptable' criteria. In the late 1960s and early 1970s, a time of governmental pride in national prosperity and political success, the Shah's regime, wishing to project a positive image of Iran and anguished about films depicting the country's poverty, delayed the exhibition of Daryush Mehrju'i's *The Cow* (1968) and banned his *The Cycle* (1975) and Amir Naderi's *Elegy* (1975).

After the Revolution, censorship criteria remained in force, with the exception of those concerning films portraying poverty during the Shah's regime, revolt and the toppling of Western-style governments. Thus, films such as *Z*, *The Battle of Algiers* and *The Cow* were now screened in theatres and even celebrated. Meanwhile, attempts to promote Islamic morals and to prevent themes profaning the mandates of Islam proliferated. The post-1979 government continued to apply the tradition of dubbing, cutting, re-editing and banning of films inherited from the previous era, and combined this with such practices as painting over imported films which showed parts of women's bodies that should be covered according to Islamic religious codes.

The pre- and post-revolutionary governments displayed a similar concern to suppress themes of political criticism and social dissent, a continuity that demonstrates how ruling governments recognize the power of cinema. Each regime, therefore, attempted to regulate the medium in accordance with their own ideological framework. Naficy relates a telling story, indicating how the attitudes of the two governments with respect to cinema were essentially two sides of the same coin:

> In March 1983, when new-wave filmmaker Bahman Farmanara returned to Iran after an absence of four years, he was prevented from leaving the country again. His powerfully allegorical film, *Tall Shadows of the Wind* (1978), had been banned by the Forbidden Acts Bureau, and he was accused of making anti-Islamic films. Farmanara commented, 'Ironically, both the Shah's and the Islamic regime interpreted the scarecrow, which in the film terrorizes a village, as symbolizing their own rule and tried to ban it.'[7]

Following any revolution, the new government understandably needs time to stabilize itself and to solidify its grip on areas of cultural production, particularly those that can reach millions of viewers. This was indeed true of Iran after the 1979 Revolution. It is also worth emphasizing that the fate of any nation's filmmaking tradition is affected both by the degree of censorship that occurs throughout the filmmaking process and by the control of the means of production and exhibition permits; difficulties are exacerbated if this control is handled by, or tied to, the same agencies that implement censorship. Although film production in Iran went through a period of stagnation in the first five years following the Revolution, not all changes were detrimental to local film production. Indeed, after 1984, measures were drafted to encourage it. More positive developments included social security for filmmakers and entertainers, a decrease in municipal tax on local films and a tax increase on foreign films, long-term bank loans for film production and the sponsorship of films in international film festivals.[8] However, while measures were implemented to facilitate local film production, there remained – and still remains – the heavy spectre of state control through a bureaucratic labyrinth that filmmakers must negotiate.

Houshang Golmakani, editor of Iran's *Film Monthly*, summarizes the preliminary stages of production oversight that had been adopted by the early 1980s: From its inception, a film had to go through the Council of Screenplay Vetting, so that the filmmaker could attain approval of the synopsis. The next step was to go through the Council for Screenplay Inspection, which gave a green or a red light to the project. Until 1989, after approval of the screenplay, the filmmaker was required to obtain production permits that listed cast and crew, to get approval of the finished work, and to retain exhibition permits that would specify the theatres in which the film was to be shown.[9] If a script was stopped early on in the process, an alternative route was through the Farabi Cinema Foundation (FCF). Consolidated in 1983 as the executive arm of the Deputy for Cinema Affairs of the Ministry of Culture and Islamic Guidance (MCIG), the FCF would discuss the problems and offer practical solutions for preparing the script to pass review by the Council for Screenplay Inspection.[10] It is noteworthy that, in addition to this mediating role, FCF has expanded its authority to become the most powerful agency in regard to local film production and distribution. It exerts considerable control over obtaining and allocating production equipment and raw stock. FCF also monopolizes the acquisition of rights for imported films. It plays important roles in issuing loans and subsidies for local projects, as well as in the export and submission of films to international film festivals and markets.

In 1989, the necessity for script approval in the preliminary stages of film production was removed. It was soon replaced, however, by new requirements in pre-production that subjected the fate of a filmmaker's project to a rating of his previous work. A director whose previous film had been given a 'C' grade needed both script and synopsis approval, a director who had made a 'B' grade film needed synopsis approval only, and a director with an 'A' grade film needed neither. This form of rating system, initiated through FCF under the leadership of Mohammad Beheshti and implemented in 1987, ranked finished products according to three loosely defined categories of content, aesthetics and technical aspects. The rank a film received would determine access to commercial advertisement, ticket prices and the duration and location of the film's public screening. The system later evolved to include viewers' ratings of the script, actor, director, producer, cinematographer etc., which were polled during the annual Fajr Film Festival, and which both the management at FCF and the deputy for cinema affairs considered the final verdict.[11]

In 1993, however, a pre-approved script once again became mandatory for all film projects seeking a production permit.[12] In more recent years, even though censorship seems to have intermittently loosened its grip or undergone changes, the ideological expectations of filmmakers and the dependence of their careers on state agencies have not lessened. As Naficy suggests, the relaxation of censorship standards in 1989 was indicative not only of the government's self-assurance and sense that now it could afford to open up cultural discourses, but also of its confidence that finally its ideological demands and Islamic values had been sufficiently inculcated.[13] A question worth raising here is whether the removal of a step in ideological control entails, let alone guarantees, more freedom of expression. Naficy thus points to a trend of increasing self-censorship.

Mohammad Beheshti, who served as the managing director of FCF until 1995, refers to controversial and sensitive social issues as 'circles of perturbation'. If a filmmaker wants to touch upon matters relating to 'circles of perturbation', then s/he inevitably has to take sides. Alluding to the dangers and risks involved in touching on sensitive subjects, Beheshti exclaims, 'Are filmmakers prepared to go under the spotlight? If they are, they can go ahead and make films on controversial subjects.' Of course the question remains: will the film be released? With respect to social criticism as the subject matter of films, Beheshti adds,

> Criticism is not forbidden; there are transgressors in all walks of life … But when a filmmaker introduces a miscreant, a police officer, or a teacher, let us say, it has to be clear whether he is criticizing an individual or the system as a whole. If the latter, then he must be stopped.[14]

Thus, given the high cost of film production and the highly subjective process of identifying political allusions and interpreting subjects as 'circles of perturbation' – which can in turn provoke more rigorous control over the works of artists during both production and exhibition – many filmmakers choose to avoid controversial themes entirely. In other words, filmmakers have been led to refrain from making confrontational and socially critical films for fear of being held accountable for making anti-system or anti-establishment statements through their work. This repressive situation fosters self-censorship in ways that become additional impediments to the creative activity and critical expression of filmmakers. Bahram Beyza'i, whose filmmaking career spans decades of experience with both pre- and post-revolutionary governments, speaks of the predicament of the Iranian filmmaker who must compromise in order to make films: 'Stopping the filmmaking process means the bankruptcy of those involved in production, stopping the distribution means having to endure the heavy burden of loans, and resistance means witnessing your entire future career melting away.'[15]

Two further points concerning censorship are worth emphasizing. First, while this discussion centres around cinema in Iran, it does not presume that censorship is a phenomenon particular to Iran or other non-European and non-American countries.[16] Comparisons between national cinemas, however, may lead to the pitfall of justifying a particular characteristic in one in light of its presence in the other. A comparison between Iran and the US, for example, tends to disregard the two countries' incomparable differences, justifying the flaw in one because it also exists in the other. Still, comparative studies can be compelling if they account for differences and lead to constructive criticism. For example, one may note that censorship in US cinema was institutionalized and enforced for about three decades – from the early 1930s with the founding of the Production Code Administration (Hays Code) to the mid-1960s, when the code was replaced by the Motion Picture Association of America Rating System. Although these changes did not completely eliminate censorship from the institutional structure of the US film industry, it was no longer maintained in any official capacity.[17] In contrast, censorship in the Iranian cinema has existed in one form or another from as early as the 1920s, having survived both monarchy and theocracy. Still, a study of how the Hays office denied its seal of approval to films that did not meet its moral criteria, or case studies of US film directors and scriptwriters who lost their careers, were blacklisted, or were exiled from the US during the Hollywood 'red scare' and the McCarthy era, could provide comparative grounds to appreciate the conditions of anxiety, struggle and compromise with which some filmmakers in Iran have been grappling.

Secondly, by foregrounding self-censorship as a problematic consequence of state control in Iranian cinema, I am not suggesting that creative activity and critical expression are only possible in the absence of (self-)censorship, nor do I hold it to be the duty of filmmakers to be politically conscious and openly critical of society in their work. Tight circumstances often have the ironic blessing of further motivating artists to invent indirect means of expressing their ideas and creatively to seek metaphors and allusions. This, however, does not mean that censorship is good because it makes artists more creative.[18] A discussion of creativity under censorship should be accompanied by an emphasis on its inherently repressive logic. Furthermore, filmmakers may wish not to deal with politically or socially sensitive matters in their work, regardless of the presence or absence of censors. However, because filmmaking is an expensive art and depends on the support of either the private or the public sector, it can often be caught in a situation in which filmmakers are led to avoid sensitive subjects if their careers are to survive.

Restrictions and Outlets: International Film Festivals

An implicit hypothesis of the preceding section is that developments within recent Iranian cinema show a continuity with, as well as a transition from, both the pre- and the post-revolutionary years of cinematic production. A separate and extended scrutiny of the history of film censorship in Iran may well eventually indicate that, although compliance with the Shi'ite ideology has been an ever-present censorial concern since the inception of cinema in Iran, this concern has been interwoven with – if not subordinated to – the ruling political pragmatism of the time. My discussion in this section will situate Iranian cinema in a web of global economic and political relations, and will delineate how recent developments in filmmaking in Iran relate to the festival phenomenon.

Golmakani mentions that 1991 was announced as the last year of cheap film production in Iran, as subsidies were to be removed by 1992–3. Film production showed a 40 per cent increase in 1991 over the previous year, and then decreased. The average production cost of a film jumped from six million rials in 1990 to forty million in 1998. With the bleak prospect of inflation, higher production costs and less government support, Iranian filmmakers increasingly considered using international markets mediated through film festivals. The problem is that Iranian filmmakers cannot independently submit their work to international festivals and film companies. This task is handled by Iran's public and private sectors through the ultimate authority of FCF, which is under the umbrella of the MCIG. As Ahmad Talebi-Nezhad notes, FCF's thriving promotional outreach caused the annual international screen appearances of Iranian films to jump from an average of 35 between 1979 and 1988, to 88 in 1989 and 377 in 1990.[19] With a slight drop in the two subsequent years, the international appearances of Iranian films reached 429 in 1994 and 744 in 1995.[20] After a decline to 640 in 1996, the figure rose once more in 1997, to 766.[21] In 1999, this annual presence reached a high of 849, compared to 616 in 1998.[22]

The international popularity of Iranian films resulting from their festival screenings has not only brought an expanded market for film exhibition and therefore a higher financial return for filmmakers, but has also increased the chance of foreign investment in local film production. In Kiarostami's case, for example, the popularity among French cinéastes of his *Where is the Friend's House?* (1987) enabled him to make his subsequent films with partial or full French financial support.

Mojdeh Famili, an Iranian journalist who writes for the French media, reports that several French production and distribution companies, such as MK2 and CB2000, have shown interest in the (co-)production, promotion and exhibition of Iranian films. Because of inflation and the drop in the value of the rial, investment in Iranian films by European companies has indeed proved rather lucrative. For example, the funds that MK2 put into Mohsen Makhmalbaf's *Gabbeh* (1996), which would have been enough to make a 15-minute film in France, produced a feature film which has been exhibited worldwide, to which MK2 now owns the rights.[23] Thus, while European festival programmers and film distributors can pride themselves on the discovery of other cinemas, they have also benefited from the cultural and economic returns of the films they promote. This point demystifies film festivals as the profit motive driving them is brought to the foreground. Several people associated with European film festivals visit Iran's annual Fajr Film Festival in order to choose films to screen in international festivals. Some of them have direct involvement with production or distribution companies, hence tying their production or distribution interests to the publicity and support films and film projects gain through festivals.

A telling example is Marco Muller, who from 1991 to 2000 headed the Locarno International Film Festival, where the 1988 screening of *Where is the Friend's House?* brought the film five prizes including the Bronze Leopard and initiated the escalation in the presence of Iranian films abroad. Muller has co-financed over 100 films; his first production was with the Chinese director, Zhang Yuan, who won the Best Director Award at the 56th Venice Film Festival, a festival in which Muller served as a consultant from 1981 to 1992. Muller also supervises Fabrica Cinema, a Benetton-backed production company created in 1998 which co-produces films taking part in European film festivals. He co-produced Samira Makhmalbaf's *Blackboard* (1999), which competed for the Palme d'Or in the 2000 Cannes Film Festival and won the Jury Prize.

The growing attention given to Iranian cinema in the West must also be linked to recent attempts to develop diplomatic ties and promote cultural exchange between Iran and the West. Cultural exchange can prove a neutral ground and therefore a suitable first step to embark on further diplomatic relations, one which may often demand subtle and yet key interventions. A controversy emerged, for example, around the curious admission to the 1997 Cannes Film Festival of Kiarostami's *The Taste of Cherry* (1997), which was banned in Iran and initially barred from entering the festival. Although the film missed the entry deadline for official competition, it was shipped to France at the last minute and allowed to be shown with other competing entries, eventually sharing the Palme d'Or with Shohei Imamura's *The Eel* (1997). According to *Gozaresh-e Film*, the Iranian foreign minister, Ali Akbar Velayati, came to realize that the film's presence at Cannes would have a good impact outside Iran. He therefore mediated its entry in the festival through negotiation with Gilles Jacob, the festival director.[24]

A historical parallel is worth noting here. In 1971, a US table-tennis team visited China. Soon after, Henry Kissinger, Richard Nixon's security advisor, travelled to Beijing for a secret meeting. What became known as 'ping-pong diplomacy' paved the way for the normalization of relations between the US and China, which lasted until 1979. While Iran and the US may still have many issues to resolve before achieving a similar rapprochement, this parallel is worth contemplating in light of a sample of recent diplomatic and cultural activities.[25] Kiarostami's *The Taste of Cherry* won the Palme d'Or at Cannes in 1997, the year that Khatami was elected Iran's president, his image as a moderate leader circulating in the Western media. In 1998, the Iranian soccer team played the US team at the World Cup in France, and a former US hostage met his Iranian captor in Paris. That was also the year when US wrestlers visited Iran amidst the most hospitable of environments, and when Khatami spoke before the UN, calling for cultural exchange, dialogue and people-to-people relationships between Iran and the West. In 1999, Majid Majidi's *Children of Heaven* (1998), the first Iranian film finally to be allowed to enter competition for the American Academy Awards, was one of five nominees for Best Foreign Film. It is noteworthy that only two years earlier, *The White Balloon* (Jafar Panahi, 1995), which by 1999 had the highest commercial gross among Iranian films in distribution in the US, was pulled out of official competition in the Academy Awards at the request of Iranian authorities.

The recent activities of the Search For Common Ground (SFCG) provide a striking example of an organized negotiation between Iran and the West through cinema. SFCG, founded in 1984 in Washington DC, co-operates with the European Centre for Common Ground; it has devised and implemented extensive policies and programmes aimed at the resolution of conflict and a call for dialogue, understanding and cultural exchange between Iran and the West. In conjunction with the Gulf 2000 project, SFCG organized a meeting to plan the 'US–Iran Cinema Exchange' that took place in Cannes in 1998. On 25 May 1998, following the conclusion of the Cannes Film Festival, a group composed of film industry professionals from the US and Iran met to 'share information and discuss potential co-operative cinematic projects'.

According to the report,

> Participants agreed that film can be a powerful and effective means to bridge differences and increase cultural understanding between Iran and the US. Participants recognized that American and Iranian film festivals and programs have, for years, showed films and invited film personalities from each other's countries. What is new is that a window of opportunity is now open, making possible cinema activities of much higher impact.[26]

The meeting resulted in the following agreements: American participants and a US film personality to attend the Iranian National Film Day in September; Iranian Women's Delegation to attend film events in New York and Chicago; young Iranian filmmakers to be featured at the Sundance Film Festival in January 1999; a high-profile US delegation to attend the Fajr Film Festival in February 1999; the range of filmmakers and films available for exchange and festivals to be extended; film student exchanges to be promoted; co-productions; entry visas for both countries' film personalities to be facilitated.[27]

With the collaboration of Iran's House of Cinema, SFCG arranged a second meeting of Iranian and US film personalities in Cannes and Antibes in May 1999. In a series of meetings, conversations were held about possible joint projects and other co-operative efforts, some of which reflect attempts to ease inter-cultural tension and negative public opinion. For example, there was discussion of a blueprint for co-production of a film about the life story of Howard Baskerville, an American Princeton graduate who visits Iran for missionary purposes in the early twentieth century, but ends up fighting on the constitutionalist side against the Qajar Shah and finally dies a 'martyr'. According to the SFCG report, 'it was thought that a film about this *American Lafayette*, who gave his life for revolution in Iran, would shatter stereotypes'.[28] In a business meeting, the idea of an exchange of documentaries was also discussed, in which

> [it] was felt that an Iranian documentary on a subject such as Islamic customs in America might make a positive public statement in Iran. In addition, Iranian participants suggested that American documentaries about values and religion would be well-received in Iran.[29]

Points agreed through the 1999 US–Iran cinema contact included the activation of a finger-printing waiver for SFCG programme participants travelling to the US; the exchange of US and Iranian directors to participate in their respective film programmes; an increase in the participation of Iranian filmmakers in US film festivals; the facilitation of timely invitations of US film personalities to the Fajr Film Festival in Tehran; a visit to Iran of a major Hollywood star; an exchange of film critics; negotiations on the possibility of the US building multiplex theatres and an IMAX planetarium-style theatre in Iran. The prospect of donating state-of-the-art equipment to Iran was also raised, as were ideas such as seeking an exemption from the trade embargo and arranging for equipment donations from a third party, possibly Japan.[30]

SFCG no longer perceived the necessity of a third meeting in 2000, as enough relations had already been established; in March 2000 Madeleine Albright announced the lifting of the ban on imports of Iranian carpets, pistachios and caviar, apologizing to Iran for past interventions. While the exchanges over cinema cannot be considered the cause of these political manoeuvres, they are certainly symptoms of a need, or simply timely tools, for easing tension and bringing Iran–US contact to the surface through this 'neutral' and 'cultured' medium.

In linking the new attention paid towards Iranian cinema to the recent escalation of diplomatic ties and economic negotiations between Iran and other countries, particularly the US, I am neither denigrating the artistic merit of the films that are sent to festivals, nor suggesting that Iranian directors have much of a say in the initiation of these policies, though this may be the case. Rather, I emphasize that, in the midst of utmost economic hardship and cultural anguish, filmmakers may resort to different means of resisting challenges and surmounting obstacles to their filmmaking careers. It is also necessary to point out that, while cinema can be used to facilitate circumventions of the economic embargo, and to replace the Iranian image of the US as 'Great Satan' with one as patriotic fighter, or the American image of Iran as hostage-takers with one as humanists and artists, the cinematic activities of only a handful of filmmakers may prove to be useful in this venture. In sum, only a select few have their films endorsed for entry in international film festivals, and are showered with publicity and honoured with retrospectives which tour the world, while others whose work is equally compelling are excluded.

The Iranian media themselves have been open to raising such questions and concerns. For example, a short report in *Film International*, a quarterly

Iranian publication in English, noted that the 16th Turin International Film Festival in November 1998 screened Samira Makhmalbaf's *The Apple* (1998) and hosted the distinguished actor Fatemeh Motamed-Aria as a jury member. The report added, however, that Beyza'i's attendance at the Festival as a jury member had been cancelled for unknown reasons. Furthermore, it also stated that the festival director, Alberto Barbera, who, for a 'second successive year' had announced a film retrospective of Beyza'i, for which brochures had been printed and distributed at the Cannes Film Festival, cancelled it for an obliquely stated reason – he had 'failed to collect copies of Bayzai's films'.[31]

Similarly, *Gozaresh-e Film* published a piece on the controversy about the incomplete screening of *Tales of Kish* (1999), an Iranian entry in the 1999 Cannes Film Festival. The film was about Kish Island, with episodes by several different directors: Beyza'i, Mohsen Makhmalbaf, Naser Taqva'i and Abolfazl Jalili. Beyza'i's episode (*Dialogue with Wind*) was omitted from the finished film when it arrived at Cannes.[32] Included in this article is an open letter by Farmanara to festival director Gilles Jacob, who gave the unsatisfactory explanation that Beyza'i's episode did not cohere in spirit with the film as a whole. In his letter, Farmanara encouraged Jacob to resign because of this 'big embarrassment' for the prestigious festival. He also condemned the 'disrespect shown to Iranian cinema', stating that it would have been better if Kiarostami had written this letter and returned the festival award which he had received in 1997.[33]

In a Long-shot: Recent Iranian Cinema and Abbas Kiarostami

In the 1990s, Kiarostami and his films came to epitomize recent Iranian cinema. But he is certainly not the only filmmaker to have placed Iranian cinema on the international map: the films of directors Ebrahim Golestan, Beyza'i, Sohrab Shahid-Saless and Mehrju'i were recognized and applauded in international film festivals during the 1960s and 1970s. However, the recognition that Kiarostami has received outside Iran since the late 1980s through festival circuits, articles, anthologies and TV programmes far exceeds that of the others, making his position unique and worth special study.[34] Kiarostami's image oscillates between that of a celebrated director of the new Iranian cinema and an *auteur* in the arena of world cinema.

The picture painted here is intended to historicize and problematize aesthetic values and to subject them to critical consideration. My discussion aims to situate Kiarostami's highly regarded works within a broader context. Here, I will recount some of the key characteristics of his cinematic texts which reflect and comment on this very context in unique ways. Kiarostami's involvement with the Centre for Intellectual Development of Children and Adolescents since the beginning of his career as filmmaker partially explains his attention to subjects relating to children. His focus is mainly limited to children of the urban middle and lower classes and to rural children. In his later films, his thematic concerns extend to other villagers, the disaster-stricken and people on the outskirts of urban settings. In the light of the unspoken rules of censorship previously discussed, these subjects indicate a rather safe genre that would allow both local and international distribution.

Kiarostami's films bypass the most highly censorable themes, such as political or social criticism; as for the portrayal of women, he simply avoids the issue, by using only a few female characters. As mentioned earlier, filmmakers tend to avoid 'circles of perturbation'; consequently their films, simplistically put, are either apolitical or propagandist. However, as Talebi-Nezhad indicates, past experience has shown that pro-IRI propaganda films have little chance of success in film festivals.[35] This gives a filmmaker with an eye on the international market an additional reason to avoid sensitive subjects. In other words, the political escapism in Kiarostami's films is a facilitating, rather than a debilitating, choice, one which caters to the film festival taste for high art and restrained politics.

The state's imposition of 'Islamic' dress codes and restrictions on women's screen appearances does, however, make the production of Iranian films with women on screen an extremely challenging task. To conform to these restrictions, besides wearing *hejab* women should not look attractive or appear in colourful clothes, nor should there be close-ups of their faces.[36] Despite the strong pressure to limit the roles that women can play and the ways in which they can appear in front of the camera, the implementation of these conventions on the screen has to a large extent been naturalized. For example, while highly unrealistic in the real world, the on-screen veiled appearance of a woman in front of her family, at home and even in the bedroom, is understandable to the Iranian viewer. Yet, to a non-Iranian, this could indicate the backwardness of Iranian society and repressive, 'fundamentalist' rules of behaviour. Ironically, village women are less subject to this constraint than their urban sisters, as there have been fewer restrictions on their cinematic appearance and representation in traditional colourful costumes.

Additionally, village themes and location shooting in rural landscapes not only take viewers away from urban politics, but also reinforce the exotic look of Iranian films – and increase their marketability abroad.

It is little surprise, therefore, that the subjects of Kiarostami's films are mainly children or men, and that the few women who do appear are either villagers (*Where is the Friend's House?*, *The Wind Will Carry Us*, 1999) or older women (*Close-Up*, 1989). An exception is *Through the Olive Trees* (1994) in which, in addition to village women, there is also a woman production assistant in the film, who plays an arguably but problematically strong role. In his construction of female roles, Kiarostami keeps conservatively in line with the religious belief that allocates a marginal position and a subordinate gender role to women. Female roles in his films are depicted either as over-sentimental and therefore blameworthy (the absent mother in *Homework*, 1987), or as cold, aggressive, unaffectionate and thus tolerable (*Through the Olive Trees*). This exclusionary approach is also reflected in the almost total absence of women in *The Taste of Cherry*, and in Kiarostami's substitution of a male teacher in *Where is the Friend's House?* for the kind and compassionate female teacher in the book upon which the film is based.[37] In *The Wind Will Carry Us*, several village women appear, but the film offers a dichotomous characterization of city and village women. The absent wife and the female producer of the 'engineer' in charge of the funeral shooting expedition both make impatient phone calls that are unnecessary and comically troubling. The nuisance of these absent urban women is thus set against the exoticism of village women, rendered through their mysterious silence, outspoken wisdom and magically maternal and resilient struggles in life.

A structural composition common in Kiarostami's filmic style is the insertion of a mediating character through whom the viewer disavows an equal exchange and a compassionate involvement with others in the film. This makes Kiarostami a yet more powerful figure for the Western intellectual and the distant observer. The closest the viewer comes to the subjects (children, villagers, labourers, the disaster-stricken) is sympathy, not identification. There are scarcely any point-of-view shots of these characters in Kiarostami's films. Identifying with Kiarostami's middle*man*, the viewer becomes a detached observer, looking at his subjects as a cold and frightening authority figure (*Homework*), an inspector (*Close-Up*), a journalist/filmmaker (*And Life Goes On*), an interested and yet disengaged anthropologist/director (*Through the Olive Trees*), an Iranian version of the *flâneur*, shopping for a gravedigger (*The Taste of Cherry*) and a tourist/

reporter peeping into holes and caves while awaiting a woman's death (*The Wind Will Carry Us*). The viewer is thus protected from any shock, unpleasant encounter or guilty conscience. He can maintain his distance and remain uninvolved, be fascinated, securely appreciative of the exotic locales, as though viewing an oriental rug, whose history he does not need to untangle.

Sixteen years before *Where is the Friend's House?* the ingenious Sohrab Shahid-Saless made *A Simple Event* (1972), an unpretentious depiction of events in the life of a poor schoolboy, for whom the undramatized death of his mother is yet another 'simple event'. While it was screened and gained awards at international film festivals, *A Simple Event* was relatively unappreciated inside Iran. The film did not get a public screening, and it enjoyed little promotional and commercial success beyond festival circuits in Europe. Yet the resemblances between Shahid-Saless's and Kiarostami's films in subject matter, style, pace and even mise-en-scène, are striking. Shahid-Saless's film career did not flourish in Iran because the historical moment was not then ripe to appreciate and promote his original personal vision. Further, unlike Kiarostami's work, *A Simple Event* discloses a critical glance at society through an innovative cinematic language that was daringly combative towards the commercial ambience of filmmaking dominant in Iran at the time. It is nothing less than tragic that Shahid-Saless died in exile, his remarkable abilities left more obscured than promoted or appreciated; it is equally unfortunate that an exquisite writer, researcher and filmmaker such as Beyza'i, who chooses to remain in Iran, has found his career impeded at home. The uncompromising creator of *A Simple Event*, rather than engaging in consensual self-censorship, chose the route of self-exile, in search of another land and culture that would appreciate his art and vision. Ironically, a quarter of a century after *A Simple Event*, Kiarostami's *Where is the Friend's House?* has continued to earn international fame, awe and envy, as well as a flourishing filmmaking career for its director.

Concluding Remarks

In 1997, the new Minister of Culture and Islamic Guidance, Ataollah Mohajerani, and the new Deputy Minister for Cinema Affairs, Seyfollah Dad, made improvements in cinema affairs that distinguished them as liberal policy-makers compared to their predecessors. These measures

3. Rakhshan Bani-Etemad's *The May Lady.*

included issuing exhibition permits for a few previously banned films, and loosening censorship criteria. In 1998, the bans on Ali Hatami's *Haji Washington* (1982), Abolfazl Jalili's *Dance of Dust* (1992), Mehrju'i's *Lady* (1992) and Davud Mir-Baqeri's *The Snowman* (1994) were lifted. Nevertheless, negotiating with censors remains an unending battle for the Iranian filmmaker. Rakhshan Bani-Etemad completed her *The May Lady* (1998) in Iran and received a screening permit, in spite of the fact that the film included medium close-ups of her lead actress, who was playing a single mother and a documentary filmmaker, and that it showed brief exchanges of touch between the mother and her teenage son. Nevertheless, *Rain and the Native* (1999), her contribution to the *Stories of Kish* collection, did not receive a screening permit and was therefore not included with the other episodes, because the adolescent actress's hair was not properly covered by her veil throughout the film. The complex and evolving phenomenon of censorship demands a separate and more extensive discussion to untangle its inconsistent application as well as its hidden politics of marketability. It is worth mentioning that restrictions have occasionally encouraged the desire for products. A film that has gone through contro-versy, red stamp and cuts may well, once released, draw more of the curious public to the theatres.

The recent recognition gained by Iranian cinema has overshadowed the remarkable Iranian film tradition of the past, and ignores the current crisis facing the industry. This crisis involves issues such as the ongoing battle with censorship, the scarcity of film theatres compared to the high rate of local film production, deteriorating acoustic and optical conditions in the theatres, low box-office returns, a continuing surge in production costs and a rating system that obstructs, among other things, channels of communication between films and Iranian audiences. Besides condemning lower-rated films to less popular cinemas and lower ticket prices, the rating system sharply decreases the annual government support allocated to films according to their script rating. These regulations result in lower financial returns for the producers, damaging the filmmakers' careers.[38]

In the midst of this artistic battlefield and economic chaos, festival recognition and support from international distribution and production companies provide some hope for filmmakers. However, exported films still find it difficult to be subversive of the hegemony of Iranian society when they must also cater to festival tastes and strive to be commercially viable for international companies and markets interested in Iranian products. The sudden turn towards export of films is additionally related to Iran's shift in foreign policy, its need openly to incorporate foreign investment and to become 'visible' and positively present(ed) in the world arena. This policy shift is embraced by the Western countries, particularly the US with its decades-old interest in Iran.

The consequences of this increasing international presence are many: the popularity of Iranian films has not only brought an expanded market for film exhibition and therefore an increase in financial return for film-makers, but it has also expanded the chance of foreign investment in local film production. Besides, investment in Iranian cinema is lucrative because of the low value of Iranian currency. However, international financial support entails consequences that problematize the national address or the popular appeal of the film in terms of its local reception. For example, MK2, the French co-producer of Kiarostami's *The Wind Will Carry Us*, did not allow the film to be screened in Iran before the 1999 Venice Film Festival, where it won him the Grand Prix. Not surprisingly, the internationally adored Iranian *auteur* is not popular in his home country, where he is commonly suspected of 'making films for foreigners'. This situation underscores the problem of maintaining the 'nationalness' of a national cinema in the context of its trans-national accessibility. Further, certain filmmaking formulas are unreflectively adopted to aim for international success. Recent reviews in Iran, for example, accuse different filmmakers of making 'Kiarostami-style films', albeit more often than not unsuccessfully.

This chapter has merely touched the tip of the iceberg in linking recent Iranian cinema to its reception in the West, and in highlighting the relations between history, politics, economics and cinema via the crossroads of international film festivals. The phenomenon of the new Iranian cinema needs to be re-viewed in a complex historical and cultural context that takes into account the flow of globalized capital, economic and expressive challenges to filmmakers exasperated or eased through local interventions, (inter)national policies and diplomacy, and the impact and implication of film festivals as venues for the commercial success and critical attention gained by films. In conclusion, this study aims to prompt further research and critical debate on topics such as the contradictory politics of film festivals, the festivals' impact in welcoming films with sanitized politics, the practice of local banning of films as a promotional play to encourage the film's admission to film festivals abroad, the tension and relation between a national and an independent cinema, and finally conflicts and overlaps between the ways in which exported cinema and films made merely for local consumption each represent the nation.

Notes on Chapter 5

1.   I wish to thank Ziba Mir-Hosseini and Richard Tapper for inviting me to the Iranian Cinema Conference in London in July 1999, where I read an earlier draft of this chapter. Their constructive criticism assisted me in preparing the present version. I greatly appreciate the supportive faculty and staff at UCLA, in particular Vivian Sobchack for her inspiration and encouragement and Chon Noriega and Zareh Arevshatian for their useful remarks and suggestions. I am particularly indebted to Vivian Sobchack and Vincent Brook for superlative editing assistance.

2.   See Hamid Reza Sadr's chapter, which deals with the emerging representation of children to alter social stereotypes and create new ideals. Of interest here would be a comparison between the selection, abundance and reception of these 'children films', made not for children but about children for adults, in international markets and film festivals, and the extent of their presence and reception in Iran. The images that run through films such as *The White Balloon, The Apple, The Mirror* (Panahi, 1998), *Children of Heaven* and *The Color of Paradise* (Majidi, 1999) are informed by sentimentality and an obsessive romance with children's supposed innocence, purity and beauty. This trend, emerging prominently in the 1990s, has replaced the representation of resilient child characters in films made during or before the Iran–Iraq war, such as Naderi's *Harmonica* (in this case before the Revolution, in

1974), *The Runner* (1986) and *Water, Wind, Earth* (1989), and Beyza'i's *Bashu, The Little Stranger* (1986). In these films, children show a strong and proud presence, fighting and surviving the injustices of their surroundings. Compared to the purified prototypes of children in later films, these earlier children represent a synthesis of aggressiveness and innocence, the adult world and the child's, as well as vulnerability and pride. This contemporary shift should be linked to the emerging post-war desire to renegotiate an image of Iranian society and to counter militant revolutionary stereotypes of Iranians through representations of children.

3.   My definition here relates to but differs from Hamid Naficy's distinction of two main film trends in the Iranian cinema: a state-sponsored and ideologically defined cinema on the one hand, and a popular cinema concerned with contemporaneous social issues on the other hand (see his chapter in this volume). In a paper presented at the 1999 Society for Cinema Studies conference, I responded to this dual characterization by calling attention to and arguing for a (third) trend of filmmaking – that of making art films targeted towards festival reception.

4.   Jamshid Akrami, 'Qeychi-ha-ye tiz dar dast-ha-ye kur', *Iran Nameh* 14/3, Summer 1996, p. 459.

5.   Houshang Golmakani, 'New times, same problems', *Index on Censorship* 3, 1992, pp. 20–1.

6.   Akrami, 'Qeychi-ha', p. 461.

7.   Naficy, this volume, p. 34.

8.   Naficy, this volume, p. 40.

9.   Naficy, this volume, p. 39.

10.   Golmakani, 'New times, same problems', p. 19.

11.   'Goft-o-gu ba Mohammad Mehdi Dadgu dar bareh-ye seyr-e darejeh-bandi-ye keyfi-ye film-ha az aghaz ta emruz', *Mahnameh-ye Sinema'i-ye Film* (henceforth *Mahnameh*) 223, Summer 1377/1998, pp. 52–7.

12.   'Darajeh-bandi dar yek negah', *Mahnameh* 223, Summer 1377/1998, pp. 58–9.

13.   Naficy, this volume, p. 39.

14.   Golmakani, 'New times, same problems', p. 21.

15.   Bahram Beyza'i, 'Pas az sad sal', *Iran Nameh* 14/3, Summer 1996, p. 377. My translation.

16.   See Agnès Devictor's chapter for a comparison of censorship in the US during the administration of the Hays office and the implementation of the Production Codes with the institutionalized control of the Iranian cinema since the Revolution.

17.   Although censorship in Hollywood cinema was at its peak for three decades, many historians and theorists have documented, discussed and openly criticized the profound and far-reaching effect it had on US cinema and have examined the commercial censorship that continues to this day. See for example Gregory Black, *Hollywood Censored: Morality Codes,*

Catholics and the Movies (New York, Cambridge University Press, 1994); Richard Corliss, 'The legion of decency', *Film Comment*, Summer 1969, pp. 24–61; Charles Lyons, *Movies and the Culture Wars* (Philadelphia, Temple University Press, 1997); Alice Goldfarb Marquis, *Hope and Ashes: The Birth of Modern Times* (New York, Free Press, 1986); Frank Walsh, *Sin and Censorship: The Catholic Church and the Motion Picture Industry* (New Haven, Yale University Press, 1996).

18.　Mohsen Makhmalbaf's *A Time to Love* (1991) is a good example, illustrating the possibility of creative expression in spite of censorship, and distinguishing censorship from self-censorship. Instead of explicitly showing sexual attraction or love-making scenes, Makhmalbaf creates powerful moments of erotic contact in two episodes of the film, the story of a love affair between a married woman and her lover told in three versions. In the first version, they are in a carriage together, their scarves entangled in the wind, inter-cut with a close-up tracking shot of horses' feet running. In the second version, the woman and her lover are in the claustrophobic environment of a bus, and a medium close-up of the woman looking is juxtaposed with her point-of-view shot of the man squeezing the juice out of a lemon in his hands. These creative moments in the film – alluding indirectly to sexual contact or erotic desire – may be traced to the self-censorship embedded in the text, though it is equally true that these choices could have been made regardless of censorship. Nevertheless, the film was banned – i.e. censored – in Iran, because it dealt with illicit extra-marital affairs.

19.　*Dar Hozur-e Sinema: Tarikh-e Tahlili-ye Sinema-ye Ba'd az Enqelab* (Tehran, Farabi Publications, 1998) pp. 105–6.

20.　Mohsen Beig-Agha, 'Deep waters: Iranian Cinema 1995 in the market place', *Film International* 4/1–2, Winter 1996, p. 110.

21.　'Merry go round: the award it won in 1996', *Film International* 5/1, Summer 1997, p. 36; Mohammad Atebbai, 'Iranian films and international scene in 1997', *Film International* 5/3–4, Spring 1998, p. 17. The decline in 1996 is linked to changes within the government institutions in charge of cinema affairs after Beheshti's resignation in 1995. Beheshti is known for his allegiance to Mohammad Khatami, the liberal-minded Minister of Culture and Islamic Guidance, until his own resignation in 1992. Ali Reza Shoja Noori, who worked under Beheshti, has been credited with fostering the presence of Iranian films in international film festivals and distribution markets until he resigned and moved to Sima Film after Mohammad Rajabi came to power. See Talebi-Nezhad's last chapter of *Dar Hozur-e Sinema* for a brief sketch of recent changes in the leadership of the Iranian cinema industry. For an attempt to link tensions within cinema to those within political factions in the Islamic Republic, see Sussan Siavoshi, 'Cultural politics and the Islamic Republic: cinema and book publishing', *International J. Middle Eastern Studies* 29, 1997, pp. 509–30.

22. 'Sinema-ye Iran va arse-ha-ye beinolmellali dar 1999', *Mahnameh* 247, 1999, p. 26.

23. Mojdeh Famili, 'Esteqbal-e faransavian az sinema-ye mo'aser-e iran', *Iran Nameh* 14/3, Summer 1996, pp. 427–8.

24. 'Ta'm-e shirin-e gilas: Cannes 1997', *Gozaresh-e Film* 92, 1997, pp. 68–84.

25. The comparison is also made by Thomas Omstead, among others: 'Wrestling with Tehran: U.S., Iran go to the mat in a replay of ping-pong diplomacy (Pres. Muhammad Khatami's attempt to thaw US-Iranian relations through sports exchanges)', *U.S. News & World Report* 124/8, 2 March 1998, pp. 44–6.

26. 'Report of the Planning Meeting on US-Iran Cinema Exchanges' (Cannes, France, 25 May 1998): http://www.sfcg.org/iran/Exchanges/Arts%20&%20Literature/report_of_1998_cannes_meeting2.htm.

27. 'Iranian cinema today: Irano-American contacts, but in cinema', *Film International* 6/1, Summer 1998, p. 6.

28. See SFCG website: http://www.sfcg.org/iran/Exchanges/Arts%20&%20Literature/report_of_1999_cannes_meeting2.htm (9/22/99).

29. *Ibid.*

30. *Ibid.*

31. 'Turin Festival without Bayzai', *Film International* 6/2, Fall 1998, p. 9.

32. *Tales of Kish* was originally planned with episodes by six directors, including Rakhshan Bani-Etemad and Daryush Mehrju'i. Beyza'i was the first to finish his segment, whereas Mehrju'i's was not completed by the time the film was to screen in the annual Fajr Film Festival – the mediating road to a film's entry to the local exhibition market and international film festivals. Bani-Etemad's episode was not included for reasons mentioned below. Thus, in a meeting in the presence of the film's producer and production manager, a consensus was eventually reached to consider the four episodes by Beyza'i, Makhmalbaf, Taqva'i and Jalili as the complete *Tales of Kish* which could eventually enter festivals.

33. 'Che kasi janjal-e jashnvareh-ye kan-ra beh-pa kard?', *Gozaresh-e Film* 127, Summer 1999, pp. 19-23.

34. For a list of retrospectives, tributes, festival competitions and awards that Kiarostami received up to 1996, see Zaven Qowkasian, *Majmu'eh-ye Maqalat dar Naqd va Mo'arefi-ye Asar-e 'Abbas Kiarostami* (Tehran, Nashr-e Didar, 1996), pp. 345–51. Articles on Kiarostami in key film journals include: Pat Aufderheide, 'Real life is more important than cinema', *Cineast* 31, Summer 1991, pp. 31–3; Marc Glassman, 'An introduction to Kiarostami', *Brick* 59, Spring 1998, pp. 64–9; Philip Lopate, 'Kiarostami's Close-Up', *Film Comment*, July/August 1996, pp. 37–40; Laura Mulvey, 'Kiarostami's uncertainty principle', *Sight and Sound*, June 1998, pp. 24–7; Godfrey Cheshire, 'Abbas Kiarostami: a cinema of questions', *Film Comment*, July/August 1996, pp. 34–6, 41–3.

35. Talebi-Nezhad, *Dar Hozur-e Sinema*, p. 108.

36.   Restrictions on women's screen appearances loosened to some degree in the late 1990s when some pro-reform manoeuvres took place within local cinematic production. This has encouraged the development of the cult of stars inside Iran and enhanced the exoticism resulting from Iranian film exports.

37.   Elham Khaksar, 'Zan, zendegi va zeytun', in Qowkasian (ed.), *Majmu'eh-ye Maqalat*, pp. 60–1.

38.   For a report on a sit-in by the producers of 'C' grade films and for other articles discussing the damage generated by the rating system in its attempt to control people's taste, see 'Alef, Beh, Jeh: darejeh-bandi, arreh ya kheir?', *Mahnameh* 223, Summer 1998, pp. 48–59.

6

Politics and Cinema in Post-revolutionary Iran: An Uneasy Relationship

Ali Reza Haghighi

Politics, as a dynamic and complicated matter with wide appeal, has always been part of cinema. Further, individuals have often sought to express their political objectives through this well-established medium. The main argument of this chapter is that since 1983, when the administration of cinema in Iran became centralized and regulated, the Iranian film industry has been unable to reflect significant elements of realpolitik. Political themes depicted in films are either past events (such as the crimes of the previous regime) or marginal issues (such as anti-revolutionary groups) after they have been resolved and are no longer a concern of society. In other words, cinema has not reflected the contemporary Iranian political scene. Iran is currently going through a stage of transition, having witnessed many ideological confrontations in the last two decades, which have opened up new vistas. These confrontations have deep-rooted links with political criticism, hence they are primarily of a political origin. In this respect too, Iranian films have failed to represent the ideological scene, while books and the press have succeeded in portraying both political and ideological scenes to the extent that current debates often originate in these media.

Background

It is 30 July 1977 in Shiraz, in the south-central province of Fars; 10:30 pm. Some students from Pahlavi University (now known as Shiraz University) are holding a special ceremony in a mosque to mark the fortieth day after Dr Ali Shari'ati's death. As the speaker concludes his talk, the young audience walk out, chanting 'Hail to Khomeini!' repeatedly, inaugurating the first public demonstrations in Iran which led to the victory of the Islamic Revolution some 19 months later. As the students continue their march, about half an hour later, they reach the Capri Cinema, where a festival of 70mm American films (including *Spartacus, Ryan's Daughter, Funny Lady, The Wild Wild West, Ben Hur* and *El Cid*) is being held; they break the glass in the windows of the cinema. When film-goers go to buy tickets the following morning, they are amazed to see the pictures of Kirk Douglas, Barbra Streisand, John Wayne and Omar Sharif staring at them through broken glass. The cinema owners attribute the event to a drunken brawl. They do not know that this marks the beginning of a new age of revolution.

Over the years that followed, in the course of the Islamic Revolution, 195 of the existing 525 cinemas were demolished. The Revolution's discourse criticized cinema as one of the sources of the cultural and political dominance of the Pahlavi regime. Hardly any other cultural institution of the regime was subject to such hostility. Perhaps for this reason, while revolutionary Muslims had succeeded in producing works in other fields of culture and art, they left cinema alone.

In the face of the dominant discourse of the Pahlavi regime, there did exist a minor domain of resistance in cinema too. The genre, known as intellectual cinema, developed mainly in the 1970s and attracted some public attention. Most of its criticism was directed at social issues, however, since overt political criticism was rare and highly unconventional before the Islamic Revolution. In fact, a political cinema did not develop under the previous regime for three main reasons.

First, recognizing the popularity of cinema, the Pahlavi regime's propaganda machine was very sensitive about the representation of any kind of critical approach – even non-political in nature – and would not allow such films to be screened. Most of those films offering a directly critical view of social issues that did get a licence managed to do so through the filmmakers' personal relations – a major parameter in the political structure of Iran. Such filmmakers had to pay a high price, both socially and politically.

The second reason concerned the narrative structure of these films. Since an explicitly political cinema was not possible, filmmakers who wanted to articulate a critical view resorted to such complex metaphor and symbolism that, in practice, they could not communicate fully with their audience, and they never succeeded in having a political impact on public opinion – unlike in other fields of art, such as literature.

Finally, few of those active in the Iranian film industry had any specific ideals, which explains why the film directors and actors were the only social category to produce no political prisoners.

From among the intellectual opposition who used the cinema as a medium, no specific genre emerged that could influence public opinion. In other cultural realms, some among the Islamic and leftist opposition managed to find a large audience. Islamic intellectuals became more prominent in the resistance, and eventually their cultural products acquired greater acceptance throughout society. But the absence of Islamic intellectuals in the film industry meant that no revolutionary forces emerged there in support of the Revolution, and this effective medium was ignored. Public interest in cinema, however, was such that it could not continue to be neglected. Although the culture of appreciating visual concepts was not deep-rooted in Iranian society, people's fondness for melodramatic film and their sensitivity to visual images revealed the popularity of cinema and filmic images. All in all, cinema came to be considered one of the ambiguous issues in the Revolution, and foreign journalists in Paris would sometimes mention cinema when asking political questions of Ayatollah Khomeini.

Cinema and the Ideology of the Early Years

Following the Revolution the above-mentioned factors brought the film industry to a halt, since, as stated earlier, there were no Islamic filmmakers, and the revolutionary and ideological atmosphere of the period –much like that of other revolutions – called for a cinema concordant with the concept and spirit of the Revolution. These two parameters, and the fact that cinema was associated with the previous regime's cultural dominance, meant that a completely sceptical attitude prevailed towards filmmakers, who accordingly were practically unable to work.

The powerful new perspective which promoted the integration of politics and religion now became the measure to distinguish acceptable films from unacceptable ones. Revolutionary agendas and identities were expressed through religious issues. Here, the cinema faced another problem. Unlike many other forms of art, which have a long history in the Islamic civilization of Iran, film was a new art form which the religious elite had ignored and even boycotted: going to the cinema was considered an indecent act. While revolutionary trends were adopted in other forms of art, cinema was left behind in this regard. Consequently, between 1979 and 1983, very few films were produced in Iran: between 3 and 21 per year.

After the victory of the Revolution, however, there was an accelerated debate about the usefulness of cinema and what an Islamic cinema could be. The newly established Arts Centre (Howzeh-ye Honari) of the Islamic Propaganda Organization was the first place where a number of individuals who supported the Revolution gathered to discuss their ideological understanding of an Islamic cinema, sensing, of course, that they needed to come up with a totally novel design. In practice, however, they failed to produce anything interesting in those years.

Ayatollah Khomeini and other religious leaders emphasized that they approved of an educational cinema, that is compatible with the healthy scientific and moral growth of society. They considered an acceptable cinema to be one that served the Revolution or the divine mission. The fact that the film industry was seen as the cultural institution of the Pahlavi regime which, more than any other, had influenced the younger generation, was so important that Khomeini referred to it in his first speech upon his return to Iran, while discussing the most important political issues of the day: 'We do not oppose cinema, we oppose decadence'. Despite such general comments, there were in practice many ambiguities and divergent views, and more than one body inside the country in charge of decision-making concerning cinema. As a result, licensed films were sometimes banned by clerics in some cities. In June 1980, Ayatollah Khalkhali notoriously banned *Qeysar* (Massoud Kimia'i, 1969) in Tehran; in the same year all film theatres were closed for seven days. Subsequently, a council was set up to deal with the cinemas.

Given the potential of the Revolution, the formation of a revolutionary political genre within cinema, as happened in most revolutionary societies, was expected. But this did not occur. Between 1979 and 1983, years of dearth in Iranian film, some opportunists made the Revolution the theme of their work, which was basically rhetorical. Prominent examples of such films are *In Limbo* (Iraj Qaderi, 1982) and *The Cry of the Mojahed* (Mehdi Ma'danian, 1979), the plots of which are based on the atrocities of the

Shah's notorious secret police and disasters of the feudal landlord system. Unlike other cultural products, the release of such political movies required connections with influential groups. The two main difficulties were official suspicion towards veteran filmmakers and the lack of a new generation of directors.

The Nature of Political Film

The victory of the Revolution led to fundamental changes in the political structure of society. In the first few years after the Revolution, Iranian society witnessed the formation of various political factions, which had a constraining impact on social relations. The new political system was intent on realizing an utopia. In an attempt to create new sources of legitimacy, it introduced new features into the realm of politics, which political analysts have variously described as ideological, charismatic, populist and authoritarian.

If we accept that the basic essence of a political film is an engagement with the most important political issues of the time, and if we assume that the fundamental political issue in Iran is the above-mentioned characteristics of the structure of political power, then we find that Iranian cinema has not engaged with them. Not only was there an absence of films examining the structure of power from a critical angle; pure propaganda films about the new structure of power were not even produced. In other words, no specific genre took shape in this respect – only a few exceptional films, such as *Wedding of the Blessed* (Mohsen Makhmalbaf, 1989) and *The Glass Agency* (Ebrahim Hatamikia, 1998). Even though the war cinema addresses the ideological, charismatic and populist characteristics of the political system, these are raised in the context of war, not as political criticism. In effect these films belong to the war genre rather than a political genre.

In countries where the political system places restrictions on the public screening of films, directors commonly employ symbolism to express their political opinions. This has rarely been attempted in Iran. Nevertheless, it is interesting to note that, because of the agitated political atmosphere of the country, many films were considered political. This was because people were searching for symbolism when analysing these films.

The reasons for avoiding political issues are numerous. First, after 1982, film production was financed by either the allocation of government funds or the grant of long-term loans, in line with the FCF's authoritarian policies. Naturally, the conservative attitude of this institution prevented it from financing serious political films. Loans would only be granted to producers who managed to get licences for their films; needless to say, screenplays with political themes rarely received approval. This is probably why few political scenarios were written in the first place. In order to maintain their position, the FCF authorities obviously tried to promote a non-political film industry. Consequently, filmmakers who took less interest in politics gained more recognition and success.

Secondly, a filmmaker would have had to pay a socio-political price for the production of a political film: it was quite likely that a political film would be banned, or that the film's director and/or producer would end up being marginalized.

Thirdly, apart from a few directors who started making films after the Revolution, such as Mohsen Makhmalbaf, Behruz Afkhami and Hatamikia, most Iranian directors have not had any specific political commitment that would motivate them to make such political films.

Finally, compared to books and the press, cinema has a much larger audience and thus a stronger impact on the masses. At the same time, this industry has enjoyed more financial support from government, which is why it has been so carefully supervised over the years. In order to be allowed to continue their careers, it has become common practice for directors and producers to accept this monitoring, which may range from the elimination of a few seconds of a film to a complete restructuring of the story.

Besides failing to portray the current political scene in Iran, the film industry has also failed to represent the ideological scene of the nation. This scene is currently characterized by intellectual developments within society that, on the one hand, have themselves originated from political developments and, on the other, are greatly affected by them. A political cinema should not neglect these developments.

Intellectual life has flourished significantly in Iran during the 1990s. The major features of this new efflorescence have been a promotion of intellectual debate around issues remaining from previous decades, and the rise and spread of two new sets of discourses.

Throughout the last century, Iranian intellectuals were by tradition involved with two important and relevant issues: progress and the West. Alongside these issues, discussion of religion is of course inevitable. Hence, these three issues – progress, religion and the West – have formed the general agenda of intellectual debates in Iran in the past. Over the last two decades, a major change has occurred, the consequences of which are now clear; that is the promotion of a new kind of intellectual dialogue caused by a change in both the social origin and the standpoint of the new generation of intellectuals.

A prime indicator of the promotion of intellectual discourse in Iran is the changing vocabulary regarding the issue, in which the questions of 'progress' (*taraqqi, pish-raft*) and 'the West' (*gharb*) are now labelled 'development' (*towse'eh*) and 'modernity' (*tajaddod, moderniteh*) respectively. Furthermore, these two concepts have been integrated to form a deep bond with the issue of religion, a bond which evoked neglect, denial or confrontation from previous generations of intellectuals. These linguistic changes are gradually establishing the replacement of a literary –metaphorical language with an academic–scientific discourse. The changes have brought the adoption of two different yet relevant discourses in the intellectual circles of Iran: a discourse on democracy and a discourse on a new generation of religious intellectualism. In these two newly-adopted discourses, political reform, which plays an essential role in solving the issue of religion, is considered the prerequisite to both social progress and economic development. Iranian religious intellectuals are commonly of the belief that the political arena can be significantly reformed only through extensive research on religion, which guarantees a correct perspective towards this issue. This is the rationale underlying the attempt to integrate these two discourses with the transition of Iranian society from tradition to modernity.

The Iranian film industry, it seems, has neglected these new developments. Filmmakers are still preoccupied with the older intellectual debates; 'modernity' has not yet replaced 'the West' in Iranian films. As a result, not only is the issue of modernity downgraded to the level of the issue of the West but it is also treated as a trivial matter, as if modernity is all about copying the West. Films that betray this viewpoint include those with plots based on emigration to the West, a critical approach towards material lifestyles and similar themes. There are, of course, a few exceptions, such as *Hamoon* (Daryush Mehrju'i, 1990) or *Bread and Poetry* (Kiumars Pourahmad, 1994). The concept of development is usually dealt with in films commissioned by the government, and this is probably why they tend to advertise the progress of the country according to industrial or agricultural criteria rather than portraying the obstacles that have postponed development in Iran in the last few years. The issue of religion is at best limited to films with moral themes, a cinema which itself limits morals to moral obligations. There are again a few exceptions, especially if one overlooks that they are primarily films of the war genre; *Birth of a Butterfly* (Mojtaba Ra'i, 1998) is one such instance.

Conclusion

Iran is currently experiencing a profound social and intellectual transition. The Iranian film industry, broadly speaking, has failed to illustrate the main processes of intellectual development in Iranian society in the last two decades. The best one can say is that Iranian cinema has succeeded only in portraying some social aspects of this transition, neglecting the intellectual domain which has been necessarily integrated into practical politics. The rather weak political films of Iran shed little light on the intellectual issues of society and their integration into politics.

I have expressed my views on the weaknesses of political cinema in Iran. I end the chapter by recalling my memories of the past. It is true that many film theatres were demolished in my country, but our cinema lived on, because it existed and could go on existing. There was, however, no political cinema to be destroyed in the first place. Ironically, such a cinema has yet to be established, although the previous regime has long passed away.

7

Dead Certainties: The Early Makhmalbaf

Hamid Dabashi

In his 1955 essay, Heidegger analyses the essence of technology to be Enframing as Destining as 'standing reserve', that is the categorical reduction of things, including the human, to their use-value. This he finds to be the most pernicious danger inherent in the very project of Technological Modernity. As a way out of this *cul-de-sac*, towards the end of the essay he detects a saving power evident in Technological Modernity itself and as such rooted in the Greek conception of *technê*, this time in the sense of *poiêsis*. For turning man into an irresistible agency of useful ordering, he sees an antidote in that ordering itself.[1]

This is a critical point in European self-reflection on the crisis of Technological Modernity, and only a slight modification of its evident Eurocentricity makes this passage extraordinarily revealing for the state of art among the rest of us, at the receiving end of the project. For us, technology did not come from the Greek *technê* but out of the long and extended barrels of European vernacular guns; Heidegger's 'art was simply called *technê*' assumes a significance far beyond its European vicinity. For us, the brutality of the colonial reception of Technological Modernity has been intrinsic to our creative revolt against it. Consider the glorious materiality that Heidegger ascribes to art at this presumed primal moment:

4. Mohsen Makhmalbaf.

'The arts were not derived from the artistic. Art works were not enjoyed
aesthetically. Art was not a sector of cultural activity.'²

He could very well be speaking of our art, post/colonial³ art, the saving
power against the *danger* of Enframing inherent in Technological
Modernity. All we have to do is place ourselves where we are, at the receiving
end of the project, at the colonial site of Capitalist Modernity, at the
tropical outposts of the polar centres of the European Enlightenment. For
all 'traditions' in our arts that we have had to invent, there is no understanding our art, as there is no escaping our politics, without a preliminary
reading of this Modernity.

At our poetic best, in Mahmoud ˙Darwish, Nazim Hikmet, Pablo
Neruda, Ahmad Shamlu or Feyz Ahmad Feyz, we revolt against the colonial
consequences of Technological Modernity. The moment that Heidegger
has called 'the frenziedness of technology'⁴ is the colonial site, the location
of its most naked accomplishments, and yet invisible at the polar centres
of Technological Modernity until the Holocaust – when the criminal
atrocities at its colonial peripheries came home to roost. The 'frenziedness
of technology' has wrought havoc on us *en masse*, and in our art we could
not but speak in the anxiety of that frenziedness. For us, the technological
was also the mysterious. We did not know how it worked and yet we were
at its mercy. We on the post/colonial periphery were at the mercy of the
Technological, twice removed in terror from the European centres. The

European had unleashed the monster and was riding it, while it was riding us.

Art was no aesthetic act of pleasure for us, but a primal gasping for air. Thus we hear the ring of truth in Heidegger's words:

> Because the essence of technology is nothing technological, essential reflection upon technology and decisive confrontation with it must happen in a realm that is, on the one hand, akin to the essence of technology and, on the other, fundamentally different from it. Such a realm is art.[5]

No. One move is missing here. Such a realm is not art. It is the sub-Saharan continents of colonial catastrophes that Technological Modernity entailed, and only then comes the art that is created on that realm. What does it exactly mean that the essence of technology is not technological? If we bracket for a moment Heidegger's proclivity to trace everything to its Greek origin, in this particular case tracing technology to a mis/reading of the Greek *technê*, and place the German philosopher himself squarely in the context of a moment of crisis in the post/Enlightenment anxiety against which he launched his philosophical project, then there is something in that European project itself, in the very *idea* of 'Europe' as a colonizing (self-raising/other-lowering) invention, which is the ideological fore-grounding of Capitalist Modernity, and which is the *essence* of technology, and thus not technology itself. That *essence* is to be detected in the cataclysmic changes in the very subjectivity of human agency ushered in during the course of the European Enlightenment and its twin project of Capitalist Modernity. Once we go that far, there is only one step we need to take towards the colonial conclusion of the project, and once on that site, the essence of technology as the categorical reduction of things – including the human – to their use-value need not be, for us, persuasively argued. It is there. We – the post/colonial subjects – are it. Thus colonialism *is* the essence of technology, directly consequential to the twin projects of the European Enlightenment and Capitalist Modernity.

Heidegger postulates both an 'essential reflection' and a 'decisive confrontation' with the essence of technology. 'Essential reflection' on the essence of technology has of course been an entirely European proposition. The deceptive monster was born there and has only been *essentially* reflected on precisely on that site. But when it comes to 'decisive confrontation' with it, then we must be on a site which is 'fundamentally different from it'. Europe, except in its moments of crisis, is *not* that site; the serious site can only be the colonial realm, its categorical denial, its civilizational Other.

Heidegger rightly saw the problem of art, in achieving the task he was stipulating for it, to be its over-theorization into the aesthetics. '[I]n our sheer aesthetic-mindedness we no longer guard and preserve the coming to presence of art.'[6] The radical theorization of the work of art into an aesthetics is almost exclusively an act of the post-Enlightenment practice. Cultural Modernity, as Max Weber realized and Habermas underscored,[7] broke down what Weber had called 'substantive reason' and placed it within the prerogative of the sacred imagination into three autonomous spheres of truth, normative authenticity and beauty. As science claimed the truth and morality the normative authenticity, aesthetics assumed an exclusive jurisdiction over the beautiful, autonomous of both truth-claims and morality. It is only in reaction to the disastrous consequences of the Enlightenment that Adorno later tried to retrieve for the work of art its inherent truth-claims.[8] Thus Heidegger's diagnosis of the superimposition of aesthetics between the post-Enlightenment European and the work of art is exclusively limited to that polar centre of Technological Modernity and entirely absent in the case of the post/colonial art and confrontation with the work of art.

Here, we must avoid the trap of 'traditional art' that both Technological Modernity and its nativist detractors – strange bedfellows but nevertheless in active coalition with each other – have concocted for post/colonial art. What we have produced on the post/colonial site is not 'traditional' but a perfectly modern response to the predicament of our place at the colonial end of the twin projects of the Enlightenment and Capitalist Modernity. Kant's assertion that we in the African and Asian outback of modernity were constitutionally incapable of the sublime,[9] helps us here to keep our art at the necessary arm's length from European aesthetics which, as Heidegger rightly suggests, is an Enlightenment proposition. The nakedness of technological aggression at its colonial ends, one might thus argue, has made post/colonial art particularly immune to European aesthetics. European aesthetics, in turn, have been the necessary distancing measure that Technological Modernity has exacted in order to keep the eyes of the European 'wide shut' to the truth of the Enlightenment.

What is particularly applicable to the colonial site in its creative moments is Heidegger's suggestion that 'the closer we come to the danger, the more brightly do the ways into the saving power begin to shine and the more questioning we become'.[10] The post/colonial has lived that danger, and thus he is that danger. There is no site closer to the danger of

Technological Modernity than its colonial consequences, where the brutalities of the fatal attraction to the 'Enframing as Destining as standing reserve' had no Enlightenment sugar-coating. In fact, quite to the contrary, we have been the civilizational Other of the project of the Enlightenment. But even Heidegger's philosophical critique of Technological Modernity was no ordinary theoretical undoing of the project. He emerged from the very depth of a moment of crisis at the heart of Capitalist Modernity, and that is why his destruction of the project of modernity appeals so thoroughly to our predicament at the colonial end of the crisis.

Closest to the Danger: An 'Islamic cinema'?

Any critical reading of our successes and failures to dwell poetically in, and thus rebel against, our state of coloniality must begin with an equally critical awareness of the structural affinity that exists between moments of crisis at the heart of Capitalist Modernity and the intrinsic crisis at the colonial extension of its logic. The poetic way out of the predicament of Technological Modernity is far more evident in a post/colonial condition, where 'Enframing as Destining of things as useful and expendable' is inherent in this very condition. It is quite understandable that Ancient Greece would constitute a Golden Age to which the Heideggerian generation of Europeans disenfranchised from Technological Modernity would turn. Whether at the polar centre of Technological Modernity or at the tropical outskirts of its colonial extensions, constructions of mystical and imaginary Golden Ages seem to be the first, dangerously fictive but nevertheless necessary, step towards the transformation of the substance of the danger into the poetic material of rebellion against it. It is precisely here that we see the affinity between the mythical components of both National Socialism and the Islamic ideology. They are both necessary and inevitable mythical responses to identical moments of crisis at the receiving end of the project of Capitalist Modernity, for Germany at a moment of crisis at the centre and for Iran as a structural conditioning at a post/colonial periphery of the globalizing project. Heidegger's destruction of the Enlightenment project and his disdain for Capitalist Modernity appeals to the coloniality of our condition precisely because he too spoke from a moment of crisis like the one that is intrinsic to us.

On the site of the post/colonial production of our material reality, we have been closest to the *danger* inherent in Technological Modernity. At the best moments of our self-re-creative emancipation, we have managed to do far more than merely to resist ideologically the colonial extension of the inner logic of Technological Modernity, and to constitute artistically a mode of subjectivity for ourselves beyond the reach of that colonially crafted identity. Our ideological resistances to colonialism have been, *ipso facto*, a negational reflection of the colonial project itself. We could not resist colonialism except with ideologies that it made possible. The 'Islam' of our political practices is one particularly poignant counter/colonial construct. Islamism, as a liberation theology, has been a form of ideological resistance to the colonial extension of the project of Technological Modernity, in which we have invested all of our ancestral faith in exchange for a site of ideological resistance to colonialism, and thus it is in its entirety a colonial product. Islamism, both the saving power and yet itself the very nature of the danger, was a particularly powerful ideological apparatus, not because it was so radically different from colonialism, but because it was so thoroughly rooted in it.

What is an 'Islamic art', as in 'Islamic cinema', in the context of the ideological Islamization of resistance to colonialism? In this context, Islamic art, the perturbed spirit of our moral resistance to colonial subjection, is nothing but a further Islamization of ideological resistance to colonialism as the extended arm of Technological Modernity. It is to this notion of 'Islamic art' that Mohsen Makhmalbaf, along with any number of other Muslim activists, squarely belonged when he began to take pictures with his camera, cut close-ups with long-shots, and try to tell an 'Islamic' tale. Neither the Islam that was conducive to the reign of the Pahlavi monarchy nor the Islam that was in the Orientalist production of subjectivity on behalf of colonialism, meant anything to this generation of Muslim activists. Islamic art of the sort useful to them was conceived and executed on the ideological site of a David-and-Goliath battle against the onslaught of Capitalist Modernity, a helping hand given to the cultural constitution of resistance as *ipso facto* 'religious', 'traditional', or 'authentic' in its claims to legitimacy.

At the commencement of their activities, Muslim ideologues-turned-artists such as Makhmalbaf do not recognize that their ideological mode of resistance to cultural colonialism is itself the most effective form of self-colonization. From Frantz Fanon to Ali Shari'ati, a fundamental feature of such resistance has been this categorical failure to recognize the formation of the so-called 'native' or 'traditional' mode as something of itself deeply colonial. Fanon went so far as to consider veiling Muslim women as a counter-colonial barrier, guarding a territory that colonialism could not transgress. Shari'ati of course went much further and sought radically to *ideologize* his received conception of Islam into nothing but an anti-colonial ideology. But an anti-colonial ideology *is* a colonial ideology. It is the colonial subject in his most agitated moment of political anxiety who goes to the memorial remembrances of his ancestral legacies in order to concoct an ideology of resistance to the colonial onslaught. So long as he remains an ideologue, he cannot but be colonial in all his acts of both compliance and resistance; in acts of ideological resistance in particular, his subjectivity having been constituted by the very act of colonization, he cannot but further colonize the traces of his ancestral memory in search of an ideology of resistance. When, as a post/colonial subject, the Muslim ideologue turns into an artist, initially he cannot do anything but further cultivate the site of resistance to colonialism in what he now considers to be 'artistic' terms. He may think he is an artist, but he is still too much in the sun of ideological resistance.

Makhmalbaf: The Beginnings

The first phase of Makhmalbaf's cinema, roughly from 1981, when he wrote *Someone Else's Death*, to 1983 when he made *Two Sightless Eyes*, is squarely at the service of Islamic ideology as a site of revolutionary resistance to both imperialism and its domestic consequences.

At the commencement of his artistic career, Makhmalbaf was still very much a revolutionary Muslim activist. He had formed his own urban guerrilla organization, small but serious, as early as 1972, when he was about 15 years old. By 1974, he had taken his vocation as a Muslim revolutionary so seriously that he actually took up arms to fight against the Pahlavi monarchy. After a failed attack on a police officer, Makhmalbaf was arrested and jailed in August 1974; he was not immediately executed because at 17 years old he was a minor. From then until 1978, when he should have graduated from high school and passed through college, he spent four most productive and crucial years in the company of other political prisoners, almost all of them decades senior to him.

Makhmalbaf was released from the Pahlavi jail in October 1978 under the pressure of the revolutionary momentum; he emerged an even more dedicated Muslim revolutionary, and until the start of his cinematic career in 1981 was totally devoted to the Islamic Revolution and its ideals. On his release, he married Fatemeh Meshkini, and began to write and fight for the Revolution: one year later their first daughter, Samira (Zeynab), was born. Meanwhile, in January and February 1979, they had witnessed the Shah's departure from Iran and Ayatollah Khomeini's triumphant return, scenes no Iranian of Makhmalbaf's generation ever thought possible. Less than a week after his return, Khomeini had appointed Mehdi Bazargan as prime minister of the transitional government, and less than a week later he had forced the last remnant of the Pahlavi monarchy – Bakhtiyar's government – to resign and go into hiding. By the end of March, Khomeini had ensured that millions of Iranians came to the polling boxes and gave their unconditional support for an Islamic Republic. Makhmalbaf must have seen the failure of the secular left and liberals to resist the Islamization of the Revolution as a categorical condemnation of the whole universe of corruption with which the *ancien régime* was now identified.

By the summer of 1979, the Constitution of the Islamic Republic was already being drafted: its final draft was ratified under the smoke-screen of the American Hostage Crisis that began in November. Everyone, secular or religious, was now living in an Islamic Republic. The next year, an Islamic Republic took root in Iran, and Makhmalbaf served it enthusiastically in his writings and activities. In September, the far more serious and bloody process of Islamizing the Revolution began. The devastating war with Iraq was the most enduring act of consolidating the Islamic Revolution as the defining moment of Iranian political culture. One year into the war, the Makhmalbafs' son Meytham (Ayyub) was born. Another year on – three years into the Islamic Revolution – he found himself behind a camera, a committed ideologue commending himself to his faith.

Radicalized to the point of rebellion by age 17, followed by four years in the Pahlavi dungeons, then four more of revolutionary participation in an Islamic Republic, on that momentous occasion in 1982 when the 25-year-old Makhmalbaf stands behind a camera for the first time, in order to make his first feature film, he thus has a plethora of revolutionary experiences under his tightly-fastened belt.

When Makhmalbaf commences his cinematic career in 1981, he does so with the perfect intention of a committed ideologue to put his creative urges at the service of the Revolution. His early cinematic endeavours – the writing of *Someone Else's Death* and *The Sixth Person*, and the directing of *Nasuh's Repentance* (1982), *Two Sightless Eyes* and *Seeking Refuge* (1983 based on *The Sixth Person*) – are entirely devoted to substantiating the metaphysical foundations of the theocracy he has helped to bring to power.

Makhmalbaf's turn to art – generic yet experimental – is thus a natural continuation of his ideological commitment to the Islamic Revolution. Now that the Revolution is politically successful he sees its achievements as threatened by the cultural forces of the *ancien régime*. So he begins his artistic career with the stated purpose of helping buttress its cultural foregrounding by preventing non-Islamic art from being used against the Revolution. Early in the Revolution he joins the staff of Iranian National Radio and becomes part of the propaganda machinery of the young Islamic Republic. Very soon he joins the Centre for Islamic Thought and Art, which was later renamed the Arts Centre of the Islamic Propaganda Organization and brought directly under the jurisdiction of the propaganda machinery of the Islamic Revolution. He becomes its chief ideologue, committed to translating ideological concepts into artistic expressions.

Makhmalbaf squarely denounces pre-revolutionary art in general – cinema in particular. His targets, first and foremost, are secular artists and filmmakers, whom he categorically identifies with the 'evil' monarchy, even demanding that they be publicly tried. He believes that when people burned the cinemas in the course of the Revolution they were expressing their categorical condemnation of pre-revolutionary art. Makhmalbaf prefers to be identified as a 'Muslim artist', viscerally dismissing all those who fail to meet his standards of revolutionary piety. His conviction at this point is categorical, emphatic, Manichean, with a clear cosmo-vision of Good and Evil. Islam is good, un-Islam is bad: he is reported to have said, 'I would rather sweep under the feet of the weakest Muslim director or actor than co-operate with the most distinguished non-Muslim artist.'[11]

At this time, Makhmalbaf believes that there is no theoretical statement as to the nature of an 'Islamic Art', and single-handedly seeks to create such a statement. He writes short stories, novels, plays, scripts and even critical essays on the nature and disposition of 'Islamic Art' and commentaries on its reconstitution. For Makhmalbaf, at this stage, Islam is a categorical imperative, it has a truth and a philosophy, and 'Islamic Art' has to reflect that truth and that philosophy. He is angry, and scarcely literate in matters of art, philosophy or even Islamic learning beyond the most rudimentary preaching of the popular proselytizers and whatever he could have read in jail. He has had no formal or informal training either in scholastic or in modern education, and knows no language but Persian. And yet he reads and writes in Persian ferociously, with absolute conviction, with totalitarian tendencies and always with a vengeance against those artists who had worked under the Pahlavi regime. In his *Moqaddame'i bar Honar-e Islami*

(*Prolegomena to Islamic Art*), he seeks to outline a new and revolutionary description of what exactly constitutes the nature and function of 'art' in an Islamic context. His writing in this period is prosaic, bordering on banality. But there is an urge in him, a relentless pursuit of something that his blind dedication to Islamic ideology prevents him articulating, let alone probing.

Makhmalbaf's cinematic career commences in a context of almost frenetic religious fixation with revolutionary ideals. What sorts of films are produced in this period? In 1980, Iranian films were by and large and for obvious reasons almost exclusively concerned with revolutionary and religious themes. Taqi Keyvan Salahshur's *Flying Towards Minu*, a typical film of the year, follows the fate of a worker who is dismissed from his work because of his political activities. He ends up working at a bookshop and then becomes a revolutionary. Another typical example of the films of 1980 is Reza Safa'i's *Uprising*, about the atrocities of a feudal landlord. In *Blood-rain*, Amir Qavidel tells the story of three soldiers in the Shah's army who join the revolutionary movement. Asghar Bichareh's *The Living Document* examines contemporary Iranian history from Reza Shah to the Islamic Revolution. In *Long Live*, Khosrow Sina'i follows a young revolutionary who seeks refuge with a family and gradually converts them to the cause of the Revolution. Akbar Sadeqi's *Satan* adopts *ta'ziyeh* leit-motifs for a contemporary examination of Good and Evil. Aman Manteqi's *The Soldier of Islam* explores a love affair between a Muslim revolutionary and the daughter of a member of SAVAK.

Makhmalbaf is no exception to this cinema of self-mortification. *Justification* (1981), the first feature film directed by Manuchehr Haqqani-parast, based on a play by Makhmalbaf, reveals the types of issues that preoccupied the young ideologue. An urban guerrilla organization assassinates an American diplomat during the reign of Mohammad Reza Shah, and plans a series of explosions in the capital. The disagreement between two of the guerrillas and their doomed fate centre around the cliché-ridden debate also whether the end justifies the means. The characters of Ali and Behruz represent opposing sides of the political agenda of subversive revolutionary activity. Ali finally kills not just the SAVAK agents sent to capture them but Behruz too. In *Fortress in Fortress* (1982) and *Someone Else's Death*, both written by Makhmalbaf and directed by Mohammad Reza Honarmand, we see little change. *Someone Else's Death* examines the nature of evil via a Bergmanian appearance of Death to force a general on the verge of a major military campaign to face his criminal past. At this point Makhmalbaf is very much preoccupied with matters of morality in any kind of political choice. Here we see him mostly in a self-examining struggle. His mind is still in prison, his soul agitated by the revolutionary upheaval, his ambitions set alight by the infinite possibilities he sees ahead of him. He is as innocent of any cinematic culture as he is unclear where exactly to take his passionate fixation with the possibilities embedded in film and fiction. He is still immersed in flat ideological investigations of Death and Destiny. In its best moments, *Someone Else's Death* becomes an occasion for anti-military reflection. But Makhmalbaf is still too raw, too flat, too visually pleonastic to see anything, very much like that general, imprisoned in the bunker of his own ideological limitations, convictions and certainties. His principal problem at this point is that he is on a wild goose chase after an 'Islamic Cinema', a figment of his own perturbed ideological imagination which even he himself cannot quite identify. He knows that an 'Islamic Cinema' has to be revolutionary and anti-secular. But these are negative features. What precisely this cinema should be in positive terms neither he nor his revolutionary cohorts have a clue. But what is still lurking beneath all this pompous emptiness is a restless mind. Makhmalbaf's creative body is captivated by a spell. He does not know it, but he is in labour.

1981 – the year *Justification* was made – was no ordinary year. The American hostage crisis finally came to an end on 19 January. The Iran–Iraq war was raging. Bani-Sadr's beleaguered presidency ended on 1 June when he went into hiding in fear for his life. The clerical opposition to his presidency found fault with his handling of the war. The Mojahedin-e Khalq Organization wrought havoc on the Islamic Republic: on 27 June the attempted assassination of the then Supreme Council member, later President and Supreme Leader, Ali Khamene'i, in which he lost the use of his right arm, was a clear warning sign that opposition to the Islamic Republic was there to stay, with the Mojahedin at the forefront. The following day, they blew up the headquarters of the Islamic Republic Party; among the dead was Chief Justice Ayatollah Beheshti. A massive crackdown against the Mojahedin ensued. Amnesty International reported the execution of thousands of Iranians on various anti-revolutionary charges. On 30 August, newly-elected President Mohammad Ali Raja'i and his Prime Minister Mohammad Javad Bahonar were among those killed in yet another massive explosion in the capital. A reign of terror was evident in Tehran and other major cities. Iranians were being killed in their hundreds in bomb blasts and executions, and in their thousands in the war. Shortage

5. Mohsen Makhmalbaf's *Nasuh's Repentance* (1982) featured his own mother, Esmat Jampour.

of food in major cities was rampant. Bomb blasts at train stations and department stores denied civilians an iota of security. Islamic codes of dress and conduct turned Tehran into Calvin's Geneva. Women and religious minorities were the principal victims of these circumstances. In October, Khamene'i became President and Mir Hoseyn Musavi his Prime Minister, but no sign of peace was in sight.

What kind of films are produced in these circumstances? Corrupt land-lords, brutal SAVAK agents and immoral military personnel are usually pitted against young revolutionaries and devout Muslims. Mohammad Baqer Khosravi's *The Condemned* (1981), for example, featuring the veteran actor Parviz Fanni-zadeh, is a farce about SAVAK, CIA and MOSSAD, all fooled by a man who shoots at the Shah's picture on banknotes. Hoseyn Aqa Karimi's *America is Destroyed* (1981) explores American colonial designs in the region. In *Besieged* (1981), Akbar Sadeqi depicts a member of the Shah's army whose entire family is devoted to monarchy, except one son who joins the revolutionary movement. The perturbed spirit of the Islamic Revolution knows no rest.

Makhmalbaf, too, was deep in the Islamic phase of his filmmaking. In *Nasuh's Repentance*, Lotf Ali Khan, a bank employee, reminiscent of Scrooge in Dickens's *A Christmas Carol*, is taken for dead but rises from his death-bed and, guided by his benevolent friend Us Yahya, seeks to atone for his evil past. With a script adapted from the writings of two revolutionaries,

Ayatollahs Motahhari and Dastgheyb, *Nasuh's Repentance* narrates Lotf Ali Khan into the very fabric of Islamic moralizing. The central theme focuses on the moment when he attends a public gathering of his friends and acquaintances and asks for their forgiveness. Meanwhile one of his sons and his son-in-law try to embezzle his property. His other son, having devoted his life to the cause of the Revolution and the subsequent war, comes to his rescue. The film then turns into an examination of the difficulty of a conclusive repentance from sin. Makhmalbaf is a preacher through and through, in this as in much of his early cinema. He is still sorting out the anger he had accumulated in prison against an immoral life, and particularly against secular intellectuals. His cinema is didactic, his visual diction sermon-laden, his attitude moralizing. He feels himself presiding over a moral moment when the entire constitution of Iranian cultural identity is being reconfigured.

Makhmalbaf's innocent sentimentalism here matches his political and religious concerns. In *Nasuh's Repentance* he is simply working out his own juvenile moralism. He has been prematurely politicized, to pick up arms to oppose tyranny. His target is correct, but his political awareness is extraordinarily childish and idealistic, with no historical consciousness. In religion he has found a haven, a place of secure moral judgement. Cinema was forbidden to Makhmalbaf's earliest religious sensibilities. He feared it as one fears a taboo. He approaches it by throwing mud at it, by kicking and screaming his morality, by reciting the Qur'an, the prophetic traditions and any other kind of incantation one recites in the presence of a danger which is at once repellent and attractive. 'Cinema' for Makhmalbaf is a classic case of a forbidden pleasure, both feared and yearned for.

Thus Makhmalbaf's earliest attraction to cinema recalls the way that Muslim Hajj pilgrims, as part of the ritual, throw stones at a symbolic representation of Satan; the harder they throw, the more sinful is their conscience of their own deeds. Makhmalbaf's earliest work is thus an exorcism of the demonic forces of his own inner anxieties, fears, hopes and aspirations. The 25-year-old director, who has spent his life fighting for a just 'Islamic' society, now pontificates about the morality of a pious life. He is bewildered by this cinematic medium. But like a sleep-walker he is attracted to it almost involuntarily. In the depth of this prosaic banality, this celebration of vacuous piety, something is brewing in him. It is true that all these early films, up to *Boycott* (1985), could be safely trashed and nothing would be missed of Makhmalbaf's brilliant cinematic career. But there is much archival evidence in them to justify their continued relevance. Lotf Ali Khan, the chief villain of *Nasuh's Repentance*, is an evil character that Makhmalbaf must exorcise from his own creative imagination before he can dig deeper and begin to be more serious about his art. To Makhmalbaf himself, more than to any critic, these characters appear empty, shallow, flat, pointless. Yet they are signs of the growing pains at the core of his creative body.

What was happening in Iran in 1982, as Makhmalbaf made *Nasuh's Repentance*? What sort of audience was expected to go and see these films? Iranians were being massacred in their thousands at the front, in revolutionary executions and anti-revolutionary assassination attempts. The endeavours of Olaf Palme, the UN special envoy, to end the war were futile. The arrest on 10 April of the former foreign minister Sadeq Qotbzadeh, and his execution on 14 August on charges of plotting to assassinate Khomeini and overthrow the Islamic Republic, marked the beginning of a new, even harsher reign of terror. In June, the Iranian government missed an opportunity to make peace with Iraq. The abuses of citizens' rights were so rampant and pervasive that by December Khomeini himself issued a warning against the abuse of power.

The situation of cinema that year is equally hapless. Beyza'i makes *Yazdgerd's Death* (1981) about the last days of the last Sassanid king before the Arab conquest, the point of its antiquarian demodulation of Iranian historical mythologies totally lost at this time of naked brutality. Hasan Hedayat makes *The Jungle Messenger* (1982) about Mirza Kuchek Khan Jangali, the revolutionary leader of a movement in northern Iran early in the century. Ali Hatami makes *Haji Washington* (1982) about the first Iranian ambassador to the US and his collapse into madness. Naser Mohammadi's *The Devotees* (1982) is among the first films to begin to explore the sacrifices of Iranian youth in the course of the Iran–Iraq war. Time, in manner and matter, reality and fiction, is out of joint.

In *Two Sightless Eyes*, Makhmalbaf continues to exorcize the political demons inhabiting his still-agitated imagination. The targets of his pontificating anger are now a leftist teacher and a greedy merchant: the teacher lacks principles, the merchant is sub-human. Salvation is to be found in Mashhadi Iman and Seyyed Abdollah, two pious Muslims, their names crudely reminiscent of what Makhmalbaf wants them to represent. The puritanical sentiment in *Two Sightless Eyes* is equally evident in Makhmalbaf's oft-quoted statement from this period, that he was unwilling to be caught 'even in a long-shot' with secular filmmakers, Beyza'i, his main target, being dismissed as 'Satanic' (*taghuti*). At this period, the term was categorical, sweeping, exclamatory, anti-secular. In 1983, when *Two Sightless Eyes* was released, the Islamic Republic launched a major anti-communist campaign. Leaders of the Tudeh Party were arrested and discredited. Relations with the Soviet Union deteriorated. Meanwhile, the war with Iraq continued, peace attempts by the UN and Islamic countries producing no concrete results. The explosion at a US marine headquarters in Beirut on 23 October further aggravated US–Iran relations. Both the US and France intensified military aid to Iraq for fear of an Iranian victory which might result in further agitation in the region while strengthening the military prowess of the Islamic Republic. The Islamic Republic, in a state of siege, felt justified in attributing 'Satanic' characteristics to actual and fictive enemies. In the cinema of this period we see more war films, more depictions of SAVAK atrocities, more corrupt landlords and more rich, pro-American anti-revolutionaries.

Seeking Refuge is by far the most disastrous of Makhmalbaf's early films, exhibiting symptoms of a formal but formless mysticism that, had he not immediately cured himself of it, would have resulted in a far more deadly case of cine-mysticism. In the film, Makhmalbaf completely abandons the social scene and opts for what he terms 'Philosophical Man', a vast, empty abstraction constructed – in a script based on a late-medieval religious text, Majlesi's *Bahar al-Anwar*, and a text by a contemporary religious revolutionary, Ayatollah Dastgheyb – in order to examine the nature of Evil. Five 'Philosophical Men' – a ghastly notion that would frighten any mortal man out of his wits – encounter Evil in five convergent episodes, each simulating one of the pitfalls of the Carnal Soul. The first four encounters are won by Satan; only the fifth and final encounter results in a decisive victory for Man, predicated on his having achieved Purity. In search of salvation and victory over their carnal souls, these five Philosophical Men seek refuge on a remote and mysterious Island. Satanic temptations do not leave them alone there, and four of them succumb: one dies from drinking sea water, the second drowns in the sea, the third hangs himself, the fourth falls into his own trap. The only path to salvation, the fifth and final Man realizes, is to seek Refuge with God.

It is terrifying to imagine what effect *Seeking Refuge* had in the Iran of 1983. Under Khomeini's chilling puritanism, with the culture plunged into a pool of martyrological mysticism, the war raging full blast and Iranian youths being slaughtered in battle in their thousands, this ghastly metaphysical examination of the 'Nature of Evil' is itself a very epitome of evil. Five nameless, shapeless, characterless Men get into a Boat and sail to an Island in the middle of Nowhere. Four of them perish in battle with Satan; the fifth survives through Rectitude and Righteousness. Makhmalbaf's Manichean mind is still dividing the world between a shapeless Evil and an afflicted Good, engaged in a fateful, cosmic battle. The film plumbs the depths of Makhmalbaf's imagination at this period. It is nothing short of a miracle that he could save himself after such a malignant catastrophe. But these catastrophes are not entirely his. They are the roster of a cultural register of mental malaise which has afflicted us Iranians as a people for ages. What Makhmalbaf gives to these mental afflictions, this psychopathological impotence to face the real, is a new lease on life, a fresh, radical contemporaneity. The vertiginous anthropophobia in the fake Biblical/Qur'anic narrative of *Seeking Refuge* makes the film simply unwatchable.

Makhmalbaf, however, had to pass through this valley of dead certainties to reach the salutary summit of living doubts, before his own creative imagination could bring him to the glorious conclusion that there are more things in heaven and earth than can be dreamt of in his 'Islamic' philosophy. In *Seeking Refuge*, with all its petrifying abstractions, we still see Makhmalbaf seeking a kind of ethical theodicy, preoccupied as he is by the nature of Satanic forces within historical agencies. There is a struggle here, constant yet varied in form, between the Carnal Soul and the innate Goodness Makhmalbaf sees in man. The finality of a victory of Good over Evil is transected by an almost ironic (but never articulated) suggestion that no victory of Good over Evil is final. There is of course a Manichean determinism in the bifurcation of Good and Evil, still active in Makhmalbaf's moral imagination. He is still, in his mind, in prison, trying to sort out the various ideological claims on Truth. Yet we can already detect signs that he has moved beyond categorical identification of social types with Good and Evil by actively engaging in reflection on the nature of the two. Equally evident in this phase of Makhmalbaf's cinematic training is his attribution to man of an active – though implicit – agency, of an instrumental role in the outcome of a dialectical opposition between the possibilities of Good and Evil.

In his prison notebooks, Gramsci quotes Guicciardini: 'two things are absolutely necessary for the life of a state: arms and religion.'[12] He adds, 'This formula of his can be translated into various other, less drastic, formulas: force and consent, coercion and persuasion, state and Church, political society and civil society, politics and morals.'[13] On trial in these early Makhmalbaf films is the very idea of Modernity in its post/colonial implications. Collapsing into a medieval dogmatism that informed the ideological context of his revolutionary disposition, Makhmalbaf moralizes and preaches with a vengeance born of his cruelly shortened youth. Assured of the military success of the Islamic Revolution against its political enemies, he now seeks an artistic extension of its religious veracity. But – and there's the rub – with all the crude pontificating evident in the young Makhmalbaf's films, with all the political and fanatic uses to which they could easily have been put by the propaganda organs of the Islamic Republic, they also show evidence of a preoccupation with principles such as truth, morality, conviction, social commitment and a proclivity towards philosophical abstraction. The result is immediate ideological benefit to the Islamic Republic's propaganda machinery, yet a massive corrosive dismantling of that very metaphysical claim, located in the bosom of the creative consciousness it harbours. Unknown to himself and his ideological cohorts, Makhmalbaf is a Trojan Horse.

The Decisive Moment

The rise of Makhmalbaf from the very depth of ideological resistance to colonial domination has fortified his art with the danger intrinsic to Technological Modernity. As he begins his creative career he cannot help but see artistic activity as a mere extension of his insurrection against tyranny. What he, along with his gurus such as Ali Shari'ati, fails to see at this juncture is the quintessentially colonial nature of all ideological resistance to colonialism. The result is the production of a mode of debilitating cine-mysticism that plunges the dominant political culture further into a frenzy of self-mortification and abstraction, all informed by dead and deadening certainties. Ghastly as this early period of Makhmalbaf's cinema is, we can see him systematically exorcizing his ideological demons. It is as if he had to exorcize them from his creative body and project them onto the screen to see their monumental emptiness for himself. These films thus cure him of his afflictions. They are so therapeutic precisely because they are so poisonous. Out of the *danger* in which Makhmalbaf and his nation at large were living and dying, emerges its own therapeutic antidote, its chemical antitoxin, its remedial medicine.

The fate of 'Islamic Cinema' thus coincides with that of 'Islamic Ideology'. Both were colonially constituted responses to the onslaught of Technological Modernity, both incapable of coming to terms with the over-riding logic of a phenomenon unprecedented in human history. The decisive moment comes, however, when the reality of art as a phenomenon *sui generis* seizes the ideologue and transforms the site of his resistance from merely *political* to substantially *poetic*. Having emerged from the very heart of *danger*, Makhmalbaf has felt the saving power intrinsic in the colonial extension of the project of Capitalist Modernity. Of course, he does not recognize the transition in specifically mutational terms. But the key factor is that he is constantly agitated by a relentless dissatisfaction with what he achieves. From the heart of the *danger*, from the ancestral faith of a people colonially moulded to an ideology of resistance to colonialism, thus emerges first an art, an Islamic cinema, bringing forth in effect the Muslim ideologue's subjectivity from a colonially constituted identity in an emancipatory direction. It is in the very nature of the post/colonial poetic to resist over-aestheticization, which it cannot afford. Makhmalbaf's art is particularly powerful because it emerged out of the Islamic ideological response to colonialism. That art has been closer to its *danger*.

Makhmalbaf has had to pass through that *danger* in order to reach the poetic *saving* power now paramount in his cinema. The danger of cine-mysticism is not limited to Makhmalbaf or the assumptions of an 'Islamic cinema'. In fact, a historical collapse into essentialist mysticism is a far more universal trap. More experienced and accomplished filmmakers in Iran have fallen squarely into it and never escaped. The most illustrious example is Daryush Mehrju'i, whose most recent films, concluding with *The Pear Tree* (1998), show the disastrous consequences of an attraction to cinematic mysticism. The crucial difference between Makhmalbaf and Mehrju'i, however, is that Makhmalbaf began his cinematic career with this inevitable affliction with cinematic-mysticism and very quickly recovered from it, whereas Mehrju'i seems to be signing off an otherwise brilliant cinematic career with the disease.

Clearly the Revolution, in effect one massively orchestrated, ideological Islamization of a constitutionally polyvocal culture, has been chiefly responsible for this artistic turn to the metaphysical. While Makhmalbaf was ideologically bred into a metaphysics of mystical convictions and gradually allowed the aesthetic realities of his art to lead him to auto-nomous judgement, Mehrju'i was artistically born into that multivocality but gradually submitted to the overwhelming authority of the mystical, now fully supported by a triumphant theocracy. Mehrju'i's best films were the result of close collaboration with one of the most brilliant Iranian dramatists in modernity, Gholam Hoseyn Sa'edi. Sa'edi's suicidal urges in the aftermath of the Revolution, which ended in 1985 in his deliberately drinking himself to death, undoubtedly left Mehrju'i morally and psycho-logically depleted. Most of Mehrju'i's films after Sa'edi's death have inclined to a fatalistic mysticism from which he has never recovered. Mehrju'i's case clearly illustrates the attraction of Persian mysticism for a range of creative artists. But whereas superior artists like Beyza'i have been able to contain this urge and, with impeccable creative discipline, channel it in constructive directions, in weaker hands and minds the attraction has indeed been fatal. Makhmalbaf is a spectacular example of relentless honesty, with the real literally pulling the artist out of the mystifying misery of casting a metaphysical gaze on an already brutalized world.

To understand these false moments of ideological liberation from the onslaught of Technological Modernity on its post/colonial outpost, we must also understand the moments of genuine despair at its polar centres. A good recent example of this is Stanley Kubrick's spectacular failure, *Eyes Wide Shut* (1999). The sad, spectacular fate of art at the end of the twentieth century and at the polar centre of Technological Modernity, as evident in one of its greatest visual theorists, is just this turn to *false* mysticism at a moment of *genuine* despair. This example from outside the purview of Iranian cinema both illuminates the case of the early Makhmalbaf and points to a larger attraction to cine-mysticism as a particularly powerful pathological trait, albeit for different but nevertheless symptomatic reasons. Moments of genuine *despair* at the polar centre of Technological Modernity correspond to false moments of *liberation* at its post/colonial tropical outposts.

The task of a filmmaker like Makhmalbaf at the post/colonial frontier of Technological Modernity is to reach for genuine *liberation* from genuine *despair*, escaping the danger of *false* liberation through *false* ideologies. Having concluded a creative exorcism in his early 'Islamic cinema' by a successful visualization of his innermost religious anxieties in his first three films, he is ready to move. He recognizes the poverty of his visual 'literacy' and begins to read and watch extensively the classics of his chosen profession. He recognizes that he has opted for far too serious a medium, and that he is far too serious about it to use it in a cavalier way.

Bagh-e Bolur, 1984–5

By the summer of 1984, one year into his success as an Islamic filmmaker and four years into the war, Makhmalbaf is born again, though not in a film but in writing a work of fiction. *The Crystal Garden* begins with a painful description of an excruciatingly difficult childbirth.[14] The birth of Setareh, already fatherless, might as well be the birth of an artist in Makhmalbaf, from the very depth of his religious and revolutionary convictions. Setareh was conceived before her father Mansur was dispatched to the front to be killed in action. Her mother Layeh is now a martyr's widow. Makhmalbaf himself was conceived in the course of a marriage that lasted only six days: his parents were separated and divorced before his birth. He too was born to an absent father – a self-made child, as it were. Years later, in 1996, he reminisced about the circumstances of his birth with good humour:

> And so my father comes along and marries my mother, and after six days his first wife comes and grabs him by the ear and takes him back, and so the story ends. I'm the outcome of those six days [laughs]…which is to say, if my father hadn't fallen in love, and they'd not spent those six days together, well, who knows what really would have happened to Islam and blasphemy… After I was born, I lived with my mother.[15]

The description of Layeh giving birth is unusually detailed and poignantly graphic. Makhmalbaf describes it as if he were giving birth himself, in himself, to himself. By 1984, Makhmalbaf and Fatemeh Meshkini had been married for six years; he had witnessed the birth of their children, Samira in 1979 and Meytham in 1981. His mother was also a nurse by profession. The description of Setareh's birth in the first chapter of *The Crystal Garden* is thus biographically placed within Makhmalbaf's own experiences.

But something far more enduring, far more significant, is also taking place in this chapter and in the entire book. To come from watching those ideologically overburdened films to reading this gem of a short novel is a miraculous revelation. In *The Crystal Garden* we read an artist in the making, with no sign of Makhmalbaf the religious and revolutionary ideologue. What happens is Makhmalbaf's metaphoric return to an internal birth-point. In the first two chapters he recreates not just the world of Layeh, widowed mother of three young children, but the cosmic expanse of a universe of emotions into which he has been born and on which he can now draw. In this book he goes back to basics and there, in the simplicity of poverty and the brutality of the real that he sees, feels and lives, he gives birth to himself.

By the third chapter, the surreal Makhmalbaf is in full, fantastic view. His description of Layeh's nightmarish insomnia, her fears and anxieties in facing the prospect of caring single-handed for three young kids, is a premonition of the later cinematic Makhmalbaf of *Once Upon a Time Cinema* (1991) and *Gabbeh* (1995). It is hard to believe that the author of *The Crystal Garden* is the same ideologue who about a year earlier made *Seeking Refuge*.

The Crystal Garden has a simple plot. It takes place in the house of a rich family which fled the country in the aftermath of the Revolution. Such houses were typically confiscated by the revolutionary government and given to the families of those who had perished in the course of the Revolution and the war. The narrative revolves around the fate of four families gathered in the old servants' quarters. Khorshid and her husband Qorban Ali were the servants before the Revolution and continue to live there. The widowed Layeh has just given birth to Setareh and has two other children, Sareh and Meytham. The third family is that of Mashadi and his wife Aliyeh, whose son Akbar perished in the war; they live with their daughter-in-law, Akbar's widow, Suri and her two children, Samireh and Salman. Mashadi and Aliyeh's other son, Ahmad, younger brother of the martyr Akbar, also lives with them. Young Maliheh and her husband Hamid, paralysed from the waist down in the course of the war, make up the fourth family. Maliheh married Hamid from a religious commitment to care for a hero of a just war. Because of his condition, the couple cannot have any children.

Writing a work of fiction, as opposed to making a film, involved an entirely different set of creative urges for Makhmalbaf, a psychological disposition that would soon transform his entire creative mood. If we consider, as one among many examples, the scene where Layeh, after her childbirth, goes to the public bath in the company of her friends and neighbours, the event, as Makhmalbaf describes it in patient and analytical detail, is almost tangible in its unburdened physical realism. Here his descriptive power leaves no room for any intrusion by ulterior motives. It is as if, in the 'privacy' of these pages, he has no chip on his shoulder. He does not have to prove himself to Beyza'i or any other prominent pre-revolutionary filmmaker. No trace of the committed revolutionary or the fanatic Muslim is remotely evident in *The Crystal Garden*. Quite to the contrary. Everything here is torn open, layer after layer, in an almost archaeological introspection. There is thus a kind of moral retreat, a reversion to the robust busy-ness of the rambunctious lives of women – wives, daughters-in-law, mothers-in-law, nieces, sisters – where life is crowded, complaints are constant, few things are actually said, and yet that is all there is. In this novel, Makhmalbaf gets lost in the bosom of the women-folk: young wives who have lost their husbands in the war, bitter mothers mourning martyred sons, pious young women married to maimed war veterans. In the midst of such miseries, however, neither Makhmalbaf nor any of his characters are remotely ideological, revolutionary, committed or even political. Politics is almost absent from *The Crystal Garden*. But the consequences of politics are not. These people just live, and their lives are crowded, lost to all grand illusions, major highways of salvation, monumental solutions, abstract convictions, metaphysical certainties. These women are Makhmalbaf's way back to the insurmountable ephemerality of the real in its magnificent cruelty, its detailed minutiæ of small hopes, long before and beyond its distortions into one grand illusion or another.

In *The Crystal Garden*, Makhmalbaf reaches for the hidden corners of cultural catastrophes, realities that are ordinarily hidden from the blinkered eye of moral formalism, political absolutism, ideological conviction. His description of the inner anxieties of Hamid, the young war veteran, for example, is brutally suggestive, reaching for paralysing pains beyond name and recognition. Though not a word is mentioned about sex, Makhmalbaf's awareness of Hamid's sexual paralysis and anxieties toward his young wife is culturally cataclysmic. Hamid is relentlessly – almost obsessively – conscious of Maliheh's religious reasons for agreeing to marry a half-paralysed and totally useless man. Makhmalbaf gives full narrative swing to the young veteran, without ever collapsing into moral evaluation of the reasons for or consequences of his sacrifice. He simply dwells on the moment of a wasted youth, the *cul-de-sac* of a life come to nothing. The result is a tortuous passage through an awareness of realities that defy categorical ideologies. The ferocious reality Makhmalbaf must face in order to describe it forces him in effect to abandon all ideological formulations and reach for their earthly details.

Practically all the criticism aimed at the early Makhmalbaf has focused on his naive, flat, early films and ignored what is happening, almost at the same time, in his fiction. *The Crystal Garden* is not the work of a committed ideologue: a far more serious intelligence is at work here, probing and discovering realities beyond the bland, tedious and insipid emptiness of all ideologies, Islamic or otherwise.

Not much happens in Makhmalbaf's fiction. He is certainly no Hushang Golshiri, the Iranian master of miniaturesque attention to narrative detail. He is no Mahmud Dowlatabadi, the other Iranian master of the glorious epic narrative. In fact, Makhmalbaf is not much of a storyteller. He is a well-digger, an archaeologist of latent emotions, forgotten anxieties, hidden horrors, inarticulate hopes. *The Crystal Garden* is much less a novel than a patient record of an excavation into subterranean realities ordinarily lost to the mundane matter-of-factness of living. What Makhmalbaf does, in chapter five for example, when he unfolds the inner trepidations of the young widow Suri, is to map out the topography of conflicting, at times eloquent, at times mute, emotions. The flat certainties of Makhmalbaf's characters in his early, 'Islamic', cinema here give way to a universe of painstakingly sculpted characters, the living memories of a culture in crisis.

Neither here nor later in his best films does Makhmalbaf attempt a logical narration of interrelated events. He has always pursued the virtual veracity of the real more than its actual or factual. Many of the characteristic features of his later films are anticipated in *The Crystal Garden*, where narrative movement is always virtual, at a time when his cinematic record is nowhere near the depth of emotional investment paramount in this short novel. *The Crystal Garden* is thus of central significance in detecting the earliest moments of Makhmalbaf's later cinematic penchant for virtual realism, one of the characteristics which has led to the global celebration of Makhmalbaf as a filmmaker.

If Makhmalbaf was ideologically afflicted early in his creative career and his first three films are symptomatic of that malaise, the earliest signs of his robust recovery and a full recognition of a turn to emancipatory release are fully evident here in *The Crystal Garden*. The initial reason for the rise and constitution of his creative character in fiction rather than cinema is sociological. Makhmalbaf came from a family both lower-middle class and fiercely religious. He was neither highly educated nor a deeply cultivated intellectual. The most prominent members of the Iranian cinematic establishment, people like Beyza'i, Mehrju'i and Kiarostami, came from secular upper-middle-class backgrounds, cultivated in both substance and manner. That substance and that manner created awe and anxiety among the class that Makhmalbaf best represented.

The Revolution had of course a fundamentally class-based component. Much of the so-called Islamic code of conduct forced on the public at large was an expression of lower-class resentment against the upper-class air of superiority. Twenty years later, a profoundly class-based cultural distinction is still paramount in Iranian cultural politics. It is often distorted by a dichotomization of 'traditional' and 'westernized' components in society, but the schism is far too serious to be represented by this bogus dichotomy. Economic at base and cultural in disposition, it is rooted in the semi-colonized state of Iran during the nineteenth and the twentieth centuries.

Makhmalbaf's search for an 'Islamic' cinema is equally rooted in this categorical search for an alternative cultural expression to defy the domineering air of the pre-revolutionary filmmakers. His famous statement about not being pictured with them, 'even in a long-shot', rests precisely on this sentiment. The term *taghuti* ('satanic'), applied to pre-revolutionary filmmakers, also expressed this attitude of resentment against everything that had survived the brutal cut of the Revolution.

By 'Islamic' cinema, Makhmalbaf intended far more a revolutionary than a religious cinema. But the historical fact of the Iranian polity at this juncture was that a revolutionary cinema must also be religious. In effect, what Makhmalbaf does in his early cinema is thumb his nose at pre-revolutionary filmmakers, proving to them that he can be both a Muslim revolutionary and a filmmaker. It is crucial to remember that much early revolutionary anger was manifested in bombing and burning film theatres. It was in one such attack that hundreds perished in the southern city of Abadan.

In the 1970s, the Tehran Film Festival was an occasion for Iranian secular intellectuals to rub shoulders with world-renowned filmmakers. The festival had phenomenal consequences for the Iranian cinema of the 1970s, but at the same time it was deeply alienating to millions of the poorer residents of the capital. They could hardly afford to attend the events, let alone share in the air of cultural superiority evident in their theatricality. It is sad but nevertheless undeniable that much of the secular culture of Iran in the 1960s and 1970s – as expressed not just in the Tehran Film Festival but even more offensively in the Shiraz Art Festival – was sponsored by, and gave cultural credence to, the Pahlavi monarchy. To be sure, pre-revolutionary Iranian filmmakers like Beyza'i or Mehrju'i were as innocent of collusion in the Pahlavi tyranny as Makhmalbaf and a score of other filmmakers have been of involvement in the atrocities the Islamic Republic has committed against its own citizens. But the unfortunate state of the pre-revolutionary art was such that, in order to see the work of even Amir Naderi or Mehrju'i, two of the most progressive filmmakers at the time, one had to sit next to the Pahlavi ruling elite.

Makhmalbaf of course soon realized the absurdity of his position and began to remove himself from the corner he had blindly painted himself into. But the result of this passage through a revolutionary determination against the *ancien régime* is that in his creative imagination there is a solid material base in Iranian realities that defies the counter/colonial constitution of all revolutionary ideologies, including Islamism, and a search for a kind of subjective emancipation that does not issue creative cheques that it cannot materially cash. The fundamental problem with Iranian art of the twentieth century – its quintessential disjunction from its material conditions – is here solved by an excruciating passage through the material hell of that society. To be sure, the pre-revolutionary art against which Makhmalbaf revolted had not altogether yielded to either the colonial or the nativist parameters alternately placed on its path. The Persian poetry of Yushij, the fiction of Hedayat, the drama of Sa'edi and certainly the cinema of Beyza'i, all had profoundly liberating and emancipatory thrusts in them. But Makhmalbaf did not emerge from the 'secularist' response to cultural colonialism. He had been specifically a Muslim activist and as a result his art had to conquer its own particular demons.

The political tide of a massive, radically Islamized revolution had given Makhmalbaf the historical opportunity to express his at once Islamic and revolutionary charge against pre-revolutionary art. In 1981, while the Iran–Iraq war was raging and violent opposition broke out at home, the Islamic Republic's grip on power was only further strengthened by crushing all forms of opposition. In these circumstances, with secular artists in a state of fright, Makhmalbaf was triumphant.

Or was he? By far the most visible signs of the active Islamization of revolutionary Iran were the women. Almost half a century into their active incorporation in state-sponsored modernization under the Pahlavis, they were now forced into far more restricted social roles. Women are also of central concern to Makhmalbaf in *The Crystal Garden*. The novel is in fact dedicated to 'Women, the tyrannized women of this land'. Who are these women? The casualties of a culture. Widowed at a very young age and with infants to care for but no steady source of income, they are at the mercy of the revolutionary zeal to which their young husbands have lost their lives. Evident in these women are both the enduring stigma of widowhood and the ephemeral respect of marriage to a 'martyr'. Makhmalbaf is quite clear in his diagnosis of the enduring calamities of being a woman, and totally dismissive of the momentary 'respect' they are offered. Layeh, whose husband has died in the war with Iraq, has three children to raise. Suri, who has also lost her husband to the war and has two children, has to endure the indignity of living with her in-laws. Maliheh, who married a partially-paralysed war veteran out of pity and piety, now mourns her wasted youth and frustrated desire for children. These women, in their mundane, numbingly pitiful lives, represent realities that defy and persist through revolutions and wars. Straight out of post-revolutionary, war-torn Iran, they in effect cure Makhmalbaf of his convictions. While people with far fewer revolutionary credentials now hold high office, Makhmalbaf is increasingly drawn away from the Revolution, its ideology, and even its metaphysical certainties. What he sees in these women, whom he portrays with astonishing realism, is the persistence of a moral, cultural and social malaise beyond any ideological cure.

Far simpler and more palpable realities now reveal themselves to Makhmalbaf, realities that in both their enduring miseries and their hope of redemption have the ring of truth that no ideological movement in contemporary Iran has addressed, let alone changed. In Sareh and Salman, Layeh's orphaned children who have lost their father to the war at a very young age, Makhmalbaf invests the vast innocence of birth, wonder and discovery – the very alphabet of his emerging realism.

> 'What's this, Layeh?' asks little Sareh.
> 'An earring.'
> 'What's an earring for?'
> 'It's to hang on your ear. It's for beauty.'
> 'Beauty?'
> 'Yes, dear, beauty.'
> 'What's beauty for?'
> 'Beauty? It's for happiness.'
> 'Happiness?'
> 'Oh for God's sake, my dear, I don't know! Put it back, you'll spoil it.'[16]

In an unnecessary attempt to account for various chips on his shoulder, Makhmalbaf has repeatedly boasted of the number of books he has read or films he has seen or paintings he has carefully studied and analysed. But he has achieved the most solid and enduring education of his lifetime through *writing* these stories, the very act of sitting down and relentlessly digging deep into his own, and through that into his collective, sub/conscious. In these servants' quarters of a rich family who has fled the wrath of an Islamic Revolution dwell characters and consequences from which 10 Islamic and 100 non-Islamic revolutions cannot escape. This is a goldmine of pre-ideologized realities that defy the crooked and callous instrumentalities of all ideological convictions. All categorical imperatives lose their relevance and effectiveness in these servants' quarters and gradually make of Makhmalbaf the Muslim ideologue an artist with a world of misery and hope at his creative disposal.

When Makhmalbaf lets his ideological guard down, as he does fully in *The Crystal Garden*, he cannot but see and show the realities that in their very material irreducibility make a mockery of all those ideologies and demand a far more serious attention to their particular place on the cultural constitution of a society. In *The Crystal Garden*, Makhmalbaf is almost clinically aware of this irreducibility of the real, and disarmingly analytical in his unravelling of the tyranny perpetrated on Iranian women, one particularly poignant example of such realities. The novel, as a result, can be read as an archæology of grave injustices that have culturally and socially conditioned the status of women in all patriarchal societies. It is not just the cultural construction of femininity that becomes evident in *The Crystal Garden*. By examining Hamid's inner anxieties about his unconsummated marriage, or Layeh's second husband Karim Agha's masculinist trepidations, Makhmalbaf assays the topography of gender-constitution, both masculinity and femininity. Placing these deeply wounded and permanently scarred adults next to the young Sareh, Salman, Matham and Samireh, Makhmalbaf's story becomes a panoramic view of the very process of socialization through which culture and society inculcate their enduring miseries in young and impressionable children. Ten PhDs in social sciences and humanities, and a train-load of self-congratulating and highly cultivated secular intellectuals and *literati* who ridiculed – and continue to ridicule – Makhmalbaf could not and did not do any better. Makhmalbaf's art is superior because it emerged from the dirt and mud of a culture and then, by the sheer power of creative imagination, reached for emancipation in terms domestic to the miseries of that culture.

Over all his characters, without any exception, Makhmalbaf pours a cascade of love and affection, understanding and sympathy, and that is the singular superiority of his auto-didactic rise from the depths of his shallow ideological convictions. For example, when he looks at Mashadi, Aliyeh's husband, father-in-law to Suri, father to the martyred Akbar and his younger brother Ahmad, and grandfather to Samireh and Meytham, he unpacks this pious, prematurely old man into the diverging sum of emotions that make him possible and prompt him to act. It is precisely this overwhelming outpouring of Makhmalbaf's love for his characters that enables him to reach a far richer and more fulfilling conception of them and their moral and cultural predicaments. He could not have this grasp of reality and continue to issue those ghastly ideological statements about 'the Fate of Man' or 'the Battle of Good against Evil'. By and through *The Crystal Garden*, Makhmalbaf is freed: from the dual Manichean dungeon of his Persian prison, from the labyrinth of Islamic meandering made all but inevitable by his fight against Pahlavi monarchy, and through it the very constitution of colonial subjectivity. In that freedom, Makhmalbaf does not pull any punches. He goes for the jugular when he has to.

There is something of that youthful 17-year-old revolutionary in Makhmalbaf's art, especially when it gets nastily transgressive, as when Mashadi arranges for a marriage between his son Ahmad and his young daughter-in-law Suri, who used to be married to his older son Akbar, and has two children from that marriage, Meytham and Samireh. The moment is transgressively powerful. When Akbar was alive, Suri was like a sister to Ahmad, yet now that Akbar is dead Ahmad is both religiously and socially eligible to marry her. The match is so logically perfect that it loads the transgressive moment with a daunting sexual overtone, without the slightest narrative suggestion to that effect.

Such suggestively transgressive moments make Makhmalbaf's narrative particularly receptive to his female characters, by far the most anxiety-provoking thematic for an Iranian male novelist. In *The Crystal Garden*, Makhmalbaf shows an uncanny ability to penetrate the deepest thoughts, doubts and anxieties of the women. His portrayal of Layeh is particularly powerful. Makhmalbaf spent his childhood in the company of three extra-ordinary women, and, until his mother remarried, without a father figure. His mother was a strong-willed woman, married to his father for only six days. After her divorce, she pursued a nursing career, assisted by her mother and sister in raising her son. Makhmalbaf's maternal aunt was an equally impressive woman, who assumed responsibility for educating her young nephew. But by far the most influential character in his early life was his grandmother, a deeply devout woman who left an indelible mark on the young boy. He spent his early childhood at home in the protective care of these three women, and in fear of being kidnapped by his father. This is how Makhmalbaf remembers these formative years:

> After my birth, I was looked after by my grandmother, as my mother worked nights in the operating room at the hospital. She paid our bills. My father refused to get a birth-certificate for me, and the two of them fell into the sort of petty games of humiliating and holding grudges against one another...and so, my mother paid our bills until she was suddenly dismissed. She got into

an argument with the hospital administrator, and he cancelled her nursing certification. She could no longer work as a nurse, just because he made a pen mark across her certification card. She couldn't even get a job anywhere else. And so, because of this situation, she was forced to file a complaint and try to get child support from my father. When she went to make the complaint, she had him arrested, naked that is, with a loin cloth, and had him taken to the police station. This episode humiliated my father [laughs] and so he decided to kidnap me, since my mother refused to let him be my guardian. And since I'd only seen my father once or twice, I only knew that he was really fat, I was afraid of him ... and at this point he decided to kidnap me ... I was about five years old. My dad hired a thug to wait at the head of the alley, and my father paid his wages for two years to look out and kidnap me whenever I should venture out the door of the house and into the street. And so I spent two years in jail right there in my own house [laughs]. I had an aunt who was a schoolteacher. She lived with us and loved me quite a lot. She taught me to read and write. Before I even went to the first grade I was already reading detective stories... My grandmother, mother and aunt, we all lived together then. My aunt taught me to read and write, and my grandmother, since she couldn't just leave me at home alone, would take me with her to the mosque... [This went on until] my mother met this lawyer while dealing with our legal problems. He was a young man, had recently come from Qom, was a follower of Khomeini, a religious and political person, and she married him. And so these three people, my grandmother ... well, my father had the effect of scaring me, driving me from the life of the alley which was more or less the real world, and entrapping me in a house where three important people tried to take care of me. One was my grandmother, who introduced me to religion. One was my aunt who made me literate. The last was my stepfather, who made me political. My character was thus moulded by these three in the first three decades of my life.[17]

Partly because of these experiences, Makhmalbaf's female characters come straight out of Iranian urban reality. The autobiographical monologue of Khorshid in chapter 11 is an exceptionally brilliant narrative of the life of a young peasant girl, married first to a tribal chieftain, then to a wandering pilgrimage leader, and finally in an endless succession of temporary marriages (*mot'eh*) – a perfect portrayal of the terrors and tribulations of her gender and class. By far the most colourful and courageous character of the entire novel, a woman who constantly defies her fate and turns the abused status of women in patriarchal cultures to her advantage, Khorshid is in effect engaged in one religiously sanctioned form of prostitution after another. Within her limitations, she is an extraordinarily resourceful and assertive woman, changing husbands as often as a slight improvement of her lot may require. She becomes something of a philosopher, with a profoundly perceptive notion of life in general, men in particular.

But what can I say? As they say, a woman with no husband is like pure gold, but hidden in a drawer. Unless you put her on display in the window, no customer will notice her. Will they? Someone has to tell the rat what's in the barn, you know. But say what you will, eyes deceive before ears can hear. In my case it was the landlady who kept my market hot, she did. She was a noble lady, she was. But so was I, wasn't I? Of course I was. Thanks be to heaven that not once did I lay my hand on something forbidden. Not once did I look at a man in a sinful way. God forbid! Don't you believe for a moment that I was particularly happy. No. I married about a hundred men, one worse than the next. When a woman is put on and off like a garment, even her soul gets worn out. Just like her body, it ages. I have never lived in comfort. But, hey ... I saw the world, and pretty much figured it out. The whole world is run by men. The whole world has been created for bastard men. It has. Whoever they want, they marry. Whoever they don't want, they divorce. If they are good, they collect every good thing for themselves. And if they are bad they do the same with the bad things. All over the world, men want women for one thing and for one thing only: to play doll with them and have them serve them, mother them, you know? Once I married this fellow ... [18]

Khorshid also has the great virtue of being in love with cinema. The highest expression of her piety is always the most sincere moment of her love for cinema: 'In the morning I used to go to the movies. In the evening I went to the holy shrine as a humble pilgrim.'[19] Indian musicals are her favourites. Speaking of one of her favourite husbands, she says:

When he came home that night, he had made himself up again to look like Raj Kapour ... He said to me, he said, 'Let's go out to see a movie'. He used to put a comb and a piece of paper in his mouth, just like a harmonica, and then sing in this nasal voice: 'Gunia, Guni, Gunia, Gunia mo Saghia'. I said to him, I said, 'What madness is this? One day you mourn "O My Martyred Lord Abelfazl!" and the next you sing 'Gunia Guni Gunia'!?'[20]

Makhmalbaf creates in Khorshid a manifesto for the veracity of cinema as art. Speaking of yet another husband, Khorshid reports:

We used to go to the cinema too. But mostly I went to the movies by myself. Once every blue moon he would take me along with him to see a movie. *Ali Baba and the Forty Thieves* we saw, *The Famous Amir Arsalan, Yusef and Zoleikha, The Return of Abu Antar*. Only God knows how terrified I was when Abu Antar put on this pair of dark sunglasses and did all those weird tricks. When I left the cinema, I saw the world differently. Once I made it a condition of my temporary marriage with the fellow. I said to him, I said, 'Your rights and privileges as my temporary husband, all good and dandy. But I have to have my right to the movies.' He said to me, the bastard, he said, 'I won't marry a woman who doesn't care about the forbidden and the permissible and goes to the movies.'

I said to him, I said, 'You can go to hell. I won't marry you.' The ugly bastard. It was hard enough to bring myself to marry the hideous thing and now he was adding insult to injury. Pretending to be more Catholic than the Pope, he was. I know these bastard men inside out, I do. Once I saw a movie, there was this man in it, a kind of foreign spy, you know. He had come to another country to have a temporary wife, I am quite sure of it. Then he was secretly putting the poor woman up to all kinds of tricks to report to him about this, that and the other. Finally they were both caught. They killed the poor woman. But the man, who was from some other part of the world, was returned to his country. When I tell you all over the world womenfolk are just plain stupid, here is an example. To hell with the bastard. He didn't deserve me anyway. When the time of my temporary marriage with him was over...[21]

No-one, especially not Makhmalbaf, could withstand the unsettling effect of such an outpouring of the unconscious on metaphysical, let alone ideological, convictions. All his religious and revolutionary convictions, evident and flaunted in his early cinema, collide head-on with his brilliant portrayal of Ahmad and Suri's wedding night, even more effectively than in Khorshid's soliloquy. The (im)possibility of these two young people consummating their marriage puts into the balance everything Makhmalbaf holds sacred. The memory of Suri's dead husband haunts and paralyses the newly-weds. Makhmalbaf of course cannot see them having sex under the gaze of the martyr, even if Aliyeh, Suri's vigilant mother-in-law, has removed her son's picture to her own room. His simple, ingenious way out of this impasse is to send the newly-weds off on pilgrimage to Mashad, there to absolve themselves of their 'sin' and who knows what else.

The sudden, bewildering, news that Akbar is alive and a POW (prisoner of war), in Iraq gives his parents a shock of both joy and fear, throwing Makhmalbaf's own narrative off balance:

> Aliyeh seemed not to hear. She was seated, talking to her own shadow on the wall. Suddenly she would get up and run from her shadow to the other side of the room. As for Mashadi, he didn't even have a shadow. He was standing in the dark, behind the window, looking at the yard that was being covered again with snow. Overnight he had shrunk to a shadow. He was going mad with sadness and joy: 'What's right. What's wrong. Day of Judgment. Akbar. Ahmad. God. Suri. Aliyeh, I'm leaving.'[22]

Mashadi has been instrumental in marrying his daughter-in-law to his younger son, thinking that her husband was killed in the war. Ahmad and Suri are now in Mashad on honeymoon, and he discovers that his martyred son is actually alive. He is paralysed by a combination of joy that his son is alive, the 'sin' that he has committed by giving his daughter-in-law to his other son, and his inability to tell his first son. He leaves for Mashad to prevent a catastrophe.

Meanwhile in Mashad, Ahmad and Suri, in the company of Suri's children, are trying to redefine their relationship from brother and sister to husband and wife. They succeed. They break the barrier. They make love. Suri becomes pregnant and begins to learn to love her new husband.

There are very few chapters in the long and magnificent history of modern Persian fiction that can compete with chapter 15 of Makhmalbaf's *The Crystal Garden*; the concluding chapter of Dowlatabadi's glorious epic, *Klidar*, is the first to suggest itself. What Makhmalbaf does in this chapter simply defies description. Mashadi, Aliyeh, Ahmad and Suri are of course completely numbed by the news that Akbar – their son, brother, and husband – is alive and a prisoner of war in Iraq. They do not know whether to be happy that he is alive and will be coming home soon, or to be petrified at the thought of what to tell him when he comes back to see that his wife has been married to his younger brother and is pregnant. Makhmalbaf's depiction of this moment of moral and emotional paralysis is brilliant. The gamut of the Persian ethical universe and Shi'i morality is here held at bay. Juridically, Suri and Ahmad have not erred: according to Islamic law, a woman whose husband is presumed dead can remarry, and marrying one's brother-in-law is no problem. Besides, they have added social approval since Ahmad has assumed responsibility for his brother's family, and Suri has not remarried outside her dead husband's family. But the mere possibility that her first husband is alive and soon coming home to see what has happened puts the whole spectrum of male–female and male–male relationships off balance. It literally jolts the system.

If this were not nerve-racking enough, on further investigation the family learns that there are two Akbar Soleymanis among the enlisted soldiers at the front: one they have buried in Iran, the other is alive and a POW in Iraq. Now what? Is Akbar dead or is he alive?

Ahmad and Suri immediately revert to their earlier, more formal, 'brother–sister' relationship. But what is intolerable is that they do not know whether to hope for Akbar to be alive in Iraq or dead and buried in Iran. The harsh balance between familial affection and moral propriety is put to the test. But this is one of those rare occasions, opening a universe of ethical conflicts, when the textural integrity of a culture is released from its presumed legitimacy. All emotions, relations, convictions, moralities, laws, social norms, cultural proprieties, everything is brutally and summarily suspended. For the duration of a few days – an eternity – Ahmad and Suri in particular are totally de-humanized, cut off from their vital signs of moral and cultural affiliation.

Mashadi is furious with all his friends and family who did not let him see his son's face when they buried him. But what can he do now? 'We'll exhume the body!' he announces to his son Ahmad. There is only one way out of this calamity, this debilitating state of uncertainty. They have to dig up the body to see if it is Akbar's. Even if the face is not recognizable, they can measure the length of the body. If it is 170cm, it is his, if it is 153cm, then it is the other Akbar Soleymani's. The commotion the family goes through to convince a grave-digger to disinter the body is only the tip of the phantasmagoric iceberg of social and religious taboos they have to transgress in order to resolve their predicament.

The scene of the actual disinterral of the body is a hideous, haunting, horrific eternity, a never-ending rollercoaster of frightful suspension of everything a person could believe in, or try to forget to believe in. Makhmalbaf's eye for detail is descriptive to a point of figural paralysis. Everybody is present at the exhumation – present, that is, in a ghostly apparition of how they would remember themselves. Mashadi, Aliyeh, Suri, Ahmad, everyone is there – even the half-paralysed Hamid has come along to witness this living hell. By midnight they have done all the necessary bribing and have mobilized all the courage they have left and brought themselves together for one final and resolute look at the body of their loved one – maybe he is, maybe he is not – in order to resolve the catastrophe one way or another, which way though, no one can tell, no one had better tell. They dig and they dig, and they fear and they dig, and they dig and they dig, and they reach the body, only to tear its shroud and expose the decayed flesh and the skeleton of a body that resembles nothing but the very picture of death. It is the wrong grave.

Is there an end to this calamity? They move to another grave, read the name of Akbar on it a million times, and start digging again. It is Akbar's. There is no way to describe Aliyeh's condition when she sees and recognizes her dead son's body, no way to know what Mashadi feels when he is at once destroyed and relieved to see it, no way to reach the depths of Ahmad's or Suri's sad and yet indescribable relief. No way to know any of this. But Makhmalbaf's narrative is electrifying, inspired.

They all go home. They are ... what? Happy? Sad? Relieved? Soon after, Ahmad returns to the war-front. Suri is hospitalized for manic depression. Mashadi and Aliyeh get busy raising their grandchildren. But soon Mashadi cannot take his sedate, wintry life any longer and joins his younger son on the battlefront. The news of Ahmad's and Mashadi's deaths reaches their family and nearly destroys Aliyeh and Suri. But the two ravaged women return from the edges of madness to take care of their children. Life goes on. It wills itself.

At the end, Makhmalbaf completely dismantles this compound household, brought together in this servants' quarters of a confiscated house by the common misery of having had a young martyr in the family. The revolutionary government returns the house to its original owner, who has returned from abroad to claim his property. Khorshid, her opium-addicted husband now dead, initially stays as servant with the original owner of the house. The other three families are all put in one room in a hotel until proper housing is arranged for them. They divide the room into three sections, one for Hamid, Maliheh and their adopted daughter Najmeh, one for the old Aliyeh, the pregnant Suri and her two rambunctious children, and the third for Layeh and her three children. Karim Agha, Layeh's second husband, disappears. But Khorshid returns to live with the rest after the owner of the house sells it to the first buyer he finds, takes his cash and leaves the country for good.

Makhmalbaf concludes his story and exits the narrative with two lasting memories, one the promissory note of how art saves reality, and the other – one of the greatest scenes in modern Persian fiction – how reality saves art. In the first, the young Samireh is listening to her grandmother Aliyeh telling her and the other children a bedtime story:

> The children were falling asleep one by one, all except Samireh who had realised that Grandmother was actually telling her her own life story, just changing the names. Samireh even knew that the girl in the story called Nasim was really her. But she didn't know why the people in the story were more lovable. She didn't understand why the grandmother in the story was more beautiful than Aliyeh herself.
> 'Why, Grandma?'
> 'Why what, my dear? Be quiet, Samireh, go to sleep!'[23]

The second scene depicts a miracle. To end the novel, Makhmalbaf is ready for one of his most brilliantly surreal moments in print, a premonition of what will later become the chief characteristic of his best films. The four families are now completely dismantled. Mashadi, Akbar and Ahmad are dead. Suri has given birth to a boy, but is now half-crazed and committed to a mental asylum. Meytham and Samireh are growing up like weeds. Khorshid has taken Layeh and her children away, no-one knows where. Hamid and Maliheh and their adopted daughter Najmeh make a meagre living. At the centre of this collapsing colony of revolutionary misery, death and destruction remain Aliyeh and her youngest grandson, who has no name, no father, an institutionalized mother, and not even a wet-nurse to feed him. The nameless baby boy is used to being breast-fed, when Layeh agreed a few times to nurse the helpless thing. He will not accept bottle-feeding, no matter how many times Aliyeh and Maliheh try to force him. Maliheh is petrified and helpless. The infant cries and screams incessantly, to the verge, at one point, of asphyxiation. There is no nursing mother in sight, no formula, no hot water and sugar to calm the infant. He cries and cries, and then he cries even harder, bitterly, edging his short and fragile life second by second to the brink of a premature death. Aliyeh, oldest woman of this small clan of calamity, widow of a warrior, aged mother of two valiant martyrs, grandmother to three surviving children, having just celebrated her heavens-only-knows-how-many-eth birthday, sole remaining pole of this collapsed tent, grabs her nameless, fatherless, motherless, youngest grandson and runs in desperation into the middle of the court-yard, frantic, wild, bewildered, mad with rage, confusion, despair.

> In the half-dark, half-lit courtyard of the hotel, there was no-one in sight. The sky was full of stars. The moon was sliced thin, a narrow crescent of light. The baby was implacable. Aliyeh walked him, patting him on the back. 'Ala la la lalalala, A la lalalala, A lalalala . . .' The baby did not get calmer. Aliyeh became desperate, she scratched her face furiously. She sat down and tore her dress. She put the baby on the ground and began to beat herself. Her veil fell off her head. She beat herself again. The baby was about to pass out again. Aliyeh grabbed some dust from the ground and poured it on her head. She beat her knees and her breast. Her legs and her breast burned. The baby's voice was about to die out. Aliyeh's whole body, in this bitter cold, was on fire. Involuntarily, she grabbed the baby and put one of her breasts into his mouth. She held the baby's legs in the middle and squeezed them. The baby took Aliyeh's breast in his mouth and suckled. Crying and suckling gave his voice a rhythmic tone. Pain ran wild from the skin of Aliyeh's breast to the very depths of her heart. The baby chewed on her. Aliyeh was aflame and burning. Her heart and guts were churned up. The baby released her breast and cried:
> 'Un-na. Un-na'.
> 'Calm down, my dear, calm down! For God's sake, calm down. That's enough.'
> It was not enough. Aliyeh bared her head and put her breast once more into his mouth. The baby wouldn't take the nipple in his mouth. He would-n't be fooled. Aliyeh got up. She raised her head to the sky and bit her lips. Blood rushed to her face, and under her lips she roared:
> 'God, where are you? Don't you exist?'

Something inside her began to flow. Her heart began to palpitate. Involuntarily she stood up and ran. The infant had put all his remaining strength into his lips and was suckling at her breast. Aliyeh's heart was beating madly. The veins in her neck were swollen from frustration. Something burned her from within. It boiled from the depth of her heart and gushed forth towards her breast, burning and cutting through. Fresh milk streamed into the infant's mouth.

The whole earth had become young. What's the time? Where is this place?[24]

Notes on Chapter 7

1.   See 'The question concerning technology', in Martin Heidegger, *The Question Concerning Technology and Other Essays*, translated with an introduction by William Lovitt (New York, Harper Torchbooks, 1977), pp. 14, 34.
2.   Heidegger, 'Technology', p. 34.
3.   My use of the specific term 'post/colonial', needs careful understanding. Though Iran was never officially colonized in the way that much of Asia, Africa, and Latin America was by the British and the French, chief among other Western European colonial powers, it was squarely located within the hegemonic parameters of colonial interests in the region. The entire course of nineteenth-century Iranian history is grafted smack in the middle of the colonial interests of the British, the French and the Russians. My use of the prefix 'post/' does not mean that I believe Iran or the rest of 'the Middle East', Asia, Africa and Latin America is in a postcolonial condition simply because India received its independence from Great Britain in 1947 and a slew of brilliant theoretical articulations of postcoloniality were proposed by intellectuals of postcolonial India. Nor do I believe that post-Second World War neo-liberal economics, facilitated by such instrumental agencies as the World Bank and IMF, have successfully disguised the relation of economic and political power between the advanced capitalist economies and the rest of the world. Colonialism salvaged its dominant characteristics by turning the earliest forms of commercial colonialism into active capitalist colonialism, and now the same logic is equally present in the rapid globalization of capital. But the same globalization of capital and the rapid labour migration it has occasioned have generated a form of global insurrectionary consciousness which I point to and celebrate by the slash ('/') inserted in the post/coloniality of our condition. This metamorphic sign is thus there to point to the continued relation of power that exists between advanced capitalist economies (the G7) and the rest of the world, while underlining the necessity of active opposition to a globalized condition of coloniality. As much as we are all indebted to the Indian experience of theorizing their particular condition of postcoloniality, the careless universalization of their particulars has done grave damage to the necessity for a careful

understanding of the rest of the colonized world. That perhaps permanent slash ('/') is the vigilance we need to keep between our actual condition and our potential emancipation.

4. Heidegger, 'Technology', p. 35.
5. *Ibid.*
6. *Ibid.*
7. See Jürgen Habermas, 'Modernity: an unfinished project', in Maurizio Passerin d'Entreves and Seyla Benhabib (eds), *Habermas and the Unfinished Project of Modernity* (Cambridge, MIT University Press, 1997), p. 45.
8. See Theodore W. Adorno, *Aesthetic Theory*, newly translated and edited, with a translator's introduction by Robert Hullot-Kentor (Minneapolis, University of Minnesota Press, 1997).
9. Kant's aesthetics categorically disqualified and excluded us from serious consideration (Immanuel Kant, *Observations on the Feeling of Beautiful and Sublime*, translated by John T. Goldthwait, Berkeley, University of California Press, 1960, p. 111). He has more charitable things to say about Arabs, 'the noblest man in the Orient', Persians, 'the French of Asia' (p. 109), and Japanese, 'the Englishmen of this part of the world' (p. 110).
10. Heidegger, 'Technology', p. 35.
11. Gholam Heydari, *Mo'arrefi va Naqd-e Film-ha-ye Mohsen Makhmalbaf* (Tehran, Espark Publications, 1372/1993), p. 26.
12. Antonio Gramsci, *Further Selections from the Prison Notebooks*, Derek Boothman (transl. and ed.), (Minneapolis, University of Minnesota Press, 1995), p. 17.
13. Gramsci, *Further Selections*, p. 17.
14. Mohsen Makhmalbaf, *Bagh-e Bolur* (Tehran, Nashr-e Ney, ninth printing 1374/1995); The English translation (Mohsen Makhmalbaf, *The Crystal Garden*, Minou Moshiri [trans.], Tehran, Ney Publishing House, 1989) is unfortunately not successful. Because of its serious shortcomings, all translations in this chapter are mine; but all page references are to the original Persian text.
15. Excerpt from a conversation with Mohsen Makhmalbaf, October 1996.
16. Makhmalbaf, *Bagh-e Bolur*, pp. 95–6.
17. Excerpt from a conversation with Mohsen Makhmalbaf, October 1996.
18. Makhmalbaf, *Bagh-e Bolur*, pp. 149-50.
19. Makhmalbaf, *Bagh-e Bolur*, p. 137.
20. Makhmalbaf, *Bagh-e Bolur*, p. 142.
21. Makhmalbaf, *Bagh-e Bolur*, p. 135.
22. Makhmalbaf, *Bagh-e Bolur*, p. 185.
23. Makhmalbaf, *Bagh-e Bolur*, pp. 250–1.
24. Makhmalbaf, *Bagh-e Bolur*, pp. 261–2.

8

A Ghost in the Machine: The Cinema of the Iranian Sacred Defence

Roxanne Varzi

The history of cinema is a long martyrology.[1]
Gilles Deleuze

It was the victory of faith over unbelief.[2]
MCIG

A pair of hands ties together loose wires on a row of coloured lightbulbs that dangle in the dark night. Eerie music plays as the camera pans below the festive rows of wedding lights to Da'i, who is busy tying ribbons and flowers to his car. A man dressed in a brown robe passes by. For a second he turns. He looks like Da'i.

He asks Da'i, 'Are you preparing for the return of a POW [prisoner of war]?' He is referring to the festive lights and decorated car.

Da'i is visibly surprised; shaken, he replies, 'A wedding.'

'Do you have a POW?' the man asks.

Da'i nods yes; 'Do you?' he calls after the man. 'Is he on the Red Cross lists?' Da'i starts to cough, he cannot finish his sentence: 'Be assured he will re—,' he tries to say.

But the man is gone.

The bride sits alone in the middle of a circle of family and friends. She is dressed in white. The traditional wedding mirror, Qur'an and sweets surround her. Nearby is a framed picture of the absent groom. The telephone rings, but no-one is on the line. The long drone of a cut telephone line suggests an absence, but it also presents a ghostly presence or a sign that someone or something is trying to speak.

The telephone rings again; this time it is the groom, calling from abroad. A man with a camcorder moves around the room, recording the wedding. The camera closes in on another framed picture on the wall, of another young man, Yusef, whom the bride would have married had he returned from the war. The framed pictures mark a double absence created by Yusef's flight into war and the groom's flight away from war. They are exiles and POWs waiting to return. Being waited for.

A woman places a large-framed picture of the groom in front of the bride and nonchalantly hits the speakerphone button. The groom is now present in image and voice. He is far away, but locatable. The bride puts the receiver to her cheek, as though she were having a private conversation. She seems unaware that everyone is listening, waiting for her to exchange the wedding vows with the man on the telephone.

The voice of the groom asks her, 'Are you still in love with Yusef? Are you marrying me because you want to, or because Yusef's father, Da'i, wants you to?'

She does not answer, the line is cut, and the electricity goes off. The crowd claps, as if the vows were exchanged. The camera moves to Da'i's face. He looks guilty, sad. The camera moves behind him toward the dark night. They waited all day for the call. Outside, festive, brightly coloured wedding lights blow in an increasingly gusty breeze – as if a ghost is moving through them. A lightbulb pops. Inside, everyone is silent, it is dark. Waiting. There is the sense that something beyond human perception is at play and that the empty night is charged with invisible energy. Ghosts: *khiyal,* feelings; *ruh,* spirit; *shabih,* similar, like a shadow of one that was.

In the next scene, at the airport, the bride is about to walk through the Departures gate to go abroad to meet her groom. She turns back for a final glance at Da'i, to catch him mesmerized by a screen showing the evening news, with buses of returning POWs.

The bride comes to his side and asks: 'What are you after? When the dogtags were returned to us, I got my answer from Yusef.'

'Do you love your new groom?' Da'i asks.

'Why?'

'Do you love him? I have to know.'

6. Ebrahim Hatamikia's *The Scent of Yusef's Shirt*.

'Yes.'

'Well, then, give me the tags,' he says, referring to the dogtags she is holding in her hands.

'You never wanted them, please don't take them from me,' she says.

'Give them,' he says.

She puts the tags in his hands, and before walking through the gate, she says, 'I too believe in miracles, but only ones my size.'

On the way home from the airport, Da'i gives a ride to a young Iranian woman, Shirin, who has returned to Iran after 15 years in Paris. She has come back to find her brother, Khosrow, whom she believes to be among the POWs released by Iraq. The film, Ebrahim Hatamikia's *The Scent of Yusef's Shirt* (1996), documents the friendship between Shirin and Da'i and the very different yet similar ways each deals with mourning and the ambiguity that surrounds those who are MIA (Missing in Action) but not positively known to be dead. The film plays brilliantly on the complexities of a death that may not be physical, the problem of whether and how to mourn a missing person who may or may not be dead, and the important notion of faith. The trope of return is played out in exiles who return to Iran from abroad, returning POWs and the many ghosts who have returned to haunt the Tehran landscape.

Sacred Defence Cinema

A supply of images would become the equivalent of an ammunition supply.[3]

The war-film industry in Iran began in September 1980, shortly after the start of the Iran–Iraq war, with the inception of made-for-television documentaries, made by a team at the Islamic Republic of Iran Broadcasting (IRIB) called the War Group. In 1983, concern over the 'production of action-packed war films with poor scenarios, unable to show the truth about the Sacred Defence', led the MCIG to start a War Films Bureau at FCF. This new film initiative was created to depict the Sacred Defence, 'emphasizing experience rather than theory as a basic qualification for making movies about the war'. War filmmakers had to be Muslims who had served at the front. Over 100 films were made portraying 'the true nature of the Sacred Defence or imposed war'.[4] About 70 amateur directors were trained as war-film directors, including several – such as Mohsen Makhmalbaf and Bahram Beyza'i – who are now internationally recognized feature-film directors.

This project, which began as a move to appropriate critique of the war by re-contextualizing war images in a specifically religious and pious manner, opened a whole new arena – of post-Revolution Iranian cinema itself – where historical and contemporary social issues never before addressed could be brought to the surface.[5] In war films, the very history of martyrology and the practice of mourning in Shi'ism, and the appropriation of this history by cultural producers, work together and in conflict. In the case of Iranian cinema, the space of martyrology and mourning becomes a space of haunting. Iranian cinema is both aided and burdened by the ghosts of Shi'a history.

In this chapter I trace the move from war-era films to the post-war generation of 'war films' dealing with the aftermath of the war and the return of POWs. Concentrating specifically on Rasul Mollaqolipour's early war film *The Horizon* (1989) and Hatamikia's later *The Scent of Yusef's Shirt*, I shall discuss the roles of cinema and faith and the problem of visibility in the act of mourning.

After the inauguration of the War Films Bureau for the Sacred Defence, there was a clear move toward films that sought to represent the war as spiritual rather than military in character. This move from action to narrative films is marked by the presence of Islam, which serves to promote the war as Sacred Defence rather than a matter of cold-blooded strategy.

In the first action films made about the war, it is virtually impossible to differentiate between Iraqi and Iranian soldiers.[6] The soldiers rarely mention Allah or the Imams, let alone Hoseyn, who, as the most important Shiʿa martyr, became the emblematic Imam of the war. The soldiers are clean-cut and freshly shaven, unlike the bearded revolutionaries who will later come to mark Iran's war. Films made after the Sacred Defence film programme was put into effect mark a clear departure from the earlier 'action' films by providing the space for the 'sacred' in defence. These films emphasize the role of martyrdom and belief in the action scenarios of the films.

The Horizon

In *The Horizon*, the Iraqis, despite also being Muslim, are relegated to the status of non-religious infidels. They are shown as clean-cut, suave, cigarette-smoking, westernized strategists who sit in their highly techno-logized war machine – a battleship equipped with massive control panels and surveillance machines – watching and waiting for the Iranians. The Iranians, on the other shore of the Persian Gulf, are portrayed as bearded revolutionaries with long, shaggy hair and red bandanas, dressed in black scuba suits reminiscent of the black shirts worn during Ashura. Their very bodies and souls oppose the traditional concept of a war machine; theirs is a war of flesh and spirit. Everything about their battle suggests its connection to that of Imam Hoseyn at Karbala. Their battalion is called the Imam Hoseyn Battalion, and their little motorboat *Ashura*.

Ashura is the defining moment in the history of Shiʿism, re-enacted annually. In order to understand fully the war films made after 1984, one must be aware of the importance of this ritual.[7] Ashura, the tenth day of the lunar month of Moharram, is the anniversary of the martyrdom of Imam Hoseyn, grandson of the prophet Mohammed, who was killed in 680CE while fighting Caliph Yazid's army at Karbala, in present-day Iraq. For Iranian Shiʿis, Karbala was the battle of believers against unbelievers; and the Iran–Iraq war was for many an attempt to reclaim Karbala.

The first 10 days of Moharram are marked by ceremonies of mourning. Men march in procession through the streets, beating their chests and flagellating their backs with metal chains. In the villages and quieter parts of the cities the traditional *taʿziyeh* plays are performed. These are re-enactments of the martyrdom of Hoseyn and his family at Karbala, passion plays in which performances of the events, although already known to the audience, remind them of the martyrdom of Hoseyn. 'It revives dormant feelings and rekindles an emotive, dormant fire.' In the plays 'a devoted warrior, inspired by the fire of his faith, faces a large army and a treacherous adversary. He is killed in battle and he is bitterly lamented. His death, however, fulfils a prophecy.'[8]

Ta'ziyeh are never actually performed in the films I reviewed. Yet, the thematic use of Ashura in the war, and again in cinema, is an attempt to make the war itself a performance of *ta'ziyeh*, doubled in the cinema, which re-enacts the re-enactment, bringing many mimetic layers to the ghost-memory of martyrdom in Shi'ite mourning. It is an absent moment that history makes present in the very call to jehad: a call for martyrs.

War had everyone on the move, including the dead.[9]

Those scenes that most resemble *ta'ziyeh* are actually more like Sufi *zekr* rituals, where men gather together in a circle and move in a slow dance, bending into the circle with one arm extended then hitting their chests with the other arm. Toward the end of *The Horizon*, as the troops of the Imam Hoseyn Battalion are preparing to attack the Iraqi fleet, there is a sequence that moves completely away from the plot-driven action into a trance-like music video. It begins with a young man, wearing an Ashura headband and combat gear, seated cross-legged on the beach with his arms extended to receive a blessing – the gift of death. Just as the leader begins to rub ointment on his palms, we hear the hypnotic rhythm of *daf* (frame drums used in mystical rituals) followed by a chorus chanting Rumi's words: 'Die, die, die, go to this death, leave this earth…die, die, die.' Next we see each successive soldier receive his blessing and join the circle dance. At the end of the sequence, they are dressed in their scuba gear. Black against the black night, they pass under the Qur'an, kissing it twice as they go out into the dark water. 'People used to die for a coat of arms, an image or pennant on a flag; now they die to improve the sharpness of a film. War has finally become the third dimension of cinema.'[10]

This filmic military operation is unique in the way the divers become eerie personifications of death as they move through the water, to attack the cold, technologically advanced, un-spirited Iraqi warship with nothing but oxygen tanks and AK47s. A storm sets in as they descend into the water. If the Iranians really are closer to nature, slaves of God, then the storm can only be a prophetic announcement of death. At the Iraqi head-quarters, everyone is relaxed, certain that the Iranians will not launch an attack in bad weather. Meanwhile, the Iranians have slipped on board, unnoticed, and, like ghosts in the machine, have begun to rewire the technology of the Iraqi leviathan. The first sign of their presence is a computer crash. 'But the radar didn't detect anything,' says the Iraqi soldier. 'The Iranians can't possibly be on board, check the radio.' Like ghosts, like the spirit of death itself, they have slipped right past the radar: a triumph of spirit over technology. When the Iraqis turn on the short-wave, a slow melodic voice chanting Qur'anic verses comes over the airwaves. The voice is a softer version of the religious music heard on shore. 'They're praying,' says an Iraqi soldier. They are fighting, and praying and presenting death in this scene, because theirs is a war of the spirit. They are soldiers of God who can slip past radar undetected, move through a storm and amplify prayer. By amplifying prayer they are announcing death. They board the ship and, like the grim reaper, start taking people to their deaths, silently, one by one. The moment a soldier sees an Iranian diver – tall, dressed in black, a masked apparition from the night – it is too late, he is dead. The Iranians have literally come out of the night, only mourning music announcing them. As Virilio says, 'War cannot break free from that magical spectacle, because its very purpose is to produce that spectacle: to fell the enemy is not so much to capture as to captivate him, to instill the fear of death before he actually dies.'[11]

Meanwhile a shot pans the dark beach, where hundreds of Iranian soldiers sit listening to the music that is being played for the Iraqis. The soldiers are already mourning their comrades fallen in battle, even before their dead bodies are washed ashore. The very call to jehad presupposes a call for martyrs (*shohada*) and mourning.

While *The Horizon* is a battle film, it strongly anticipates the problems of mourning and the legacy of war that later haunt POW films. The relationships of the head diver, Nosrat, to the partners he keeps losing, anticipate the ghosts of war and the agony caused by missing bodies that becomes so pronounced in post-war films. The story, here, is not just one of an elite underwater military operation, but of a diver's inability to deal with the death of his partners. As Virilio says, 'Rest never comes for those transfigured in war. Their ghosts continue to haunt the screens or, more frequently, find reincarnation in an engine of war – usually a ship.'[12] The Iraqi ship becomes the repository of unidentifiable Iranian bodies – ghosts that haunt the surrounding waters and feed Nosrat's nightmares.

The film begins with the surreal sound of bubbles underwater as the camera swims among brightly coloured Gulf fish. Suddenly, the anticipation of death – experienced through the sound of heavy underwater breathing

– is realized in the form of a dead diver, unidentifiable, with his oxygen mask pulled over his head. Before the audience is able to register the scene, they are back in a bedroom, where the head diver, Nosrat, has just woken from this nightmare.

The next time Nosrat enters the water, he insists on going out alone. He is forever searching for the missing body of his dead partner, Hamid, who was killed aboard the Iraqi ship. As he powers the motorboat at top speed, alone, through the winding river out to the open Gulf, his partner Ahmad follows him. Eventually, Ahmad is shot and wounded by the Iraqis. Nosrat tries to save him, but Ahmad insists that he swim away before the Iraqis come for the bodies. They both know Ahmad is dying. Nosrat says, 'How shall I dare to return without taking you with me?' It is better to return with a dead body than a ghost. If Nosrat leaves before Ahmad dies, then the ambiguity of his status, dead or alive, will forever haunt him.

It is this ambiguity or invisibility that has most concerned the war films since the end of the war. The after-effects of the war are a continuation of the war from a physical and visible battleground into the realm of invisibility. Most audience members, as they view their country on the screen, are waiting for the return of a lost person or soul. The stories are of POWs and their families, and of exiles abroad.[13] This world of lost souls replaces earlier cinema by moving the battleground from the Iraqi border and the body to Tehran and the soul. No longer do we see a replay of emotional scenes of battle or mystical scenes of trance, 'ritual', so often talked about in terms of the Iranian war-front. Instead, battle and trance are incorporated in the search for bodies, for POWs and for meaning after the war.

The Scent of Yusef's Shirt

In *The Scent of Yusef's Shirt* the surreal moments of the Ashura story are played out at the beginning of the film, when the lights go out and the wind picks up. The eerie ghostliness is reminiscent of the story of Siyavush, the hero of the *Shah Nameh* (*The Book of Kings*): 'cosmic disturbances took place when Siyavush was killed: "a violent wind began to blow, a heavy dust arose and a stagnant darkness spread." Such phenomena could only point to the sanctity of the slain hero.'[14] The gusty wind and electrical blackout point to a symbolic death, the first blow to Yusef's memory and a sign that, for one person, he must be dead. Ghosts appear when the living begin to forget. Ghosts of the dead point to a failure. They remain invisible, yet move through space the way a spirit would through a medium.

The Scent of Yusef's Shirt plays with the ambiguity that surrounds the question of death in relation to MIAs. Is he dead or alive? The question of presence and the need to have bodily proof are problematic for mourning in post-war Iran, where so many soldiers became MIAs or POWs. What is at stake – lacking physical proof of death – is visibility or its inverse, invisibility. A ghost is only present after death. Even if a particular POW is positively dead, there are enough ghosts in Iran to haunt the waiting family. With so many unidentified dead bodies and men MIA, the whole nation is easily haunted. The POW films, unlike battle films, are more about absence and disappearance than about death. The same ambiguity based on the theme of disappearance, invisibility and waiting inherent in the Shi'ite belief in the hidden Imam, comes to pass in the POW scenarios. The POWs are more than just hidden saints, they are the leftovers, the excesses of war. The ones that are most disturbing are those who leave only a trace, for whom there can be no true burial, no bodily evidence of death and only anonymous ghosts. Nameless ghosts that do not speak or identify themselves haunt *The Scent of Yusef's Shirt*.

This inability to identify ghosts complicates the processes of waiting for someone or viewing unidentifiable remains. This invisibility, inability to locate a body or identify a body, makes mourning that much harder. Derrida says, 'Nothing could be worse for the work of mourning than the confusion of doubt: one has to know who is buried where and it is necessary (to know – to make certain) that, in what remains of him, he remains there and move[s] no more.'[15] For Derrida, mourning begins by ontologizing remains, by making them present, by localizing the dead. Da'i's daughters attempt to solve the problem of locating the spirit or body at a site by buying a grave in memory of Yusef. When we see the video of the memorial service, Da'i is aloof, unwilling to participate, refusing to allow that site to be a place where he could bury Yusef for good. Yusef will remain forever in Da'i's mind, where he will continue to haunt Da'i until his body returns, dead or alive. This refusal to believe that Yusef is dead is fuelled by a doubt, which keeps him partially alive. It is doubt that haunts, regardless of actual death. Doubt is so unjust, so unsettling in post-war Iran. Doubt is the very injustice of war that will continue to haunt the scene.

We make sure that what we would like to see dead is dead. We mourn so that the dead will not return as ghosts; and yet they do return as ghosts if a body is not available to be mourned. Iranian war cinema does this work. The images on screen come to stand for the dead by making present what is absent. Like the video within the film, the ghost in the machine comes to stand for the body and becomes an object to be mourned. Yet, the cinematic images cannot bury or bring back the dead, but can only point to the impossibility of return.

Like a manifesto or a proclamation of death, cinema provides an image to be mourned, a ghostly presence: a hauntology of the after-war films that are created in the wake of the now-dead martyrs. The media, neither living nor dead, neither absent nor present, spectralizes.[16]

While Iranian war cinema consciously provides a visual image for the mourning audience, within the film, video unconsciously creates a ghostly image of the missing person. In both of his POW films – *The Scent of Yusef's Shirt* and *From Karkheh to Rhine* (1993) – Hatamikia uses video to represent a place of visual ambiguity. This he does brilliantly and controversially in *From Karkheh to Rhine* when a POW in Germany regains his eyesight and sees a video recording of the funeral of Khomeini for the first time. He grabs at the screen and begins to cry. The image of Imam Khomeini on the screen replaces the actual body. The soldier tries desperately to grab at the screen, just as other hands in the crowd infamously grabbed at the body. The sequence ends with a shot of his fleshly hand over that of the video hands reaching toward the coffin.

In *The Scent of Yusef's Shirt*, Yusef is present only as a video and photo image. Even the moments of pure mourning, when Da'i cannot hide his sadness and lack of faith, are all captured on video. It is the video of Yusef which brings Shirin out of a trance, and into a realization that her brother is dead. It is only through video that she even knows Yusef, as she watches the video sequences of Yusef and others at training camp, listening to trance music as they put on their fins. She watches the sunset with them, as they descend into the water, but is unable to follow them when the video turns blank and becomes a ghost. The next shot is of Yusef's bloody dogtags – the remains. The very dogtags they brought out of a shark's belly, thus leading Da'i to say, 'I should have named him Yunes,[17] not Yusef.' Da'i never believed he was dead. He did not watch the videos or allow them to replace Yusef in his imagination. Yusef was never a ghost to Da'i; he never spoke to him nor was present at his grave. Da'i's faith is what keeps Yusef alive – as we see in the end when Yusef returns.

When someone is missing among so many dead, confusion ensues and it becomes hard to identify individual ghosts, to claim the right spirit, just as it is difficult to claim the right mutilated body. War confuses identity.

The irony is that these video ghosts, these recreations of images, are what later help to find many POWs, by identifying them in the camps. When the soldiers return, they are confronted with the ghosts of their battalion, as family members of the disappeared, half-grieving, half-hopeful, appear with now ghostly images in the form of large framed pictures. In *The Scent of Yusef's Shirt*, Shirin and Da'i visit the home of a returned member of Khosrow's battalion. A group of villagers sit in a circle holding their large framed pictures. They drink tea and eat halva (traditionally a sweet for mourning holidays). They ask the man if he has seen their sons or witnessed their deaths.

> 'Did you see him being killed,' they ask.
> 'No, that's what happens when they are captured by Iraqis, they kill them.'
> 'If you didn't see it, how do you know?'

Without proof, without witnesses, their deaths are not positively established, nor can they be officially mourned. We know in the film that there are wayward ghosts out there, and yet these presences in the film are never named as ghosts. They are alluded to through cinematic devices – the gusty wind, the popped lightbulb, storms, eerie music – that create an effect without ever solving the problem of presence or answering the questions that drive the film: is Yusef still alive? Is Khosrow still alive? Which one of them is haunting the film, as more than just a missing person, but a returned death? Which one will return alive?

Return from the Front

Hatamikia's films deal brilliantly with the very different and unexpected types of return: the videotapes recovered from the front, dogtags, ghosts and, most interestingly, exiles from abroad. Through exiles, we come to understand the international scope of the war and that what binds a nation is so much more than land. By virtue of association, not a single Iranian could escape the mark of war. Every Iranian takes part in the act of mourning. 'We have our [ghosts], but memories no longer realize such borders by definition, they pass through walls, these remnants, day and night, they trick consciousness and skip generations.'[18] Eventually all ghosts come home.

The task of post-war Iranian cinema becomes the task of mourning itself. It is a many-layered project, which strives to use images to beautify and spiritualize a war-torn environment. It is a project in making visible the invisible, the missing bodies, without naming ghosts, without pointing to a possible injustice or crime.

It is this problem of missing bodies and of returnees who are the legacy, the mark of failed martyrdom: a martyr is meant to return in the form of a dead body. Yet, these very ghosts haunt the cinema. The return of men sent off to war to be martyred very obviously marks the failure of martyrdom. POWs present the return of something that should have remained buried. The injustice of war is written on their fragmented bodies, in the space of a lost limb (Yusef returns with one arm missing). What is at stake is visibility. What cinema does is to re-appropriate possibly critical images and memories and place them in a space of controlled mourning, where the correct effect and proper ghostly nuances are at hand. Even ghosts permeate celluloid. Ghosts of the dead point to failure, they remain invisible, but come through, the way a spirit would, to point toward a place of injustice. Here we see a partial failure of the task of concealment, because mourning is inherently critical. As Virilio says, 'If what is perceived is already lost it becomes necessary to invest in its concealment.'[19] Cinema does this by placing the emphasis in post-war films on martyrology through trance scenes. Interestingly, it is Shirin, the foreigner, who goes into trance while searching for her lost brother. It is her brother who is not found. She lacked the necessary faith to keep him alive. Her return, and her decision to stay and wait for him, point to the nationalism that cinema tries to effect in her character. It is her duty to wait, though he may never return. Cinema reinstates hope, as Da'i says, 'If you don't believe, who will?' The last shot in the film is of Shirin, back at home in Tehran, taking sweets out into the street for Khosrow's return, even though she knows deep down that he is dead. War films deflect the idea of failure and try to present an alternative image. Shirin's lack of the faith that Da'i has points to her need to become revolutionized, to see the good. Her return to Iran represents an act of faith. What is finally at stake is one's own survival and ability to move on.

While presenting the nation with its deaths in a beautiful and artistic way, war cinema opens up a whole new, safe realm for mourning. It is a project in controlling images, controlling emotion and regulating the boundaries of the nation – that place of ultimate return, dead or alive.

Notes on Chapter 8

1. *Cinema 1: The Movement-image*, transl. Hugh Tomlinson and Barbara Habberjam (University of Minnesota Press, 1986), p. xiv.
2. *The Imposed War: Defence vs. Aggression* (Tehran, MCIG, 1983), p. 63.
3. Paul Virilio, *War and Cinema: the Logistics of Perception*, Patrick Camiller (trans.) (London and New York, Verso, 1989), p. 3.
4. *Iran* (daily newspaper), 19 September 1995, p. 12.
5. This was also the case with the Centre for Intellectual Development of Children and Adolescents, which supported the careers of directors such as Abbas Kiarostami.
6. Except in the case of weapons, where some viewers will be able to differentiate the Iraqi soldiers who carry Russian guns from the Iranian soldiers with American-made weaponry.
7. A special website existed for a brief period, available to Iranians everywhere, where images of Ashura were easily accessed for 'virtual mourning': virtual images come to replace physical bodies in mourning.
8. Ehsan Yarshater, 'Ta'ziyeh and pre-Islamic mourning rites in Iran', in Peter J. Chelkowski (ed.), *Ta'ziyeh: Ritual and Drama in Iran* (New York, New York University Press, 1979), pp. 89, 90.
9. Virilio, *War and Cinema*, p. 28.
10. Virilio, *War and Cinema*, p. 89.
11. Virilio, *War and Cinema*, p. 5.
12. Virilio, *War and Cinema*, p. 61.
13. Many POWs were sent to treatment centres abroad. Hatamikia's film, *From Karkheh to Rhine* (1993) deals explicitly with this situation. His latest film, *The Glass Agency* (1998), is a controversial story about a pair of war veterans who hijack a plane to go abroad for treatment.
14. Yarshater, 'Ta'ziyeh', p. 90, quoting Tha'alibi, *Kitab al-Ghurar* (ed. Zotenberg, Paris, 1900), p. 213. Yarshater examines the Siyavash story as a pre-Islamic religious forerunner of the Ashura drama.
15. Jacques Derrida, *Specters of Marx: the State of the Debt, the Work of Mourning, and the New International*, Peggy Kamuf (trans.), with an introduction by Bernd Magnus and Stephen Cullenberg (New York, Routledge, 1994), p. 9.
16. Derrida, *Specters*, p. 51.
17. Yunes is the Qur'anic form of the Biblical Jonah.
18. Derrida, *Specters*, p. 30.
19. Virilio, *War and Cinema*, p. 4.

9

Negotiating the Politics of Gender in Iran: An Ethnography of a Documentary[1]

Ziba Mir-Hosseini

Between March 1996 and April 1998, I co-directed the documentary film *Divorce Iranian Style* with an independent British filmmaker, Kim Longinotto. The film was inspired by my book *Marriage on Trial*, which was based on ethnographic research on Islamic family law.[2] Almost the whole 80-minute film takes place in a small courtroom in central Tehran. There are four main characters:[3] Massy, who wants to divorce her inadequate husband, Ziba, an outspoken 16-year-old who proudly stands up to her 38-year-old husband and his family, Jamileh, who brings her husband to court to teach him a lesson, and Maryam, remarried and desperate to regain custody of her two daughters. This, my first exposure to filmmaking, involved me in long series of negotiations, not only with the Iranian authorities for a permit and access, but also with myself. I had to deal with personal, ethical and professional dilemmas as well as with theoretical and methodological issues of representation and the production of anthropological narratives. The film's subject-matter inevitably entailed both exposing individuals' private lives in a public domain and tackling women's position in Islamic law, a major issue which divides Islamists and feminists.

What follows is an account of these negotiations, exploring the problem of ethnographic representation generally, as well as the complex politics involved in representing 'Iran' and 'women in Islam'. The account is in three parts: first is an account of the 20 months of negotiations before we were able to make the film; second a description of the one-month film shoot in Tehran, during which we extended our negotiations to the people who came to court, and of how we edited the raw footage into the finished film; thirdly, I summarize the reactions of various audiences to the film – a final series of negotiations of meaning. Through these narratives, I aim to show the ways in which the reality of Iranian women's lives portrayed in our film came to be constructed, and how it has been interpreted by viewers.

Negotiating Access

The idea of making a film about the working of *shari'a* law in a Tehran family court was born in early 1996, when a friend introduced me to Kim Longinotto, the documentary filmmaker. We discovered that we shared the same frustration with Western media stereotypes of the Muslim world. I had seen and liked Kim's film on women in Egypt (*Hidden Faces*, 1991). She had for some time wanted to make a film in Iran, being intrigued by the contrast between images produced by current-affairs TV documentaries, and those in the work of Iranian fiction filmmakers such as Kiarostami. The former portray Iran as a country of fanatics, the latter convey a much gentler, more poetic sense of the culture and people. As she put it, 'You wouldn't think the documentaries and the fiction were about the same place.' We discussed my 1980s research in Tehran family courts and I gave her a copy of *Marriage on Trial*.

The next steps were to apply to British TV commissioning editors for funding and to Iranian officials for access and a permit to film. Kim concentrated on the first, I on the second. In March 1996 we submitted through the Iranian Embassy in London a proposal to shoot a documentary film in court in Tehran. Aware of the sensitivity of the theme, we phrased the proposal carefully. We stated that our aim was to make a film that would reach a wide audience and challenge prevailing stereotypes about women and Islam. This we wanted to do by addressing a universal theme cutting across cultural and social barriers, to which ordinary people could relate emotionally as well as intellectually. Marriage, divorce and the fate of children, we argued, provide a perfect theme for such a film.

We had two main arguments. First, in order to reach a wide audience, a film should have a story, a sense of drama. Court cases inherently involve stories and drama, which would instantly capture an audience's interest and sympathy. Stories – especially disputes – are powerful yet non-judgemental narratives; they communicate themselves, they inform and educate the audience in the human aspects of a different culture, and allow – even force – the audience to question their own prejudices and assumptions. Through such stories, audiences can gradually, without being aware of it, learn to understand and respect a different value system, which at first may have seemed remote and incomprehensible. In subtle ways, an intimate view of family disputes in another cultural context would shift the focus from cultural difference to common humanity.

Secondly, in order to challenge stereotypes successfully, and to draw the viewer into the rich and varied lives of ordinary people, the film should focus on individuals and their stories in the courts as well as in their homes. This was important, because some of the most powerful and least-questioned stereotypes of Islam and Muslims concern women and the law. In the case of Iran, for instance, many in the West understand and judge Iranian family life – and the status and position of women within it – by the accounts of writers such as Betty Mahmoody, whose book and subsequent feature film *Not Without my Daughter* (Brian Gilbert, 1991) reached a wide Western audience. This story too was about families and the fate of children when marriages break down; ordinary people could easily relate directly to these universal themes, but at the same time they absorbed a one-sided picture of the complex reality of Iranian family life. That picture has remained unchallenged, simply because there is no alternative account available.

These arguments were not enough to persuade the MCIG to give permission for the film to be made. In October our application was rejected without explanation; we learned later that FCF, which is responsible for issuing film permits, found it difficult to categorize the project, and understood it to be for a 'feature film'.

Kim and I did not give up. We were now committed to the project and were convinced of the need to tackle the topic of divorce in Iran through a film that would reach a wide audience. So we continued to lobby the Iranian embassy, attending its functions to meet visiting dignitaries and explain our project. For Kim, these meetings became a crash induction course into the official gender codes of the Islamic Republic, and it took her some time to understand and feel at ease with the embassy's gender protocol. The first time, she arrived at a reception wearing a red scarf tied behind her head – as she had done when filming in rural Egypt – and tried to shake hands with an Iranian diplomat to whom I was introducing her, almost chasing the poor man around the room.[4]

In mid-November a Shi'a organization in London convened a meeting to celebrate the birth of Fatima, daughter of the Prophet; key speakers included Zahra Mostafavi and Fatemeh Hashemi, heads of two of the most influential women's organizations in Iran, with close ties to the ruling elite. Mostafavi, daughter of Ayatollah Khomeini, was president of the Women's Society of the Islamic Republic; Hashemi, daughter of then President Rafsanjani, was head of the Women's Bureau in the Ministry of Foreign Affairs and of the Women's Solidarity Association of Iran. After attending the meeting, we had discussions with both women, arranged for us by the embassy.

We talked to Hashemi after she had given a press conference, in which she combined modernity and religiosity in both her appearance and her views. Kim and I were impressed by her performance and the way she handled the questions. She told me that she had heard of my research when she was in Oxford and saw the merits of our project, but that she found our choice of theme too controversial. In a polite and diplomatic manner, she made it clear to us that if we did not change our theme we would not get a permit to film; she would not welcome our attachment to her Association, nor would it be of any help to us. Nevertheless, she gave us her card and said she would invite us to a conference on women and cinema hosted by the Association the next February.

But we failed to communicate our vision to Mostafavi. Kim and I understood that we had an appointment to see her in the embassy residence, but when we arrived we found that she was holding a reception for a group of women. We felt awkward and unwelcome. We were not invited to join in, and were ushered into a separate room to wait. Mostafavi then came in with a young woman whom I supposed to be her assistant, and said there had been a misunderstanding: she had expected us earlier in the other building. I apologized for the inconvenience, and said that we had been told specifically to come at this time. I handed her the Persian text of our proposal, and asked for her help with getting a permit. I tried to make a case for our film and our approach, stressing our interest in portraying common humanity rather than difference. Kim and I were in a unique position to do this: I was an Iranian and an anthropologist and she was an experienced filmmaker; we had both lived and worked in different cultures, and could make a film that would reach a wide audience. But neither our aims nor our credentials seemed to convince her. She talked about the Qur'anic approach to anthropology – which she understood to be not the comparative study of culture but the study of human nature – and expressed her doubts about the sincerity of the Western world and its media, saying, 'We have been stabbed so many times.' She also told me I had lived abroad for too long, suggesting that I had lost contact with my culture. I objected strongly, defending my Muslim and Iranian identity and saying that the study of culture was my field, that I had conducted research in different parts of Iran and in Morocco, that I had been on numerous missions to various parts of Iran as a consultant with a UN organization, and that we had contacted her because we thought working with an Iranian organization could facilitate our project and would be beneficial to us all. She said she would send our proposal for appraisal to the Women's Society she headed, and promised she would let me know the result. But we never heard from her again.

After we had left, Kim drew it to my attention that Mostafavi had let her *chador* slip as she spoke to us, showing us what she was wearing underneath – something I had not noticed. I was impressed by Kim's trained eye and realized that there were many things that I took for granted and no longer noticed about my own culture; at the same time, of course, there was so much of significance that I knew and understood but Kim did not yet see. I was also becoming aware that I was not just an observer but that my debates and interactions with my compatriots were becoming a part of our project; through them, Kim was developing an insight and understanding of gender politics in Iran. If we could work together, we would be a good team.

Going to Iran: Arguing our Case

Three encouraging developments followed shortly after. We met Ayatollah Mohammad Taskhiri, head of the Organization for Islamic Culture and Communication – a body directly connected to the Office of the Supreme Leader – who had led the Iranian delegation to the 1995 Women's Conference in Beijing. He was visiting SOAS in London for a meeting with Iran specialists; Kim and I joined in, and managed to present our project to him. To our surprise, he expressed no objection to our topic and told us to contact his Organization, which could help us with obtaining a permit.

I also had a telephone call from a young filmmaker my husband Richard and I had met in Tehran in 1995; he was about to make a documentary about the Shahsevan nomads with whom Richard had worked many years before. On the phone I mentioned our project and asked his advice. A week later I had a call from Kadr-e Film, an independent film production company in Tehran. They were interested to work with us, asked for a more detailed treatment, and said they could get us a permit, assuring us that foreign filmmakers like us could work in Iran only through their company.

Finally, in December, we heard that one of our applications for funding had come through: Channel 4 was prepared to fund us to make a feature-length documentary for its prestigious 'True Stories' programme. We were enormously encouraged.

So in mid-January 1997, the first week of Ramadan, Kim and I decided to go to Tehran to follow up our permit application and argue our case in person. The trip was important for both of us, as we wanted to see whether we could work together. I especially wanted Kim to see Iran for herself, to get a feel of the place and culture. I knew she had filmed in other countries, and during our meetings at the embassy and dealings with Iranian officials in other contexts it had become clear that we shared many perspectives, but I was unsure how she would relate to the country and my family, with whom we would be staying. Kim was in her mid-forties, like me, but from a different socio-cultural background, and she did not speak a word of Persian.

I need not have worried. While she stayed with us, Kim fitted into my family and neighbourhood so well that I felt no need to mediate, to justify our way of life or to defend Iranian values and customs. She got along particularly well with my mother who, like many other Iranian housewives, was in charge of our whole household and involved in a complex and powerful network of kinship and neighbourhood activities, formed and maintained by women. During the 10 days Kim stayed in Tehran, our differences turned out to be bridges not barriers. Kim had no problem with daytime fasting during Ramadan. She easily fell in with the demands of *hejab*. Like me, Kim had a practical approach to the dress code: she observed it fully when we were in public space and did not allow it to get in the way of her work. I found this immensely liberating and reassuring. Experience had taught me that inner resistance to the dress code can make some women so agitated that it becomes a barrier, a real obstacle to what they want to do.

Every day we went to talk about our project with many people, from both religious and secular women involved in debates on women's rights in Iran – academics, lawyers, journalists – to independent filmmakers who were anti-clerical in their outlook, and officials in TV, the MCIG and women's organizations. To obtain our permit, we were prepared to collaborate with an Iranian film company or a women's group. Most of them, however, wanted us to change our theme, to film a 'politically correct' issue which reflected a 'positive image' of Iran, such as marriage ceremonies, female members of parliament or mothers of martyrs. Again and again I had to defend our choice of theme, which led to some heated discussions. I could not interpret fully for Kim, who often got anxious that we were having a serious dispute.

These discussions helped us to improve our presentation of the project, and also helped me to clarify my views on the politics of representing 'Iran' and 'women in the Islamic Republic'. We had to distinguish what we – and, we hoped, our target audiences – saw as 'positive' from what many people we talked to saw as 'negative', with the potential of turning our project into yet another sensationalized foreign film on Iran. Images and words, we argued, can evoke different feelings in different cultures: for instance, to Western eyes a mother talking of the loss of her sons in war as martyrdom for Islam is more likely to confirm stereotypes of religious zealotry and fanaticism than to evoke the Shi'a idea of sacrifice for justice and freedom. We argued that what they saw as 'positive' could be 'negative' in Western eyes, and vice versa; that one answer was to present viewers with social reality and allow them to make up their own minds; some might react favourably, and some might not, but in the end it would give a much more 'positive' image of Iran than the usual films. No single film, we argued, could show the complete reality of Iranian society, but when there were many films available people could get alternative views. If we could show women, at home and in the court, holding their own ground, maintaining the family from within, this would challenge some Western stereotypes.

We had extended discussions with three production companies. The head of Kadr-e Film, who had called me in London, was away during our stay in Tehran, and instructed his deputy to finalize our agreement. But we failed to reach any kind of understanding. A retired army man with no conception of an observational documentary, he and his colleagues first tried to persuade us to change the theme, arguing that nothing positive could be said about women and law in Iran. I found myself having to argue that the Revolution and its aftermath had empowered Iranian women by gradually opening a space for them to claim their rights within the context of Islamic law. This was obviously a view they did not share, and they took it as an argument for Islamic law and the status quo. They said that our proposal was too vague and that they would need a full script, details of our characters and locations and so on, in order to get us a permit. These of course we could not provide. We explained that an observational documentary, by definition, allows stories to present themselves to the camera, and to develop while filming; we could not define and constrain them beforehand.

Kadr-e Film told us that they had approached two quasi-governmental companies, Sima Film and Resaneh, either of which could get us a permit. Resaneh, which produces films for Iranian TV for broadcast outside Iran, had agreed to do so, but changed their mind at the last minute. Just before leaving London, I had had a call from someone in Resaneh asking for details of our project; I said we would be in Tehran the following week, and they gave me a phone number, an address and an appointment. I did not say anything of this to Kadr-e Film, as I felt unsure about their sincerity; later Kim and I decided to go and talk to Resaneh ourselves. When we arrived for our appointment, we were told that the person who had contacted us was away, and instead we were taken to see the director. But it was clearly not a good time to approach him, as he wanted nothing to do with British-made documentaries. As he put it, 'he had burned his fingers' recently with a British film, *Guardians of the Ayatollahs* (1996) by Phil Rees, which focused on the Basij, the conservative-supported voluntary militia. This film, broadcast by the BBC just before the 1996 Majles elections, proved highly controversial and cost one Majles representative his seat. The director gave us a long account of how Rees had seemed sympathetic but then made a really 'negative' film, breaking his agreement with those he had interviewed. We argued that our film was quite different: it was not about a political issue, nor would we interview any personalities, it was about ordinary people and the breakdown of marriage, a universal social issue. We wanted to make an observational film, not a current-affairs documentary with a political agenda; we were there to learn. But he would not listen to any of our arguments. Then I asked how we could get a permit to make our film. He told us that we must work either with Resaneh or another Iranian company, or get MCIG approval – which, given our theme, we never would. He had two suggestions: either we change our theme to something 'positive', such as working women or marriage ceremonies in different parts of the country, or we let Resaneh make the film for us. Both suggestions were unacceptable. The second was indeed strange, and Kim was too polite to say anything. But I said in Persian that Kim was a filmmaker who wanted to make her own film with me, and there was no way that anyone else could make a film for us, although we were prepared to collaborate.

The director then invited us to see the documentaries his company had made. He took us downstairs, introduced us to a young man who had worked on some of them, and returned to his office. The young man showed us some films, saying that one of their objectives was to present a positive picture of Iran to the rest of the world. Two of the films were about carpets. In one of them, a designer and his daughter were teaching the art of carpet-making to middle-class women, who were all well dressed, wearing makeup and showing their hair. Some of them were asked questions, which they answered to camera. The second was about making *gabbeh*, a kind of rug with no fixed pattern woven by women in some parts of Iran. The film was made following the national and international success of Makhmalbaf's film *Gabbeh* (1995), and was meant to provide information about how *gabbeh* are made. But none of the weavers spoke; the explanation was given by an 'expert' – a man – sitting at a big desk with bookshelves behind him. Kim and I asked why the women had not been allowed to speak; since they made the carpets, they could explain the process better than any man. The answer – that the women did not speak good Persian, and that the male expert was much more qualified – incensed us both, and led to a heated debate over the nature of documentary. The young man argued that the main problem with Iranian films that get to festivals abroad is that they are all about people's misery, about poverty and backwardness, whereas Resaneh wanted to show progress as well, to offer Iranians abroad a different image of their country. For instance, in a film about carpets, they would not show a child weaving, as that would give a negative impression. We said that viewers should be allowed to see the complex picture and judge for themselves; the point of documentaries is to deal with reality, the situation on the ground. It is dishonest to cut children out of a film on carpet-weaving, since this is part of the reality of the industry in Iran, as is the case in many other countries. Everyone knows that, and one should never underestimate viewers and insult their intelligence. We then spoke in detail about how we planned to make our film. At the height of our discussion the director came back and asked what we thought of the films we had seen, clearly hoping we had been impressed enough to ask him to make our film for us. I said,

'Do you want our honest opinion or a polite one (*bi ta'rof* or *ba ta'arof*)? He said, 'The honest one, of course'. This was my chance to make a point, so I said, 'They make excellent teaching material for film and anthropology courses, to show how documentaries should not be made!'

So we returned to Kadr-e Film. Our only chance seemed to be the other quasi-governmental production company they had suggested: Sima Film, linked to the conservative-controlled Iranian TV. A meeting was arranged at their offices. There we learned that Sima Film was indeed very keen to work jointly with foreign companies, and that working with them could get us a permit. Delighted, we spent a long time justifying our choice of theme and explaining our approach, but they were more concerned to clarify the form of our co-operation. They wanted a contract to make the film for Channel 4, and asked us for a list of services we needed, saying that they would take care of the equipment and provide us with an apartment and office space. We told them we had our own equipment and would stay with my family, and that all we wanted was access, but said that we would put them in touch with Channel 4. That evening our contact in Kadr-e Film – who had sat silent throughout the meeting – called me. He was furious. He told me that we could not bypass his company, and we could not do the film without Kadr-e Film, as it was they who had introduced us to Sima Film.

We did not understand what was going on, but our instinct was to avoid them all. This proved to be a wise decision. Later we found out that, contrary to what we had been led to believe, Kadr-e Film had not been in a position to help us in the first place. They had been implicated in a scandal recently discussed in the conservative monthly *Sobh*: a videotape was circulating in Tehran in which some TV presenters and personalities close to Kadr-e Film were dancing and singing songs deemed insulting to the martyrs of the Revolution. The incident cost the TV people their jobs and compromised Kadr-e Film's reputation.

By now Kim and I were demoralized, as all our efforts to set up collaboration had failed. We could not work with production companies. Women with official links were not interested in working with us, and those without such links were in more or less the same position as us. Our last remaining hope was to approach the MCIG directly, although they had already rejected our previous application. This time we sought Ayatollah Taskhiri's help, and managed to get an appointment to see him at the headquarters of his Organization. Once again, both of us on the point of tears, we put the case for our project. I said we wanted to challenge stereotypes about women in Iran, and that we were in a unique position to do so, since Kim had made award-winning films, and I was an anthropologist with substantial fieldwork experience and publications; she knew how to communicate with Western audiences, and I knew about my culture and women's issues. We could make a valuable film. This was an opportunity that the Islamic Republic should welcome, given its bad image abroad. We had a clear vision and were committed to our work; who else would have been so persistent? I added that this was the last chance; Kim was an independent filmmaker who had been working exclusively on this project for a year now, and if we did not get a positive response, she would have to give up.

Our desperation and honesty must have impressed Taskhiri. He said he would introduce us to a cultural institute, and we could make our film under its auspices. This turned out to be Resaneh, which – we hadn't known – was attached to his Organization. I said that we had already talked to them but they were not interested. He said he would try to persuade them, and phoned the director there and then. Their conversation lasted for some time. From Taskhiri's responses it was evident that the director wanted nothing to do with our film. I began to regret my lack of tact; perhaps I should not have given him a frank opinion about his mode of documentary-making.

Having failed to persuade Resaneh, Taskhiri wrote us two letters of introduction: to the head of Media Affairs at the MCIG, and to the director of the Islamic Human Rights Commission. The first was to help us get a permit to film, the second to ask the Ministry of Justice to give us access to the courts. His assistant made us appointments to see them.

The following day we went to see the head of Media Affairs in one of the MCIG buildings in north Tehran. I launched into what had become a routine explanation of our project, but he cut me short, saying we should have applied to his department at the beginning, not to FCF, as the film we wanted to make was 'reportage', and therefore fell within his department's brief, which was to facilitate and supervise the work of foreign media correspondents. I said that the embassy in London had not told us this. He told us to make a fresh application through the embassy, asking for it to be sent to his department, and they would issue us with a permit to film and appropriate visas enabling us to bring our equipment. He then sent us to talk to the head of the Foreign Media Section, who would give us all the necessary information.

The Foreign Media Section was on the floor below. A female secretary welcomed us, and asked us to wait in a room with a sofa and a couple of chairs and a nice view over Tehran. This was where foreign journalists were received. On a table there were several photograph albums, one with pictures of Tehran, the rest with pictures of war and martyrs. As we were looking through these albums, another woman came in. She was wearing black gloves – the ultimate in the *hejab* code – but was wearing slippers, and held her *chador* folded around her arms, as women often do when working at home. She asked us in English which country and press we represented. I answered in Persian that we were independent filmmakers who had come to follow up our earlier application, and that we were waiting to see the section head. She left us without a word, but after a while the first woman came back and showed us into his room. He too was wearing slippers – a post-revolutionary practice among some functionaries, like some other forms of 'casual' office dress.[5] He received us coldly, saying that his section could do nothing for us until they received our application; we must submit it through the embassy, a response usually taking six weeks. When we tried to explain about our project, he seemed quite uninterested, suggesting that even if we had MCIG approval, we still needed a Ministry of Justice permit to film in a court, and that was likely to be a major difficulty.

In the event, this proved no problem. We approached the Ministry of Justice through the head of the Islamic Human Rights Commission, who was completely sympathetic to our project. Moreover, the public relations department of the ministry was then producing a series of short educational films shot in Tehran family courts for Iranian TV. These films, called *And After* (*Va amma ba'd*), broadcast in the early afternoon as part of the 'Family Programme', showed selected cases of marital disputes in which the judge explained points of law and drew moral lessons; the few petitioners who spoke were mostly women complaining about their husbands' failure to fulfil their marital duties. The films were a clear precedent for what we wanted to do, and the ministry offered no objection to our filming.

Kim and I were now elated, as we thought our permit had been approved. The whole experience had been thoroughly instructive, and had taught me how much the MCIG was itself responsible for Iran's 'bad image' abroad. Most foreign correspondents probably either socialized with secular Iranians who were discontent with many aspects of post-revolutionary life, or saw only 'official' Iran – functionaries in slippers and gloves, and albums with pictures of war and violence. They were bound to go away with ideas of bizarre office manners, and a fanatical culture obsessed with death.

We wanted our film to get away from the official discourse and ideology of the Islamic Republic, and to show an aspect of Iran that foreign journalists seldom see. I suppose it must have been this that made the authorities uneasy. What Kim and I saw as enchanting and positive was often not 'politically correct'. Our chosen topic of divorce was also a taboo theme that threatened to undermine a central tenet of the Islamic Republic's rhetoric. At the very core of the regime's critique of the West was that family values had broken down and divorce rates had risen, while the Islamic Republic prided itself on the stability of the family. At the same time, officials knew that Western criticism of Islamic gender rules often focused on divorce – many people thought that in Iran a man could dismiss his wife just by saying 'I divorce you' three times. I understood why they wanted us to change the theme, and why it was inconceivable to them that a film about divorce, shot in a family court, could present a positive image of Iran. At the same time, I felt strongly that it was an issue that should be addressed, as divorce laws had become the most visible yardstick, after the 'Islamic' dress code, for measuring women's emancipation or oppression in Islam. Both Western media and Islamist rhetoric treated the whole issue of family law ideologically, ignoring the complex reality on the ground. It was used as a means of 'othering', and there lay the importance of addressing it.

Back in London: Waiting for the Permit

Assured, we thought, of a MCIG permit, Kim returned to London and reported to Channel 4; she went to the embassy, told them what had happened, and submitted a new application. I stayed in Tehran to spend a few more days with my family. So we got our funding and prepared ourselves to return to Tehran in March and shoot the film before the May presidential elections, while those who had approved it were still in office. In February we went to an embassy reception celebrating the anniversary of the Revolution. There we met someone from the Foreign Media Section of the MCIG who had worked on a recent documentary about the late Shah for the BBC 'Reputations' series. When he heard the story of our difficulties in Tehran, he said he would do what he could when he got back to Tehran, but that it was still very unlikely that anybody would be willing to authorize our permit, given the reaction to Rees's film. We had also made the cardinal mistake of telling everyone about our project, he said, so that there were now many people who would try to stop it.

His prediction was correct – we did not get a response to our new application. I kept calling and faxing the embassy in London and the MCIG in Tehran; nobody knew what had happened to our application. The embassy claimed that they had sent it via the Ministry of Foreign Affairs to the MCIG, and the latter claimed that it had not yet reached them. We were confused – we did not know who to believe or what to do. It seemed quite unlikely that the permit would materialize before the presidential election of 23 May. When we wrote to Channel 4 telling them that the project had to be postponed, they asked us to return the money, which demoralized us even more. Obviously they were losing faith in us.

Following the change of government and the installation of President Khatami in August 1997, we renewed our efforts. We submitted yet another application to the MCIG, now headed by the reformist Ataollah Mohajerani. Meanwhile our Foreign Media contact followed up our application and was soon able to tell us that the MCIG had accepted it and that a 'journalist' visa was ready for Kim to collect at the embassy in London. This was in effect the permit that would allow us to enter Iran with filming equipment. But Sarah Jeans, the sound recordist with whom Kim had worked previously and whose name was in our application, was no longer available to work, and Kim had to find someone else. We told the person in charge in the embassy that we would be ready to start in September, and were told that this would be all right. But when September came, we were told that we must start the whole process over again. Kim's visa had expired, as she had failed to collect it within the required three days.

We Nearly Lose Permit and Funding

We didn't know what was going on. Our Foreign Media contact assured us that the MCIG had accepted our project and it was now up to the embassy to issue the visa. Guessing that officials in the London embassy might be deliberately frustrating our project, we tried to get someone to intervene on our behalf. Through an Iranian acquaintance, Kim and I went to see the head of the Islamic Centre England, a religious and cultural outfit representing the Office of the Supreme Leader. I presented to him the arguments we had gone through in Iran the previous winter.

He then gave us a long lecture about women's legal rights in Islam and the philosophy behind the rules of marriage and divorce. We asked him to intervene with the embassy on our behalf. I don't know whether he did or not, or whether we managed to convince him of the merits of our project. Each time I called the embassy, I was told that the permit had not yet reached them.

Meanwhile Kim received a fax from Peter Moore, commissioning editor at Channel 4, saying that 'the lustre of the project' had gone for him and it was now 'like a forced marriage'; he wanted us to abandon it. This was a real blow. Kim persuaded him to have faith, but this was our last chance, we must start filming immediately. So I decided to go to Tehran to present our case again to the MCIG. Kim went into hiding in her flat, as Channel 4 thought that we were both already filming in Iran.

I arrived in Tehran on 16 October. At the MCIG I soon discovered what the problem was with our application. They had learned that Kim's most recent film, *Shinjuku Boys* (1996), was about women who live as men in Japan; they had decided that she was a filmmaker who dealt with 'incorrect' topics. I strongly defended the films Kim had made in Japan, pointing out that they had won prizes, that the Japanese themselves liked them and did not find them offensive, and that Kim was soon going there to make another film. Once again I argued our case, even suggesting that 'Iran has received such a bad press, so many negative documentaries have been seen on Western TV; even if ours does give a negative impression, it can't make things worse; but at least give us a chance, we may make a worthwhile film!'

The whole ambience of the Foreign Media Section had changed. There was an air of openness and debate which gave me hope. The new head was more receptive to our ideas. Unlike his predecessor, he was not hostile to our project or afraid of dealing critically with internal issues, and was less concerned with the opinions of the outside world. Later, I learned that he had been a POW in Iraq for eight years during and after the war, but he had no bitterness and was kind and open. Meanwhile, the pictures of martyrs had gone from the waiting room, and no-one now walked around in slippers. One day, as I was sitting in the waiting room, two young men appeared with a video camera, apparently to get clearance to send their film abroad. One of them was the young man with whom I had had the heated discussion in Resaneh on the nature of documentaries in February. He recognized me and said that our discussion had made him think, and that he now wanted to make films about real people who were allowed to express themselves. He was no longer afraid to deal with reality in his films, however it might be construed by outsiders, and thought it essential to be self-critical.

Three weeks later, visas were issued for Kim and sound-recordist Christine Felce, enabling them to bring the 16mm camera and sound equipment. On Friday 7 November, Kim fetched the passports from the embassy, but discovered that the visas were valid for only one day and would expire before their flight arrived in Tehran on Monday morning. We never discovered whether this had been a genuine mistake or a deliberate attempt to sabotage our work. Kim returned at once to the embassy, who said that it would not be a problem. Then she called me; I told her that it was a problem, she would be turned back at the airport. She was desperate, and didn't know what to do. She couldn't get an answer from the embassy, which closed early on Friday, so my sister Ruji, who lives in London, accompanied her there; they knocked at the door until they were let in, and finally a woman official there agreed to extend their visas for another day.

Tehran: The Shoot

Kim and Christine arrived on 10 November. We all stayed in my parents' house. Our team was joined by my sister Sima, who lives in Tehran, and Zahra Saʿidzadeh. Sima, as 'production manager', looked after the domestic arrangements, and Zahra, as 'camera assistant', learned to change film magazines and came with us everywhere during the shoot. Zahra, then 17, was like a daughter to me, and I introduced her as such in court and elsewhere.[6] With the aid of letters of introduction from the MCIG, Kim and Christine's visas were further extended. Then, with the help of the Public Relations Section of the Ministry of Justice, we visited several Judicial Complexes. There are 16 of these in Tehran. Each contains a number of courts dealing with cases filed by local residents. They tend to differ in nature, given that the middle classes tend to live in the north of Tehran, and the working classes in the south. This posed a problem. Our Foreign Media contact, who had appointed himself our guide, argued that we must show the diversity of the courts and the range of cases heard; we must film in courts headed by both civil and religious judges, and cover marital disputes in different socio-economic strata. But we wanted to work in a single courtroom and capture something of court life itself. We knew that in a major city like Tehran, with a population of over 10 million, no court could be representative, and we did not want to do a sociological survey on film. We wanted to focus on characters and develop storylines. We also knew that our project depended much on the goodwill of the judge and the court staff, so it was important for us to work in a court where they welcomed us, understood our project and were willing to be part of it.

Finally we settled on the Imam Khomeini Complex, the largest one, located in central Tehran near the bazaar. It housed some Ministry of Justice offices, including the Public Relations Section, as well as 33 General Courts. Two courts dealt with family disputes, both headed by clerical judges: Judge Deldar, who sat only in the morning, and Judge Mahdavi, who sat only in the afternoon. We were introduced to both judges, and both said we could film in their courtrooms.

I knew Judge Mahdavi from my fieldwork in the 1980s, when he was the head of the Special Civil Courts, which dealt with family disputes from shortly after the Revolution until 1994, when the General Courts were created. At first we filmed in his courtroom every afternoon, but we soon confined ourselves to Judge Deldar's court, which we found more interesting. As Judge Mahdavi dealt only with divorce by mutual consent – that is cases where both parties had already worked out an agreement – there was little room for negotiation. The dynamics of the cases heard were rather uniform, and couples rarely revealed the real reasons behind the breakdown of their marriage. Judge Deldar, on the other hand, dealt with all kinds of marital disputes; thus we heard a much wider range of stories and observed a more spontaneous environment. The staff in this court were also fascinating characters in their own right, especially Ms Maher, the court secretary, who had worked in the same branch for over 20 years. She was an extremely capable woman who understood our project, and she and her daughter Paniz soon became integral to the film. Judge Deldar was a pious man who ran his court with tolerance and humanity, and was so secure in his own identity and belief that he was genuinely undisturbed by the film crew. After a week, we too became part of courtroom life.

We started filming in Judge Deldar's court on 15 November, and stayed there for four weeks, resisting all pressure to go elsewhere. We had no minders, and could film what we liked, so long as the people involved agreed. To film outside in the corridors and the prayer room, we often had someone from the Public Relations Section with us, largely to facilitate our movement around the building. As an all-woman crew, we had access

7. Paniz, daughter of Mrs Maher, the court secretary, from *Divorce Iranian Style*.

to both male and female spaces, which are typically separated by a curtain, with female spaces being relatively marginal, cramped and small. An early scene in the film shows the women's lobby, shut off from the rest of the building by a torn curtain. Such a lobby is found at the entrance to every major government building in Iran. Women are checked – by other women of course – to ensure that they are observing the correct dress code and not wearing makeup; they have to submit to such checks before they are allowed to enter the courthouse, which is by definition male space. In the prayer scene depicted in the film, women are again separated by a curtain. Again they occupy the smaller space – appropriate as there are certainly fewer women than men working in the courts. Both these scenes could only be observed – and filmed – by a female crew.

Our project nearly came to an abrupt end on two occasions. In the second week of filming we were summoned to the MCIG and told that they had received serious objections to our film. We protested about the injustice and damage to our reputations if we had to stop filming once we had started. It was unfair to play with people's lives in this way: Kim was an independent filmmaker, I was an academic, and we had both put our reputations on the line, investing so much in the project that there was no way we could let it go. Finally they agreed, saying, 'You have some enemies.' We never discovered who these enemies were, but to appease them it was suggested we should have a minder. We agreed, on condition that it was a woman. Ms Tavassoli, clad in her bright blue overcoat, began to accompany us to court; she was clearly thrilled to be part of the project and became a great ally. The problem was that she would not stop talking during the court sessions, continually engaging couples in conversation and disrupting our routine. Luckily, after a week she was recalled to the ministry, as she was needed to help with a The Conference of Islamic Heads of State that was due to start shortly.

Then, towards the end of our filming, we were summoned to the Public Relations Section of the Ministry of Justice and informed that, because of the security requirements of this conference, no film crew was being allowed in Judicial Complexes anywhere in Tehran. The argument seemed rather far-fetched, and after Judge Deldar talked to the head of the complex we were allowed to film for one more week. This last week was extremely tense: every day we arrived in court we thought it might be the last. But by this time we felt that we had enough material for our film.

The Court, the People and the Film Crew

The courtroom was about 6 metres long by 4 metres wide. In one of the shorter walls was a large window, in the other, the main door opened onto the corridor. Along one long wall was seating for petitioners and a second door, leading to the court office and archives; opposite sat the judge at his desk. Other desks, including Ms Maher's, stretched as far as the main door. The film crew occupied the space in front of the window. Kim put the camera on a tripod next to the judge, with me standing next to her, facing the door and the petitioners. Sometimes she moved the camera by hand to film outside the courtroom or in the office. Christine placed a microphone stand on the judge's desk and used a boom for the petitioners, often moving around the room.

The presence of an all-woman crew changed the gender balance in the courtroom, and undoubtedly gave several women petitioners courage. Likewise, I believe the mixed nationalities of the crew helped to transcend the insider–outsider divide. The camera was another link, between the court and the outside world as well as between public and private. We meticulously observed the dress code, and kept ourselves in the background when the court was in session. We sought to keep the focus on the pro-ceedings and the protagonists, and to avoid drawing attention to ourselves. We never talked to each other except when I had to interpret remarks addressed to Kim. I did not explain to Kim what was being said or done when we were filming or when a case was in progress, saving such explanations for later in the corridor or when there was nobody else in the room. I often had to decide what to film and what not to film, touching Kim whenever I wanted her to start or stop filming. At times we became like one person. Sometimes when I was outside the room dealing with crises such as the ones mentioned earlier, Kim had to make these decisions herself. When we went through the unedited rushes in London, I was amazed how often Kim had sensed exactly when to zoom in to close-up when something crucial was being said.

Although I had never been on a shoot before, I found Kim's approach highly sympathetic: there were no fixed ideas or script, and stories were allowed to develop in front of the camera. This made me feel at ease; it was just like doing anthropological fieldwork, but with a film crew. In the first week, we filmed any case whose parties allowed it, but as the days passed and certain people kept coming back to court, we filmed less, concentrating on the development of stories we had already started filming. We had a rough idea of what we wanted to film, with certain priorities: stories with resolutions, a variety of legal issues, people from different classes, striking personalities and drama. One of our main fears was that we might not be able to follow any case in its entirety, so that we would end with only bits of cases.

The Camera and Our Main Characters

We never filmed without consent. Every morning, early, I went through Ms Maher's book to confirm what cases were due to be heard that day; before each new case, I approached the parties concerned in the corridor, explained who we were and what our film was about and asked whether they would agree to participate. Some agreed, others refused. Perhaps unsurprisingly, most women welcomed the project and wanted to be filmed. Some who had agreed at first changed their minds later and stopped us filming them. Some, like Maryam – one of our main characters – refused at first, then came round later. When we first saw Maryam, in the corridor in the first week of filming, both Kim and I were keen to have her in the film; she had a presence, a strong character and seemed very straightforward, and above all her case involved custody, a topic we desperately wanted to cover. But when I approached her, she adamantly refused to be filmed. Then one day in our second week, when the judge was out, I was sitting on a bench in the corridor, discussing as usual women's legal rights with women petitioners. That day our discussion turned on how women themselves allowed gender inequalities in the law to continue. I said that nothing would change for women unless they did something themselves; we women must ask for our rights; they won't be handed to us on a plate; we should speak out, make our voices heard, but we don't because we're ashamed of making public something we think should be private. Maryam was there; she didn't say anything, but next day, when she saw me in the corridor, she said: 'now I want to be in your film.' From then on, she accepted us as friends and confided in us, and we became her only allies in the court.

We met Massy – the woman seeking a divorce on the grounds of her husband's failure to father a child – in the first week, and talked to her outside the courtroom. She too was at first reluctant to be part of the film, but later she agreed and we followed her story. She too became a close friend: we filmed in her home, though we didn't use the footage.

We first met our other two main characters in the courtroom. Jamileh, having quarrelled with her husband, had him jailed overnight and brought to court the following day. Such 'penal cases' (*da'avi-ye keyfari*), are referred to the family court by the police, and require no prior appointment, so we had no opportunity to explain our project and ask permission to film. However, this problem was resolved spontaneously, as Jamileh turned to the camera and opened her heart to us. She was fun, had a sense of humour and was open with her own feelings.

Ziba, too, the 16-year-old who desperately wanted a divorce and to go back to school, we first met with her husband Bahman in the courtroom. There was no time to explain; I signalled to them, can we film? Both nodded. Later, we got to know them well, and they asked us to attend the arbitration session in Ziba's house. I believe that our presence there gave Ziba the courage to speak out and stand her ground. She showed herself to be incredibly articulate for a 16-year-old from any culture.

From my previous fieldwork, I had learned that marriage as constructed in law is very different from marriage as lived by ordinary people, that women can turn even the most patriarchal elements of Islamic law to their advantage to achieve their personal marital aims, and that marriage has a more egalitarian structure in practice than in law. I knew that most marital disputes that make their way to court never come to a judicial decision, and that all of them are conducted at two levels: the legal and the social (personal). Petitioners – mainly women – treat the court as a forum for negotiating the terms of marriage or divorce, using the law as a means of exerting pressure on their partners to concede their demands. Generally, cases that appear in court fall into two categories: those where the marriage has already broken down, and those where it has not yet failed but is under strain. In the first category, women come to court to negotiate the terms of a divorce settlement, to retrieve something of their investment in the marriage, in terms of youth, work, emotions, love, trust and above all their children. In the second, they come to renegotiate the terms of the relationship, to reach a new balance.

We wanted to convey these subtleties in our film, but we had no idea if people would trust us enough to indicate what they really wanted. It was easy to observe and take notes, but to capture such things on film was a different matter. In the event, women did indeed share their strategies with us, and through us with the audience. I believe this happened because they came to see us as their allies, felt that they could be themselves in front of camera and saw no need to hide their real motives for bringing the case to court.

Outside the sessions, both in the courtroom and in the corridor, I talked about our project, explaining how we wanted to make a film that foreign audiences could relate to, to bridge the gap in understanding and to show how Iranian Muslim women – like women in other parts of the world – do the best they can to make sense of the world around them and to better their lives. Because of my knowledge of the law, women often asked me for advice about their cases – just as they had when I did field-work in the courts a decade earlier. This time I felt happier dropping my mask as an anthropologist, and becoming another Iranian women who had myself been through divorce. I was open about my own position, my views about the law, and my own divorce experiences, and I often engaged in heated discussions with both men and women about the merits of our film. Some – mostly men – were opposed to the film, suggesting that nothing good could come out of filming marital disputes, which show only the worst aspects of Iranian life. One of these was a trainee judge, who tried unsuccessfully to convince Judge Deldar to stop our work. I continued to argue the matter with him to the very last day of filming; Ms Maher always took my side.

The fact that I took an active role in these discussions, speaking my mind and talking about my own divorces, broke down the barriers and made women feel at ease with the camera. The informality of the court also allowed people to talk to us. When shooting, we always stood together – I with my face at the same level as the camera – and were treated as one person. Kim, too, was open and did not hide her feelings, making it clear where her sympathies lay – though she could not follow the details. Many times during the proceedings she was moved to tears.

In effect, the people in the film took the opportunity to tell their stories and were able to play an active role in making the film. They made the film with us. This is reflected in the way they addressed the camera. Occasionally, as when Massy tells us why she wants a divorce, this was prompted by a question from me. More often, the women took the initiative and started telling us about their dispute – as when Jamileh shared with us her real reason for bringing her husband to court. At times, they ignored the camera and continued what they were doing – as when Ziba felt relaxed enough to continue blackmailing her husband into agreeing to a divorce. At times, we were drawn into the proceedings as witnesses – as when the judge asked us whether we had seen Maryam tearing up the court order during a fight with her ex-husband outside the courtroom. Note his question: 'What did you see when you were outside?' Maryam had told us she had done it, in effect confessing to an act that could bring her five days in prison for contempt of court; but when he asked us, the judge was looking for a face-saving formula to release Maryam from custody. Our response was legally accurate: we had not actually seen the act. But we were on Maryam's side, and even if we had seen the act we would have refused to be witnesses – just as those who did see the fight refused Maryam's ex-husband's demand that they testify against her.

At times what was said to the camera was a continuation of an off-camera conversation started when the judge was out – or in the corridor in our casual chat. Some of the best sequences in the film came about this way, for instance when Ms Maher's little girl, Paniz, pretends to be a judge. The origin of that particular scene sums up the way the narrative of the film came to be constructed. At first, whenever the judge was out of the room, Paniz would ask me to tell Kim to film her. So as not to hurt her feelings, we pretended to film, but she soon found out that when Kim was really filming the camera's red light was on. She confronted me: I apologized for deceiving her and explained what our film was about and why we could not film her whenever she wanted. Paniz made no further demands, but it was obvious that she wanted to be filmed. Then one day during the last week, as we were filming the judge leaving the room, Paniz chose her moment. Her mother was not in court, and as soon as the judge had left, she ran to his seat and started a mock trial. She clearly understood what the film was about and found a role in it for herself. Kim responded by filming Paniz as she presided over an imaginary case. It was sobering for me to realize how important it was to be honest and share our aims with everyone. This was the only time I had not been honest in the course of our project, though I had done it with good reason.

Another incident confirmed how far both our approach and gender shaped the film's narrative. Judge Deldar was open and welcoming and his courtroom was in the same building as the Public Relations Office of the ministry, so it was a convenient location for journalists reporting on family disputes, who joined us several times during our four-week shoot. Badri Mofidi, from the newspaper *Salam*, came every Thursday,[7] and twice we found ourselves sharing the courtroom with an all-male crew from radio and TV. We did not find Ms Mofidi's presence in court disruptive, but we could not film while the male journalists were present. One reason, of course, was that their equipment got in the way. But the main reason was their approach and their gender. The radio man, who was collecting material for a programme called *Seda-ye 'Ebrat* (*The Voice of Warning/Lesson*, implying learning from mistakes), was only interested in interviewing the judge. Whenever he asked questions of women, he was trying to make a moral point. The six-man TV crew – who were filming footage for a programme on aspects of life in Tehran – occupied the entire courtroom. They talked to the judge and were also keen to film court proceedings, but no-one would consent to be filmed. Eventually they asked me to help them get people's consent. Their presence was disrupting both court routine and our work, so in order to get them out of the courtroom I tried to persuade women to talk to them, but no-one would agree. Finally, Maryam came to our help. She put on my glasses to disguise herself, and turning her profile to the camera she told them why she had come to court.

Editing in London: Structuring the Narrative

Back in London, we assembled the rushes, some 16 hours of film.[8] It was already clear to us who the main characters were likely to be. We found we had usable material on 17 cases. For the first six weeks, Kim, Moby Longinotto – assistant editor – and I worked to produce a rough cut of each of our cases. Then Barry Vince joined us as editor. The first cut, three hours long, included 10 cases. Many agonizing decisions had to be faced in order to whittle the 10 down to the final six – only four of them fully developed – in the film. It was heartbreaking to have to abandon some very moving stories.

While sorting through this material, we tried to focus on commonalities rather than on the exotic and the different, to remind the viewer that marriage is a difficult institution, that breakdowns can be painful, that societies and individuals deal with this in different ways, and that there is no perfect solution. We also wanted to show what it is like inside a Tehran law court, and to give glimpses into the lives of ordinary people. Above all, we wanted to let the women speak, to show them as individuals going through a difficult phase in their lives and to communicate the pain – and the humour – involved in the breakdown of marriage. Although clearly some contextual information was essential, we were anxious not to over-crowd the film with facts and figures or to tell viewers what to think, but to let them to draw their own conclusions.

To help viewers understand our position and how the narrative of the film took shape, we did not cut our interventions or my questions and comments. We were aware that this might be unsettling to an audience used to films where the director is entirely hidden,[9] but it was important for us to be honest with our audience in the same way that we were honest with people in the film. We did not want to hide anything, we wanted viewers to see how we were part of the proceedings, how we did not keep an observational distance from the people we were filming. We hoped viewers would come to understand how the film was constructed, how the camera was a catalyst for the narrative and made a link between public and private, insider and outsider.

It was difficult to choose a title for the film. The problem with *Marriage on Trial* was that it did not mention the film's location. *Divorce Iranian Style* was suggested by Peter Moore, who saw it as a nice play on Pietro Germi's well-known 1962 comedy, *Divorce Italian Style*. Although Kim and I thought it trivialized our film, we could not come up with anything better.

Reactions to the Film

The completed 78-minute film was premiered at the Edinburgh International Film Festival in August 1998, and screened in numerous other festivals in 1998 and 1999, winning several awards. It had cinema runs in the US and UK, and was widely reviewed in the media. The first British TV broadcast was in Channel 4's 'True Stories' in August 1999, but a 55-minute version, cut by us for Channel 4 International, had already been broadcast elsewhere, including on the Franco–German Arte channel, which can be seen in Iran by those with satellite dishes.

The film has not been publicly screened in Iran.[10] We entered it for the Fajr Festival in February 1999, but it was not accepted, on the grounds that there was not enough time to get the written consent of those filmed, a requirement because the film dealt with private issues. As it happens, all the main characters had already signed a written consent, required by Channel 4, but I decided not to pursue the matter as I feared the film might become part of the current struggle between reformists and conservatives. We had been given a permit to film by Khatami's reformist government, so the conservative papers could have used the film as a means of condemning the policies of the Minister of Culture and Islamic Guidance, who was about to be impeached by the conservative-dominated parliament. However, the film was known, not only by those who regularly attend festivals abroad, but also by ordinary people: there were reports on it by the BBC and Voice of America Persian-language programmes, both of which have many listeners in Iran.[11]

Reactions to the film were highly varied, revealing not only the differing ways in which audiences related to our narrative but also the complexity of the politics of identity and gender. Most film critics, both Iranian and foreign, were enthusiastic. We felt that they had understood the film and that we had achieved our main goal, which was to challenge simplistic ideas of Iran as a country of fanatics and of Muslim women as helpless victims without any agency. The film had helped to humanize Iranians, who have been demonized in the West since the Revolution. Almost all Western reviewers commented on this point, some devoting a whole page to the film and the issues it raised, such as in the London *Evening Standard,* whose reviewer ends as follows:

> Five years ago in Beyond the Clouds, Phil Agland dispelled the hoary myth of oriental inscrutability by showing us that the everyday hopes and fears of the Chinese are little different from our own. Last night Kim Longinotto and Ziba Mir-Hosseini accomplished something similar for Iran...showed that there is more in an Islamic society to admire than fear. More engrossing than a soap, it humanized a people who've too often been demonised by the media.[12]

Reviews in the Iranian press – both outside and inside Iran – were also positive and encouraging. Two reviews in *Zanan* – a woman's magazine with a feminist agenda, aligned with the reformists – treat the film as an exposé of women's suffering through the legal biases of the law; Shahla Lahiji, criticizing the Fajr Festival for not screening the film, wrote:

> These authorities – who at first, with such understanding, broad-mindedness and free thinking, allowed the filmmakers' camera to document only a fragment of the tearful scenes of the civil life of women in law and in the family courts – why and how and according to what logic have they prevented the other men and women of this country from watching this documentary in a socially responsible manner? What are they afraid of?
>
> If the inadequacy of the present laws is ruining women's lives, we will get nowhere by hiding it. Although nowhere in the film do the filmmakers sit in judgment, ugliness and injustices show themselves from corners of the scenes. Covering them up is not the solution. People in other lands have seen this work and have talked about it. Permission to show this film in Iran would give us the opportunity to declare to the world: 'We recognize the suffering and we intend to deal with it.'[13]

An Iranian film journal carried a positive and insightful feature with a number of articles on *Divorce Iranian Style*.[14] Using the film as a way of examining the conditions of documentary-making in Iran and abroad, Pirouz Kalantari begins:

> After seeing *Divorce Iranian Style* once, probably the most salient question is: how could a foreign film crew – with such ease – be given such a free hand to make a film in Iran about such a sensitive (why is it sensitive?) issue? Is such a course equally open and accessible for an Iranian filmmaker too?[15]

Two other articles focus on the role of the camera and how people used it to tell their own stories, thus making their own film. There are also three translated articles: one from the London daily newspaper *The Independent* soon after the film's premiere in Edinburgh, an interview with Kim and me conducted when the film was shown in the US and my own earlier account of how we went about making the film.

The same kind of consensus, however, did not exist among ordinary viewers of the film. Whenever the film was shown in Europe and the US, I found a wide gap between the responses of Iranian and non-Iranian audiences. Non-Iranian audiences liked the film and could relate to it at a personal level, and some said that they could identify with the characters, admired their courage and drew parallels with their own divorces.

The response of Iranians abroad has been much more mixed. Academics and second-generation Iranians generally reacted positively to the film and shared our own reading of it, others either found it offensive to 'Iranian values' or used it to make a political point. After a screening, Iranians in the audience seldom spoke, and when they did it was often to protest that the film gave a distorted image of the reality of women's life in Iran and was not representative.[16] After the broadcast on Channel 4, some people phoned Radio Pars – the Persian-language radio programme in London – to express their anger and dissatisfaction with the film.[17]

In Europe and the US, Iranians who objected to the film fall into three categories.[18] First are those who identify politically with elements of the Iranian opposition abroad: they saw the film as propaganda for the Islamic Republic. The film, they argued, does not show the reality of women's oppression in Iran, and trivializes their suffering under Islamic law. In short, they find the film politically incorrect, as it does not expose the injustices and inhumanity of the Islamic regime: the judge is too nice and women are too strong.

Second are non-political Iranian expatriates, largely middle-class in background, who said that the film made them feel ashamed in front of foreigners. It should never have been shown abroad, they contended, as foreigners do not understand the complexity of the Iranian situation and think that all Iranians are 'backward'. They objected that the film did not include 'educated and cultured couples' and only showed 'shabby places', 'backward customs' and 'low-class people'.

These two groups questioned our motives in making the film. While the first group implied we had been manipulated by the Islamic Republic, the second saw a 'British hand' behind the film. During question and answer sessions following screenings of the film, we were often asked why the Islamic Republic allowed us to film, why British TV gave us money to make a film about divorce in Iran, why they were interested in such a subject, what our real motives were and what we wanted to say with such a film. Both groups agreed that the problem with the film was that it was not representative, and gave a distorted picture of reality, though they clearly disagreed as to the nature of that reality.

A third group of people, between these two extremes, not only dismissed conspiracy theories but also took issue with objections that the film is not representative. They saw the film as an indictment of Islamic law and the Islamic Republic. Parto Noori'ala – a writer living in Los Angeles – eloquently expressed this view.

> No doubt these women [in the film] are not representative of those who have been crippled by the crazy blows of their husband. Nor do they represent unaware and incapacitated women who, out of fear of their family or society

or in order to stay with their children, tolerate the suffering of living with an unwanted man. Likewise, their husbands do not represent the many biased and aggressive Iranian men, nor is Judge Deldar representative of all judges in Iran. It is not strange, therefore, that some viewers, in a hasty evaluation, accuse this film of being made to order [i.e. by the Islamic Republic] to give a kind face to the courts of the Islamic Republic and to show an unreal picture of Iranian women's fate. On the other hand, some see the film as showing the brave women who fight for their rights and obtain them.

Though conceding that, as filmmakers who made a film in Iran, we could not show the 'reality', Noori'ala seems to be suggesting that it was we who manipulated the authorities and that the film reveals the cruelty of the religious system:

> It is natural that a film that is allowed by the Islamic regime cannot display the atrocities and great problems that Iranian women face. Likewise, the viewer cannot expect such a film to show the real faces of clerical judges in the judiciary in Iran nor the usual behaviour of its employees. But the intelligent directors of the film, without resorting to slogans or overemphasizing a point, with skill and awareness, through simple images, in an unexaggerated language, with humour, succeed in unveiling the darkest and most oppressive family laws in the Islamic Republic which are based on religious laws.

She ends her review with a political point:

> This film once again reminds us that obtaining women's rights and securing social justice, equality, and protection against encroachments of cultural, religious, ideological traditions everywhere in the world are only possible when civil laws replace and correct religious laws, traditional and existing beliefs in society.[19]

Conclusion

What do my own experiences of and audience reactions to *Divorce Iranian Style* tell us about the reality portrayed in documentaries about Iranian women in particular and Iran in general? In other words, how do these narratives relate and speak to each other?

First, in making *Divorce Iranian Style*, I had to confront my own multiple identities and found myself in the uncannily familiar situation of shifting perspectives and self-redefinition. When I started the project, I was writing a book on gender issues in the Islamic Republic, based on extended discussions in 1995 with clerics in Qom.[20] With them, I had had to justify my feminist stance, while in making this film I wanted to honour the Muslim and Iranian aspects of my identity. I came to realize that the problem was also inside me. I could not integrate the multiple discourses and representations of women in Iran, nor could I synthesize my own identities and positions. I disagreed equally with Iranian and Western stereotypes of 'women in Islam', images that did not reflect a complex reality. As a feminist, an Iranian and a Muslim, I objected to how women were treated in law and wanted to change it. But my objections were not the same as those implied in Western media discourses or those aired by feminists after the Revolution: I saw women in Iran not as victims but as pioneers in a legal system caught between religious tradition and modernity. It was in the course of negotiating permission for the film and working with Kim that I reconciled these conflicting identities. Her unconditional acceptance, and her desire to understand and give voice to the women in the film, freed me from the need either to rebel against or to justify to foreigners my Muslim and Iranian identities. In this way, the film became part of the debate on women's rights in Iran with which I had been passionately involved since the early 1990s.

Secondly, the fact that much of my account concerns the process of getting a permit to film in Iran is inevitable, given the subject matter and the political and ideological circumstances. As one reviewer said: 'What is perhaps most impressive about "Divorce Iranian Style" is that it was made at all...the filmmakers' negotiations with authorities came to resemble those of the women they sought to document.'[21] Evidently, the Iranian authorities had very a different understanding from our own of the notion of documentary film and of what kind of 'reality' is suitable for filming.

We tried to show that there are different voices in Iran. The one most often heard is the legal voice: authoritarian, patriarchal and increasingly out of touch with people's aspirations and experiences. But there is also an egalitarian voice in everyday life, seldom heard by outsiders. This is the voice of women, and we wanted it to be heard. We wanted to show the anachronistic nature of the law, and how social change is daily chipping away at its monolithic authority. This is not the 'reality' the Iranian authorities wanted to be shown. Had it not been for the change in MCIG policy under President Khatami, I believe that the permit promised us by the previous government would never have materialized. Our chosen theme was a reality denied by their ideological discourse and thus harmful to the Islamic Republic's image abroad. The MCIG's concern for the image of Iran in Western media was so overwhelming that it could not allow a film to look critically at society, because it could be construed as a kind of betrayal of the Islamic Republic's ideals. But this defensive position in turn reproduces the 'bad image' the authorities fear. The matter was made more complex by the failure of our project to fit into their accepted categories: it was not a current affairs documentary, nor were its makers complete outsiders. Khatami's election brought a shift in government discourse and policies, so we were given the opportunity to make the film we wanted – to try to show 'reality' as seen by women going through divorce. The women who agreed to be in the film realized that they had an opportunity to have their voices heard. Like us, they seized it and they made the film with us.

Thirdly, we were struck by the similarity of the reactions of Iranian officials and production companies with whom we had negotiated to those of many Iranians abroad who saw the film. All objected that it did not represent the reality of women's life in Iran, arguing that it gave foreigners a distorted and wrong image of Iranian culture and society. For educated and sophisticated diaspora Iranians, in its portrayal of 'illiterate and uneducated women', the film shattered the picture of Iranian culture that they were trying to build in their host communities. Islamic officials believed that the film undermined the image of the strong family that is the foundation of the Islamic system by showing women fighting for release from unwanted marriages. Though the two objections are informed by different ideologies and political tendencies, they are both rooted in a fear of being judged and misunderstood by the 'other' – the West. While each group is happy to criticize the West – or each other – neither easily accepts any criticism of itself. Interestingly, the core objection of both groups was to the subject matter. They believed that making a film on divorce amounts to washing dirty linen in public, making public something that belongs in the private domain.

Finally, these narratives tell us how a documentary that crosses the boundaries between insider/outsider and public/private can become a mirror in which viewers can see reflected aspects of their own culture and identities. The reality that documentaries portray – or are perceived to portray – cannot be separated from our gaze, our relationship with our own culture and how we want to be seen by the 'other'. The negative reactions of many Iranians abroad speak of their ambivalence towards both their own culture and that of their host country. After all, mirrors simply reflect, but reality is in the eye of the beholder.

Notes on Chapter 9

1. A shortened version of this chapter was presented in a panel on Iranian cinema organized by the Society for Iranian Studies at the Middle East Studies Association annual meetings in November 1999 in Washington DC. I am grateful to the Society for Iranian Studies for making my participation possible.
2. *Marriage on Trial: A Study of Islamic Family Law, Iran and Morocco Compared* (London, I.B. Tauris, 1993).
3. By calling the people featured in the film 'characters' I do not mean to imply that they were actors; they were not – though of course, anyone who brings a case to court has to 'act', to put on a performance; and our characters were no exceptions.
4. Wearing red, exposing one's neck and shaking hands with men have been proscribed public actions for females since the Revolution.
5. This is a reaction to dress codes in the pre-revolutionary era, when officials were attired in the latest Western fashions. It has also come to be seen as sign of piety, to indicate that they treat the office as a mosque.
6. She had accompanied me during my 1995 fieldwork in Qom, as I have described in the preface to *Islam and Gender: The Religious Debate in Contemporary Iran* (Princeton, Princeton University Press, 1999).
7. We got on well with her and exchanged views and information. Women were happy to talk to her and she covered some of the cases we were following, including Ziba's, without mentioning names.
8. We freighted the film back to London for developing, seeing none of it until our return. This requirement was one reason it took so long to get our permit.
9. Some Iranian viewers claimed the whole film was staged: it was obvious, they said, as women were looking at and talking to someone behind the camera. Surprisingly, the same comment was made by an Indian filmmaker who saw the film at the Yamagata Documentary Film Festival; see *The Hindu Online* (www.indiaserver.com), Friday 12 November 1999.
10. As of summer 2000. There have been some private, film club and university screenings.
11. It seems too that by 1999 video copies of the film were in circulation in Iran and the US, advertised and sold on websites without the knowledge of our distributors.
12. *Evening Standard*, 24 August 1999, p. 29. Reviews in the *Daily Telegraph* and *The Times* of the same date express similar reactions.
13. *Zanan* 51, p. 25.
14. *Mahnameh-e Sinema'i-ye Film* 240, 20 Shahrivar 1378/1999, pp. 28–35.
15. 'Zanani agah na rowshanfekr', *ibid.*, p.28.
16. Jane Howard, a British writer, and Homa Hoodfar, an Iranian anthropologist, both saw the film in Tehran with a mixed Iranian and foreign audience and

found the same kind of division. There again, many Iranians were critical, objecting that the film was non-representative and that the subjects were hand-picked.

17.   Though I had spoken on Radio Pars a week earlier, to alert Iranians in London (who often do not read the English press) to the broadcast of the film, I declined to take part in the phone-in afterwards, fearing that the compere – Mr Hossein Qavimi – and others would use the film as means of attacking Islam and the Islamic Republic and thus drag me into a futile political discussion which I was trying to avoid. My refusal angered Mr Qavimi, who read a paraphrased text of my message to him, strongly rejecting the idea that his programme was political or used offensive language about Islam. But the content and nature of the phone-in justified my fears.

18.   I draw from notes after question and answer sessions following screenings of the film in the US, UK, Denmark, France, Germany, Belgium, Greece and Austria.

19.   Her review first appeared in the London *Kayhan,* 19 August 1999, p. 5 – an opposition paper – shortly before the Channel 4 broadcast. The same point was implied in Soheyla Sharifi's review of the film in a feminist opposition magazine published in Sweden: *Medusa* (*Journal of the Centre for Women and Socialism*) 4, Summer 1999, p. 48.

20.   *Islam and Gender,* see note 6 above.

21.   'Irreconcilable Differences: "Divorce Iranian Style"', by Nick Poppy, Indiewire, 9 Dec., 1998, http://www.indiewire.com/film/interviews/ int_Longinotto_MirH_981209.html. See also our interviews for 'Women Make Movies, Making *Divorce Iranian Style*', http://www.wmm.com/ advscripts/ctmnfrm.asp?source=catpgfrm.asp?rccid=454; and 'Marriage Among the Mullahs', by Cynthia Joyce, *Salon Magazine,* 16 December 1998, http://www.salonmagazine.com/mwt/feature/1998/12/16feature.html.

10

Location (Physical Space) and Cultural Identity in Iranian Films

Mehrnaz Saeed-Vafa

One of the most interesting aspects of Iranian films is the function for filmmakers and audiences of location – real places, away from studio settings. An audience's relationship with a film is often conditioned by its expectations and interpretations of the Iranian settings. For the filmmaker, location plays a significant role in creating narrative space.

A closer look at the locations filmmakers use and the way they represent them reveals their positive or negative attitude toward them. Although fragmented and rearranged in time, location manifests itself – often at an unconscious level – as an aspect of the filmmaker's psyche and identification with a particular culture at a given time.

The Politics of Location

The Audience

One of the attractive elements of Iranian films for non-Iranian audiences abroad is the locations used. On a safe, visa-free tour they can 'visit' different parts of Iran and construct a mental map of the country and its culture. At times, watching these films confirms pre-existing images or fantasies of the place as an exotic land of mystery (ancient mythical Persia) and misery (terrorism and poverty).

Iranian audiences in the US have also been fascinated by Iranian films, as they look for images of homeland in them. This was true especially during the Iran–Iraq war, when it was very difficult to travel to Iran. Many Iranians went go to see the films regardless of quality.

But for Iranian audiences abroad the experience of watching Iranian films has not always been rewarding or reassuring. They have often missed colourful images of homeland that would restore their sense of pride in being Iranian. As if exiled once more, they felt betrayed when a filmmaker denied them familiar images of childhood, youth and places of memory that would justify their sense of loss, nostalgia and longing for Iran.

Living in the shadow of negative Western images of Iran, many Iranian filmgoers in the US, Canada and Europe – particularly when accompanied by non-Iranian partners – have expressed shame and anger at the screen images they have seen of Iran, or of the capital Tehran. No matter how fictional the films might be, they believe that Western viewers take them as documentaries about life and culture in Iran. But Iranian viewers abroad have not done so, rejecting images that could pass as signs of underdevelopment or backwardness and blaming foreign festivals for promoting such imagery. For example, scenes of extreme poverty and neglected children in the films of Abolfazl Jalili, especially *Dance of Dust* (1992), or in Samira Makhmalbaf's *The Apple* (1998), Mohammad Ali Talebi's *The Boot* (1993), Alireza Davudnezhad's *The Need* (1992), Majid Majidi's *Children of Heaven* (1997) or the unsavoury landscapes of the outskirts of Tehran in Kiarostami's *The Taste of Cherry* (1997), have disappointed some Iranian audiences abroad.

Iranians whose social class has not been represented in a film may accuse the filmmaker of being naive and narrow-minded. Thus, some have criticized Kim Longinotto and Ziba Mir-Hosseini's *Divorce Iranian Style* (1998) on the grounds that the film only included low-income women and paid no attention to middle- or upper-class women who would employ lawyers to take care of their cases and would have a more 'civilized' divorce process. Those who did not like the film objected to the setting – one particular Tehran courtroom – arguing that if the camera had been placed somewhere else, or in another court, it would have captured a different class of women and, consequently, different stories.

There has been much debate among Iranian audiences abroad about what constitutes a true, authentic, undistorted representation or image of the homeland, and what should be shown in films. Regarding location, a reverse concept of political correctness is applied to Iranian films by Iranian audiences abroad, in order to avoid a 'negative image' of Iranian culture.

The Filmmaker

For the filmmaker, the choice of location is a cultural and at times a political statement, which consciously or unconsciously reveals aspects of the filmmaker's personal identity as well as his or her attitude toward the dominant culture. The location and its cinematic representation by the filmmaker constitute the world of his/her films. They reflect the filmmaker's state of mind, as well as that of the characters, and can pass as a metaphor for his or her cultural and emotional situation at the time of filming.

The majority of Iranian films are shot on location with minimal intervention or alteration by the filmmaker. This is mainly due to limited budgets, which force filmmakers to work with small film crews and the minimum of equipment and to use a semi-documentary or a semi-amateur, even experimental, film style, often referred to as 'Iranian neo-realism', in which real locations and a realistic treatment of the social environment of the characters play an important part in its definition. Such films do not aim at technical perfection or the perfect look, or depend on the common narrative structure of plot, subplot and subjective camera to dramatize the inner world of their characters. Access to the psychology of the characters is possible mainly through an examination of their exterior environments.

The emergence of increasing numbers of Iranian films with exterior scenes may also be a natural response to a growing demand by Western viewers and the international film market for depictions of the reality of Iran – real locations even more than real stories. Post-revolutionary events, such as the hostage crisis, generated political heat in the West, and subsequently a curiosity and a market for depictions of Iran.

International film festivals have honoured the realism and simple storylines of apparently low-budget Iranian films with significant political and social themes. These films include real people – non-actors – and real locations in urban or rural areas of Iran. They inform Western audiences about the land and peoples of Iran, the structure and architecture of their cities and villages, their culture, mentalities and traditions, their political and social conditions, and the appearance and private and public lives of women.

Films that meet Western expectations of a political third-world cinema have been most successful. In the 1990s, the low-budget but exotic, ideologically charged Iranian landscape locations have challenged the high-tech, digitized, computer-generated imaginary settings of Hollywood films. An abundance of realist films with minimal plots, shot in the streets of Tehran or other cities, especially in poor neighbourhoods, showing the struggles of everyday life, demonstrate the shared interest of the filmmakers and their non-Iranian – especially well-to-do – audiences in this kind of political presentation. This is not to say that Iranian directors look to Western critics for their filmmaking tastes or subjects, but a majority of them have been encouraged to follow certain styles by such Western responses.

The success of realist films such as Sohrab Shahid-Saless's *A Simple Event* (1973) and *Still Life* (1975), Bahram Beyza'i's *Bashu, The Little Stranger* (1988) and Amir Naderi's *The Runner* (1986), stimulated many filmmakers to pay more attention to the depiction of real locations and local people, their cultures, their social conditions and their struggles. In particular, the success of Kiarostami's films abroad in the 1990s has persuaded many filmmakers to fashion their films in his style. It has also prepared and encouraged international festivals to value such a genre of filmmaking from Iran, as demonstrated by the successes of Jafar Panahi's *The White Balloon* (1995) and *The Mirror* (1997), Mahmood Kalari's *The Cloud and the Rising Sun* (1997), Jalili's *Dance of Dust* and *Det Means Girl* (1994), Majidi's *The Father* (1996) and *Children of Heaven*, and Samira Makhmalbaf's *The Apple*.

Few Iranian filmmakers are immune to the forces of international film marketing, despite the partial ban since 1980 on Western – in particular, Hollywood – films in Iran. A film's artistic and economic success depends to a great extent on its success in the international film market. With high inflation and a shortage of film theatres in Iran, the film producer, for the most part, looks to the international market for a return on investment.

International film festivals and the international film market have also encouraged exoticism in Iranian films. Films that – intentionally or unintentionally – offer a kind of exotic image of Iran have been successful in these arenas. For example, Mohsen Makhmalbaf's picturesque *Gabbeh* (1995), with its colourful landscapes and tribal costumes and rituals, provides spectacular images for non-Iranian audiences.

Indeed, at times these audiences appreciate the environment and the location of the film more than its story. Kalari's *The Cloud and the Rising Sun*, with its beautiful photography of the mysterious green landscapes of northern Iran and the village house, where the story takes place, appealed to many foreign audiences and won awards at many festivals. Although the story concerns an old actor who cannot return home in time to visit his dying wife, the actual drama revolves around the production of a low-budget film. The crew carry a tree on top of the bus in the hope of finding a sunny location to shoot the final scene. The pathetic tree on top of the bus, the low-tech angel whose strings are controlled by two crew members and whose wings are later blown away in the wind, and the local couple who are going to town, these are the main elements of comedy and charm for the audience.

By revealing and acknowledging the low-budget, low-tech constraints experienced by filmmakers, this film is a conscious comment on the state of filmmaking in Iran. It includes certain elements that meet Western audiences' expectations of a modern third-world film – the way the film crew is fed by local people, the way the special effects are executed and the way in which the crew depends on the weather, the actors, the natural resources, the innocence of the local people (reminiscent of Kiarostami's *Through the Olive Trees*, 1994) and pure luck. These are all inevitable parts of the experience of film production in Iran. This kind of story is interesting mainly because it takes place in a country like Iran where – the audience may expect – in the absence of advanced technology and a big budget, the crew must depend on the environment and the innocence of the ordinary rural people in order to complete the film.

The use of real locations, treated in a realistic style, confirms and justifies an audience's assumption that there is a documentary aspect to such Iranian films. The films show real places in Iran, even if in a fragmented and fictional spatial order. When watching Iranian films in the presence of a non-Iranian audience, one notices the power of real locations, as well as the wardrobe and props. The delight of many non-Iranians in the beautiful landscapes and the costumes of the exotic tribal figures in *Gabbeh*, their surprise at seeing modern Tehran in Majidi's *Children of Heaven*, their noisy appreciation of the beautiful carpets in the bazaar scene in Daryush Mehrju'i's *Sara* (1992) and their laughter at the tree on top of the bus in *The Cloud and the Rising Sun* – these are all good examples of exotic or decorative elements that attract an audience to these films, whatever the intentions of the filmmakers.

The predominance of exterior and open spaces as locations in Iranian films is also due to the cultural notion of privacy. Many filmmakers resort to exterior scenes and public spaces – a cinematic version of *hejab* – in order to talk about their inner feelings. They shy away from exposing

8. Rakhshan Bani-Etemad's *Nargess*.

personal and private spaces, which could be sacred or profane, evil or good. This factor may be responsible for a certain one-dimensionality, or lack of complexity, in the portrayal of characters in some Iranian films. The polarization of characters as either good or bad, and the usual victory of good over evil in film plots, are interpreted as a consequence of political and cultural conditions. For example, in *Nargess* (Rakhshan Bani-Etemad, 1992), the main male character's evil habits of stealing and living with an older female accomplice are presented as a result of social ills and unemployment. The evil is in society, not in the characters. It seems that as martyrs, heroes or even victims, the characters cannot even afford to own their shadows. Their dark sides are blamed on their enemies and others, or in general on society. But the society that accommodates the unwanted culture of the other is portrayed through urban public spaces such as the bazaar, streets, traffic or administrative offices and residential buildings.

The first two episodes of Mohsen Makhmalbaf's *The Peddler* (1987) use a significant number of public spaces as an essential part of the drama. In the first episode, the film opens with a breathtaking pan over Tehran's slums: a poor couple are looking for a place to leave their child for adoption, but nowhere seems to be caring and reassuring enough. The streets are shown as inhuman, full of beggars and strangers, and the mosque is indifferent – praying men pay no attention to the crying child. Many other unsuitable locations are added to the list, finally the government orphanage, a symbol of an uncaring society where abandoned children are crying for their mothers.

At times, filmmakers self-censor their films, not only in order to save them but also to protect themselves from political or social trouble and vulnerability to prosecution. Self-censorship may go beyond the codes set by the MCIG, which define acceptable limits for the depiction of personal appearances, good and evil, women's clothing and their physical relationships with male characters on the screen, and so on. Filmmakers avoid certain topics in their films because of a concern for public opinion – especially women directors, whose concern could be a fear of disapproval by the male mentality. 'Privacy scenes' can be those that involve a female character in a male–female physical relationship or that expose characters in their own private spaces, sharing personal time with the audience. But many films lack such scenes.

Even films with no major female characters, like those of Kiarostami (except for *The Report*, 1977), are shot mainly in exterior settings. In his masterpiece, *The Taste of Cherry*, the interior of the main character's apartment is never shown. The audience has no access to his inner thoughts and the reasons for his suicidal intentions; the only private space shown is the car he travels in, alienated not only from his society but from himself, from life, and from the dominant Tehrani, urban culture. The film is set in the outskirts of Tehran, a barren landscape, an area under construction. The viewer sees only roads, hills and wastelands. The elimination of interior scenes and the exclusion of the picturesque can be read as a political, cultural and existential statement by the filmmaker.

In Kiarostami's films, his characters and their relationships with each other are defined by their surroundings and the places they live in or travel to. The extreme long-shot at the end of *Through the Olive Trees*, showing the man following his beloved woman along an endless path surrounded by trees, can be interpreted as Kiarostami's comment on life and male–female relationships. In *Where is the Friend's House?* (1987), the repeated long-shot of the boy running up the zig-zag hill path shows his dedication to his friend. And in *And Life Goes On...* (1991) the long-shot of the cracked hill shows the endurance of the local people who cross the path despite its many difficulties. In this film, the main character, the filmmaker from Tehran, is searching for the two boys who have acted in his previous film. This is the reason that he drives to a remote area of northern Iran, which has suffered a major earthquake. As he stops by the shattered villages, to observe the habits of the villagers, he is fascinated by their innocence, their instinctive, 'natural' lives and the ruined roads and houses. What he sees and notices establishes how he himself is feeling.

For Kiarostami, locations are absolutely essential to situate the meaning of his films. With his elliptic narrative style and minimal plots, location plays an important part in identifying the characters and their worlds and defining their inner space. Locations are also an integral part of Beyza'i's realistic and allegorical films. The neighbourhood of south Tehran in *Downpour* (1972) and the powerful mysterious forests of northern Iran in *The Stranger and the Fog* (1975) both define the world of the films and the social context of the characters and carry the deeper mythological and historical meanings of the films. In *Bashu, The Little Stranger*, the main characters – the traumatized black boy from the south and the self-confident, nature-attuned white woman from the north – are identified and separated by the different landscapes in which they live. The burned houses of the war-stricken southern town where the homeless boy comes from are contrasted with the sleepy, peaceful green nature of the northern village where the woman – his adoptive mother – lives. As for *Yazdgerd's Death* (1981) Beyza'i did not have the budget to shoot this film in his ideal location, so he used a small mill – in his words, a 'hole' – to create the sense of claustrophobia experienced by both his characters and his film crew. The location functions both realistically and metaphorically.

Although filmmakers choose locations based on scripts, at times locations themselves generate and justify the stories and become part of them. In this respect, a filmmaker's identification with or attachment to certain locations becomes a visual manifestation of his or her inner space. In Naderi's *Water, Wind, Earth* (1989) the windy desert with its animal carcasses and dry wells constitutes the world for the abandoned boy, and visually stands for his loss. He interacts mainly with the desert. He endlessly digs dry wells, establishing a physical relationship with the challenging earth.

Films Shot Outside Iran: Identity of Film, Identity of Location

The Split of Time and Consciousness

Films shot in Iran carry signs of post-revolutionary Iranian culture as well as intended or unintended political meanings. But when Iranian film-makers shoot their films outside Iran, the realistic locations of other countries often lose their native political and historical character and become more of a metaphorical or exotic space and image. By the same token, they reveal the filmmaker's attitude toward the politics of the story and subject.

For example, Mohsen Makhmalbaf got permission to shoot *A Time to Love* (1991), a story of love, betrayal and adultery, outside Iran: the film was shot in Turkey with Turkish actors. The adulterous woman wears a scarf – observing a *hejab* code which is not mandatory in Turkey – reminding the audience of Iran. The film not only suggests that adultery happens in other cultures, it also implies that romance takes place in other lands.

This attitude pervades even non-Iranian romantic films. In *Lovers of the Arctic Circle* (Julio Medem, 1999), the incestuous lovers – half-brother and sister – can be united only on the remote Finnish island. It seems that an unreal, distant or exotic place, far from home, is necessary for the depiction of an impossible romantic love, and to show the difference between fantasy and reality.

Iranian filmmakers have also used other countries to portray the distance between the worlds of the characters' lives and their consciousnesses. Ebrahim Hatamikia shot *From Karkheh to Rhine* (1993) in Germany. Here the location, a country in the West, is identified with a westernized woman who has abandoned her family, her country and her cultural values. Her Muslim militant brother, wounded and blinded in the war, comes to Germany for treatment. His meeting with his sister and his subsequent death cause her to return home to join the family. Here, the split between men and women – in this case brother and sister – and the cultural gulf between them are shown by the different countries in which they live. The westernized sister has to be reconciled with her radical religious Iranian brother. The film is a call for reunion, for the return of women who have been alienated by the Revolution – especially those who have physically left home for the West.

The Fantasy of Home and Homelessness

For filmmakers, home is the screen, where the world of their films and their fantasies comes to life. Each film accommodates parts of them which are expressed through different places and different characters.

In *The Taste of Cherry*, the idea of home is a transitional one. The main character's only visible personal space is his car, a mark of his identity. His final home, his resting place, is the grave he lies in. In Naderi's *Water, Wind, Earth*, the abandoned, homeless boy gives up the idea of family as home in his search for another home – his lost soul, portrayed as water. Like the unreal scene of an ocean of water, this metaphoric home is a cutaway from the endless dry wells. For Majidi in *Children of Heaven*, the idea of home is the high moral values of the poor children living in old Tehran, reminiscent of the lost world of childhood. The narrow alleys, old houses and neighbourhoods of south Tehran, a place of warm community and the values of the older generation, are contrasted with the isolating upper-class buildings of north Tehran. For Makhmalbaf, the idea of home is the lost values portrayed through the streets of Tehran in parallel to the war zone. In *Wedding of the Blessed* (1989), the main character chooses to become homeless since he does not want to fit into the greedy, corrupt world around him. The spacious house of his fiancée's rich *bazaari* family, the newspaper building where he works as a freelance photographer, and the marriage office, all convey the sense of corruption and betrayal. The film compares real homeless people and addicts on the streets of Tehran with martyrs of the war.

In the works of the major Iranian exile filmmakers, home is always somewhere else, outside the worlds of their characters. In Shahid-Saless's German films – *Roses for Africa* (1991), *Utopia* (1982) and *Diary of a Lover* (1977) – home is where the characters are not, but long to be. Or it may be a place where the absent beloved is, like the brother in Africa in *Roses for Africa*, or the disappeared beloved woman in *Diary of a Lover*. In Naderi's American film, *Manhattan by Numbers* (1993), the main character finds himself among the real homeless of New York while searching for his friend.

Cinematic Treatment of Location

The cinematic treatment of a chosen location reveals the filmmaker's attitude towards it. Camera movement, frame size and composition, lighting, editing and sound, support hidden aspects of the theme more than conscious structural elements of the story such as dialogue and plot. At the end of *The Taste of Cherry*, when the man lies down in the grave, Kiarostami fades into a video shot of the crew filming behind the scenes. This transition not only comes as a surprise or a relief for the audience in terms of the story, but is also visually shocking. The rather fuzzy video shot looks more dreamlike than real. All the video shots of behind-the-camera reality establish another world that can be as unreal or as real as the rest of the film. The change of format visually forces the viewer to question the reality of the scene and the ending of the film.

In *The Pear Tree* (1998), Mehrju'i alters the natural look of the land-scape of the past, where the adolescent's first love and erotic awakening take place. The yellow filter removes the real look of the place, giving it a more nostalgic feeling. Similarly, his garden – the place of past memories and present experience – is often shown under a heavy blue filter, with a low-angle camera movement under the fruit trees, giving it a dreamlike quality. The identification of the landscape with the boy's past erotic awakening and his present experience of loss and rigidity is formally represented by discoloured landscapes.

In his two major German films, *Utopia* and *Diary of a Lover*, Saless, with his simple but highly focused, realistic and non-dramatic style, creates a claustrophobic space by using low-lit scenes and silhouette shots of the characters, framed by windows or other structures. Exterior scenes, depicting the characters' social context, are reduced to a minimum. Slow, circular camera movements around the characters, inside rooms and hallways, create a visual trap. Intercuts of shots inside and outside the buildings emphasize the characters' isolation and define a sensation of being in prison, mirroring their repressive inner spaces. There is a desire to connect and to go beyond, without showing it. The lack of exterior scenes – and their irrelevance to the characters' dilemmas – gives an existential and philosophical quality to the characters and the part they play in creating their own predicaments.

Parviz Kimiavi metaphorically portrays a fragmented world in *The Mongols* (1973) using editing to create a fictional space to bring the different elements of the film together. The Mongol actors who are looking for the director of the film, the Mongols who are aggressive, the filmmaker who is thinking about cinema and TV, the contrasts between Western exploitation and Eastern values, the desert and the filmmaker's room, all these are juxtaposed so as to create a fictional cinematic space. The film-maker's thoughts materialize in the form of the Mongols and the deserts, and so on: he both controls their appearances and is controlled by them – a narrative rationale similar to that of *The Thousand and One Nights*.

In his earlier short films, *O Deer Saviour* (1970) and *P Like Pelican* (1972), Kimiavi uses real locations in both realistic and metaphoric styles. As well as editing, camera angle and camera movement create a metaphorical cinematic space. *O Deer Saviour* is a short documentary about one day in the Imam Reza shrine in Mashhad. The film has two parts: a subjective scene of the interior of the holy shrine and an objective, documentary-style depiction of the process of a day there. The camera, moving slowly through grand carved silver doors, looks up from a low-angle, child's point of view – for the most part excluding people – at the glorious mirrored walls and ceiling which reflect the light from the central chandelier. The many doors which are opened to the subjective, floating camera reveal and transcend a magnificent, silent and intimate space. As this visual journey comes to an end, we hear a woman crying and a man asking to be healed. The film later moves towards a more objective documentary style, depicting more people praying and those who take care of the shrine. The way the first part of the film is shot – showing nothing of the ground of the interior through which the camera is moving – and the way it is edited, give a subjective quality to the inner space, almost creating a separate reality. It evokes a sense of the divine or sacred that is absent from the second part of the film where we see people praying.

In *P Like Pelican*, Kimiavi brings to the screen another archetypal image of an Iranian collective psyche: the ruins and the old man – a reference to Iranian history and the memory of destruction, loss, poetry and madness – all in a metaphoric treatment of a realistic environment. Living among the ruins, the old man becomes them. We see a big white bird, a pool of water and a beautiful garden in the middle of desert, all far from the reality of the old man's physical environment. The editing suggests an identification between masculinity and the ruins, contrasting with the feminine asso-ciations of the garden and the deadly bird. The man shaves and dresses in white to meet the white bird but, as in a romantic love plot, his efforts to reach his beloved bring his death. At the end of the film, slow-motion shots of the walls of the ruins are paralleled to the old man drowning. The walls collapse just as he falls into the water; the film ends with a freeze-frame of him under the water, suggesting his death, understood mainly at a conceptual level. Neither the shallow pool nor the frightened bird were serious physical threats to the old man's safety, but the arrangement of shots and what they represent convey a message of death and destruction to the audience.

Kimiavi succeeds in creating a complete philosophical and metaphorical world, removed from any reference to time and history. Yet the audience finds the blurring of fantasy and reality emotionally convincing, mainly because of the reality of the old man, the charmingly innocent – non-professional – Asid Ali Mirza, and the Tabas ruins.

Conclusion

I have drawn attention to the presence and function of location in Iranian films, and the ways different filmmakers use it. Location is an important part of every film, but it usually passes unnoticed by the audience, overshadowed by the dramatic elements of the film – story, plot, dialogue, characters and music. Occasionally, location becomes noticeable when visually emphasized, as in *Gabbeh* or *The Pear Tree*. The use of real locations, an important characteristic of Iranian cinema, appealing to many viewers abroad, has promoted a sense of exoticism in these films.

From the filmmaker's point of view, location constitutes the world and mood of the film and the social and psychological environment of the characters. The same story shot in different locations would convey different meanings; that is to say, the type of location used in a film gives a definite interpretation and context to the story. The green forests of the north, the barren brown sandy deserts of central and northeast Iran, the grey, polluted, crowded, poor neighbourhoods of the capital, or its more affluent areas with their modern architecture, all provide different looks, feelings and environments for a film, giving different impressions of post-revolutionary Iran.

Similarly, open spaces or exterior settings such as roads, hills and countryside (*Through the Olive Trees*, *A Time to Love*, *Children of Heaven*) create visual, emotional and philosophical possibilities that are absent in the closed, dark interiors of buildings such as rooms, hallways and stairs (*The Peddler*, *Yazdgerd's Death*, Shahid-Saless's *Far From Home*, 1975).

The question of location is even more interesting when it comes to films shot outside Iran, where filmmakers extend their affiliation to a land and culture beyond their own. This allows, for example, the depiction of love in Turkey, in *A Time to Love*, and the identification of a westernized Iranian with Germany, in *From Karkheh to Rhine*.

The choice between urban or rural, and open or closed spaces is often justified by the story, the theme, or the psychology of the characters. But a closer look may reveal elements beyond the story that show the filmmaker's affinity with certain places and their cultural meanings, and reflect his or her attitude towards them. This attitude can be seen in the cinematic treatment of the location, through the use of lighting, composition, camera movement, camera angle, shot size, colour, sound, music and editing. Shots of landscapes, streets and buildings not from any character's point of view reveal a filmmaker's attitude toward these locations. This is especially significant in films with minimal or no plot, where location plays a major role in establishing the theme of the film, such as *Water, Wind, Earth, The Taste of Cherry* or *A Simple Event*.

Depiction of spectacular landscapes – usually accompanied by music – of, for example, the north, as in *The Cloud and the Rising Sun* and *Through the Olive Trees*, the war front, as in Hatamikia's *The Sentry*, 1988, or a poor but old neighbourhood of Tehran, as in *Children of Heaven*, reflects a film-maker's cultural harmony with those places, or a desire to identify with them and what they represent culturally.

Likewise, disparaging views of particular places can be conveyed by camera angel, lighting and composition, or by exclusion – keeping them off-screen – to show the filmmakers' alienation from those locations or their wish to dissociate themselves from their cultural values. This becomes more noticeable when a colourful location is shot at a particular season to give it a desolate cold grey look. Different urban neighbourhoods represent different classes, cultural values and traditions. By excluding the affluent parts of Tehran and the city's modern architecture, many films make a social or political comment about the filmmaker's class or class sympathies. Picturesque Tehran, the centre of mainstream culture, could be ignored in favour of its unsavoury outskirts, as in *The Taste of Cherry*, or corrupt, greedy men may be present in the mosque or marriage office – two significant institutions – as in *Wedding of the Blessed*.

When a filmmaker refrains from showing the whole image and range of views of a location, particularly by limiting shots of what the characters are looking at, that audiences usually expect, or resorts to limited close shots or partial views – in films like *The Peddler, Far From Home, Yazdgerd's Death* or *Water, Wind, Earth*, this creates a sense of frustration and a feeling of closed space. This feeling can be interpreted as the filmmaker's political and cultural attitude toward those places and what they represent.

The most interesting cinematic treatments of real Iranian locations are seen in the editing of non-realist films. Images of different places and different times are cut together to create a metaphorical world for the film-maker and the film's characters. For example, in *P for Pelican* and *The Mongols*, Kimiavi juxtaposes images of the ruins near Tabas, of the desert and desert towns with their treasures and of TV antennae, to remind the audience of a spiritual, cultural and historical loss. The non-realistic style, emphasized by editing, creates a fragmented world controlled by the film-maker's imagination. The way the different images occupy – and attack – the filmmaker's mind resembles the real historical forces – whether the

Mongols or Western culture – that colonized Iran and its culture. In a sense, by using different places in Iran for their mythological, historical, psychological and spiritual meanings and character, Kimiavi identifies himself with his homeland and what it has endured.

Bibliography

Bhabha, Homi K., *The Location of Culture* (London, Routledge, 1994).

Bordwell, David, *On the History of Style* (Cambridge, Harvard University Press, 1997).

Naficy, Hamid (ed.), *Home, Exile, Homeland: Film, Media, and the Politics of Place* (New York, Routledge, 1999).

Rosenbaum, Jonathan, 'The politics of form', in J. Rosenbaum, *Movies as Politics* (Berkeley, University of California Press, 1997).

11

Chaste Dolls and Unchaste Dolls: Women in Iranian Cinema since 1979

Shahla Lahiji

Looking at Iranian entrants in the 17th Fajr Film Festival from a psychological angle, an Iranian film magazine recently commented that the 'essence and dramatic forms of most of the films shown [at the festival] derived from the struggle between the sexes which imposed itself on the audience irrespective of the underlying motivation or instigation.' The article concluded that such an extreme attitude to sex-based conflicts, expressed in a feminist idiom, indicated the filmmakers' urge to follow the wishes of society and the dictates of the box office.[1]

The comment reveals a grain of truth which may, indeed, push the Iranian film industry of the coming decade into a kind of exaggeration of the life of women, because one of the current criteria for evaluating a cinematographic piece of work is the filmmaker's attitude to women.

This fact in itself speaks of a tension in Iranian society, which barely 20 years ago was suffering from the opposite problem – a total absence of any realistic portrayal of women's lives – a tension that neither yields readily to analysis nor betrays its inner mechanism. We only know that the public is sensitive to any works of art that offer distorted, often unrealistic and usually negative images of women: images that, whether motivated by anger or by pity, portray woman as a humble or haughty stereotype, or attribute to her an obsession – with a son or a lover – alien to the real life of women in this society. It now seems that public reaction to such images makes filmmakers aware of the risk that public opinion may call them to account as regards the roles they allot to heroines and other female characters in their films.

Judging a work of art by focusing on one aspect of it can easily amount to prejudice and bias, in which case it is not a helpful form of artistic criticism, even if it concerns a medium which is after all part of the mass media and has immense influence over the way the public view of the world takes shape. Yet it can be justified by suggesting that the whole Iranian film industry is being called to account for the wrongs it has done to women in the distant and not-so-distant past. Indeed, from its infancy, Iranian cinema has treated women with great injustice and has been responsible, more than any other medium, for distorting the image of the Iranian woman and creating a caricature of her real self.

The film industry arrived in Iran at a time when Iranian women, after a protracted period of inertia and silence, of almost total ignorance and backwardness, were about to set off on a slow journey toward an awareness of the world, intending to shed the heavy load of antiquated tradition and custom in order to receive the social status they deserved. Even though women from certain classes had played a part in the political and social changes of Iranian society in the past, the role had been discharged meekly and often – as in the case of a few ambitious women in ruling circles – in the form of 'scripts' prepared for men to articulate. Now, the modernizing trend sought to bring women out onto the social scene as women, and called on them to participate in social and economic processes as real people.

Cinema could have helped greatly to reach that goal. In a country which, at the time, suffered an illiteracy rate of between 80 and 90 per cent, cinema could have worked miracles in preparing public opinion for the acceptance of social changes favouring women. Instead, the picture the film industry painted of the Iranian woman, in its more charitable version, amounted to no more than a seal of approval on reactionary and prejudiced attitudes according to which women had only one way to salvation: to behave as second-class citizens whose main duty was to reproduce the human race, to live within the four walls of their homes and to keep house for their husbands. If they ventured outside, they were doomed to bring misery to society and to fall into an unchaste life.

This conception of women held total sway over commercial Iranian films and even managed to dominate and infest modernist and intellectual filmmakers and later on, like a chronic illness, to enter post-revolutionary cinema culture. At no time did the character and mode of life of Iranian women presented on the silver screen resemble real life.

The Iranian film industry had a late start with the production of its first film, *The Lor Girl* (Ardeshir Irani, 1933). By that time, the seventh art had already gone beyond amateur filmmaking and had entered the stage of professionalism. Iran, however, lacked the technical means to produce a film, and the *The Lor Girl* had to be made in India, at considerable expense. The story of the film was exceptional in its portrayal of how a young woman could lead an independent life in a highly volatile – even violent – social environment. The subject was a dancer in rural public tea-houses, desired by the oppressive local chief but strong-willed enough to resist his advances and preserve her independence of mind and body.

Even though the producer's concerns about the public reaction proved quite justified, in fact the film was shown to a public which had already experienced considerable social change, with the result that the traditional structures of women's lives had also altered. Besides, at that time the government had imposed certain restrictions on the power of the clergy and traditional classes, who, despite their natural opposition to the showing of such films, were unable to display open hostility.

To the filmgoers of the time, the imperfect *hejab* of the heroine was not that important. The story, emphasizing a kind of feminine power and self-reliance, challenged traditional perceptions of women's role as properly confined to the home and a life of social seclusion, but even so reports of the public reception of the film do not speak of an outcry. *The Lor Girl* was, altogether, a successful film.

The next Iranian film, this time produced inside Iran, was not screened until 1948. The long interval was due to economic problems; other films begun in India had been left unfinished for that reason. Nevertheless, during that gap of 15 years the country and the rest of the world had experienced considerable change. In Iran, a series of developments affecting women's social life, above all the compulsory public removal of the veil through the application of the order banning *hejab*, had suddenly turned women and their lives into a political bone of contention. Further developments, such as the admission of women to universities, their employment in government offices, the violent treatment of those who continued to appear in public fully veiled or even with just a headscarf, the opening of various kinds of recreational centres, severe conflict between state and clergy and the cultural and social pressures imposed on traditional segments of society which refused to bow to modernizing trends, all influenced women's lives and the way they were regarded. External political conditions too inevitably left their imprint on the whole spectrum of cultural and economic behaviour. These included the outbreak of the Second World War and the occupation of Iran by the Allies, how Iranians interpreted the occupation and Reza Shah's abdication and banishment, the accession of Mohammad Reza Shah and the weakness of central government, which revived the power of traditional and conservative social segments alongside harsh economic conditions and falling standards of living.

The first all-Iranian production, *The Tempest of Life* (Esma'il Kushan, 1948), was a tepid family melodrama devoid of the candour which had marked *The Lor Girl*. Yet it was still aware of the problem of women and took a critical – albeit crude and indirect – look at the supreme power of men in the patriarchal structure of the family. Although the Persian language used in the film was expected to attract the general public, *The Tempest of Life* and other films of the same genre produced in the following decade could hardly be described as successful. The reason was the greater attractiveness of imported films, especially Indian and Egyptian, which offered better entertainment value and were made with more advanced production techniques. In fact, the domestic film industry was pushed to the brink of bankruptcy by the general poverty, insufficient long-term investment in the film industry, and the absence of creative and talented filmmakers. This was combined with the negative attitude of traditional sections of society toward any modern means of communication and the extensive publicity they undertook against them. The situation was worsened by the introduction of dubbing, and the arrival of Italian films shown in Persian.

To confront this debilitating crisis, the few producers who were still active turned to producing *film farsi*, a genre of 'lumpen-cabaret' films that gave their name to the period. Seeing the popularity of semi-musical films imported from Egypt and India, these Iranian producers borrowed song-and-dance scenes from cabaret life and used them to spice up their films with the sex appeal of dancing women.

Although they were detrimental both to the development of public artistic taste and to public perceptions of the role and status of women in the country, these films earned good money, and for many years the Iranian film industry made nothing else. Men, suffering sexual deprivation because of traditional cultural practices, formed the main audience for these films. Their simple formula for success was to put on the screen a few obscure but young female faces, with the type of beauty that appealed to that particular class of filmgoers – sexually-deprived young men – and add good-looking, macho male protagonist, men who represented no particular social class but matched the fantasies of the penniless youths who went to see the films.

The important point is that the filmmakers of the time helped to line their pockets by neglecting, even damaging, the social status of women. We should not forget that for a long time these were the only films produced by Iranian filmmakers. That tasteless and peculiar portrayal of women displaying their bodies to satisfy poor filmgoers in no way represented the real way of life of women in Iranian society, even if it turned filmmaking into a profitable business. During the 1960s, a series of films with names such as *The Dancer*, *The Cocotte* and *The Shamed Woman* were screened, offering more or less the same kind of content. Progress was measured only by more nudity and the inclusion of cruder sex scenes, usually without artistic value or much relevance to the film's story. Thus the Iranian film industry, which, as an inexpensive means of public entertainment, could have contributed to the progress of society's cultural attributes and sense of artistic appreciation, became instead a place where men's suppressed sexual drives were satisfied.

In this way, 'unchaste dolls' came to dominate the silver screen as the sole cinematic representation of Iranian women. The screen lacked real women – and real men. Iranian films overflowed with fantasy of the most vulgar type, with no sign of aesthetic appeal. It mattered to no-one that, in this display of coarse tastelessness, the vast majority of Iranian women, who were trying to emerge from their conventional social roles and rise to a higher level of social standing, were being victimized. Such women were, as a result, in desperate need of help by the mass media, which could show some of their real-life struggles, reflect the changes that were already taking place – their entry into education and the labour market – and help to prepare traditional segments of society for further changes.

The second stage in women's sacrifice at the altar of cinematic popularity tells an even more pathetic story. Now the sacrificial knife was in the hands of the intellectuals and the so-called progressive filmmakers. Towards the end of the 1960s, the screening of Massoud Kimia'i's *Qeysar* (1969) heralded the arrival of progressive filmmaking in Iran. The storyline of the film is simple: a girl's virginity is violated by a ruffian, and she has no choice but to kill herself. Her older brother rises to defend the family honour and is killed. A one-sided vendetta begins. The younger brother, Qeysar, who had been leading a quiet, industrious life in Khuzestan, arrives to find the family faced with the ultimate catastrophe: honour has been lost and one has died in the attempt to retrieve it. He has no choice but to take upon himself the task of cleansing the dishonour with blood. Equipped with a knife, much courage and – perhaps the only exciting part of the story – a good deal of cunning, he succeeds in eliminating not only the perpetrator of the original crime but also a number of his kin and associates, by stabbing them in the most unlikely places. Perhaps as lip service to the anti-regime sentiments of the time, he is finally killed resisting arrest, the policeman appearing as representative of a structure of law and order that refuses to condone the action of a person who takes the law into his own hands by rising to take vengeance on those who rape virgins. Although the film included a number of female characters, the story could have been told without them. They included not only Qeysar's passive, rather impersonal mother, but also a cabaret woman whose only task was to satisfy the heroes' sexual impulses.

The film was a turning point in the history of Iranian cinema. It opened the doors of *film farsi* to the younger generation of the intelligentsia, and admitted these films into the review pages of magazines. Yet, this stage is also important for giving filmgoers another image of Iranian women, an image which, in the final analysis, brought them no more than disappointment, regression and seclusion. In an attempt to appeal to an intellectual audience, the New Wave films assumed a posture of confronting vulgarity and, by an insidious piece of cultural fraud, threw women off the cabaret stage and into the attic.

No matter what interpretation one puts on the political and social events of those years, the example of the few educated women who had ventured out into society 30 or 40 years before was being emulated by an increasing number of younger women – some even from traditional backgrounds – who were eager to advance their social status. They wanted to receive higher education and enter the labour market and in some cases they demanded to be admitted to some of the traditional strongholds of men, such as the army and higher levels of political and administrative decision-making. The prominent filmmakers of the post-*Qeysar* period totally ignored these woman, who were battling in the social arena to break out of the prison of antiquated and retarding traditions; taking a long step backward, they returned Iranian woman to the conditions of 20 or 30 years before.

In such conditions, and under the pretence of foregrounding indigenous Iranian cultural attributes against what they called 'imported-Western' values, filmmakers came to exalt the barren and by then partly forgotten conventions of the past. Unfortunately, because of the dominant political atmosphere, Iranian intellectuals approved of this cultural forgery as a sign of opposition to values promoted by the ruling regime.

Generally speaking, in films of this period – of which *Qeysar* is a good example – a 'good woman' was a faceless, unexciting figure who wore traditional costume and stayed in the background as an obedient housewife, or a virgin in training for the role, whose only concern in life was to make the home comfortable for male masters who wielded knives and got into fights in order to defend the honour and virginity of their female flock. These 'good women' were the crude prototypes of the 'chaste dolls' who are now all-too-common features of Iranian cinema and TV screens. The irony is that the initial design came from the progressive cinema in Iran.

Of course, the role of the cabaret-stage woman was still popular, but progressive filmmakers offered a serious rival in the shape of old mothers under their sons' patronage, with no greater ambition in life than to be taken to shrines by their lords and masters. Good women obeyed their men without question, because men were after all wiser than women. And why not? – good women would never venture from the sanctuary of the home to be stained by the villainies of a world which only men were qualified to face.

These good women offered the acceptable norm – other types of women could only wreak disorder. Other types included the leader of a smugglers' gang, or the wife of a brutal feudal lord or tribal chief, or an underhand seducer of naive rural men. Indeed, commercial cinema was quick to emulate the new concept of womanhood and, by spicing it with sex, came to create the image of the loose woman. No doubt it was during those years that the image of woman as a creature of corruption and immorality took shape in society's unconscious, to manifest itself later in political developments. We should not forget that, although many women who joined the ranks of the revolutionaries in the late 1970s wore the headscarf or even the chador as a tactical move to demonstrate their opposition to the Pahlavi regime, they had no intention of losing the little they had gained in the form of improvement in their social rights. They were well aware that, to many of their fellow revolutionaries, women who followed the Western mode of dressing could only be the supporters of the unintelligent and unreliable screen prototypes.

It would be a mistake to pass through this stage of development of the Iranian film industry without noting a few important works by directors who came to cinema from theatre. These films, appearing from the mid-1970s, took a different look at the question of women in society, but by then it was too late for the public mind to adopt a new perspective. The Revolution was underway, and films such as Beyza'i's *The Crow* (1977) and *Tara's Ballad* (1978) were never put on public show. In *Tara's Ballad*, a rural widow has sufficient authority to guide a whole village, while the heroine of *The Crow* is a teacher at a school for disabled children with much greater force of personality than the men around her. But perhaps the most famous of the films of this genre is Beyza'i's *Downpour* (1972), which depicts the rivalry of a schoolteacher and a butcher over the hand of the same girl. The girl is a normal human being, leading a normal life and left to choose one of the suitors. But despite the violence of the butcher's passion and the teacher's rather subdued approach, the audience discovers that both have essentially similar feelings and sentiments, those of normal human beings.

By the time of the Revolution, Iranian cinema had granted recognition only to the chaste and unchaste dolls. With the victory of the Revolution, many of those who had despaired of any improvement in the content of the Iranian film industry – as well as a number of theatre actors who had shunned the Iranian cinema because of its mediocre artistic value – were now able to hope that a purge of the vestiges of vulgarity from the Iranian film industry would make the environment receptive to true artistic works and, importantly, would offer a realistic portrayal of Iranian women on the screen. Domestic production had ample room to grow, in particular because of severe import restrictions on foreign films. But it soon became evident that the idea of the chaste doll, concocted by pre-revolutionary progressive cinema, would die hard; it was to continue into the post-revolutionary cinema as the lacklustre yet predominant image of women.

Thus, in the film sector, as in many other areas, all the sins committed by the fallen regime, as well as the output of vulgar filmmakers, were put on women's shoulders, ignoring the fact that women themselves had been the main victims. Women were now to pay the penalty by being banished altogether to the kitchen.

When women did appear in post-revolutionary Iranian films, they were neutral creatures engaged only in household chores, sitting by the samovar and feeding fathers, husbands and young sons – all of whom ordered them about. This appearance, however, was a concession to women, who had been totally absent from the screen in the first years of the Revolution, when the domestic film industry was driven to the brink of bankruptcy and survived only parasitically off government subsidies. At the same time, TV, backed by government finance, continued with a diet of chaste dolls, and even developed it. Women in TV films were devoid of personal identity and were only seen taking part in traditional mourning ceremonies, or washing dishes next to open ponds which had long been buried under high-rise blocks of flats. The central attraction of such films was spacious, old-fashioned rooms – almost collectors' pieces – with all members of a large family gathered around a gigantic tablecloth under the wise guidance of a patriarch. In few if any TV films of the 1980s did one see a woman returning from work, wielding a pen or working in an office or factory. A woman did not doubt, let alone oppose, the will of her husband. Women had reached the pinnacle of their assumed careers as chaste dolls.

The wartime film industry was also faced with lower subsidies and funding. Actresses who had emigrated from cinema to TV were almost all seen as figures weeping tears of ecstasy as they saw their husbands and sons off to the front. The TV screen was largely monopolized by such films, often offering little variety or novelty. Of course, a few other roles were still reserved for women: they could be faithless, treacherous hussies, opposed to the Revolution, or involved in suspicious liaisons with foreigners. These women were shown wearing a less strict form of *hejab*, betraying their lack of faith in religion and the Revolution; they were, in a sense, the successors of the negative female images of the pre-revolutionary period. Screen women could also be selfish, illogical, domineering, highly sensitive and jealous, with nothing else to do but make life hell for their wise, noble, humble and altogether lovable menfolk. More often than not, even these women were nice enough to listen to men's advice, repent, receive absolution and become chaste.

In films of the period, female 'goodies' invariably wore the chador, while female 'baddies' were attired in the more normal way, in overcoat (*ru-push*) and headscarf (*ru-sari*). Again, this was a pointed publicity weapon aimed at women who, contrary to that image, expressed a wish for more freedom to choose their own attire, even without violating the Islamic dress code. The good woman was a submissive, long-suffering, kitchen-bound creature, ever ready to sacrifice everything for her male superiors without asking questions about the results such sacrifices were supposed to bring. She took orders from men within and outside her home, and carried them out faithfully and mechanically.

In 1988, when I published *The Image of Woman in Bahram Bayzai's Works*,[2] I never foresaw that the image of women in the Iranian film industry would one day become the subject of heated and significant social debate and the criterion for evaluating filmmakers' work. That book was merely my personal reaction to the degradation of women in the visual media. The book was detained by the censor, but at the end of the war with Iraq it finally received a printing licence. The end of the war also signalled a change in direction for the Iranian film industry. Soon, a number of good films by respected pre-revolutionary directors were screened, such as Beyza'i's *Bashu, The Little Stranger* (1988) and *Maybe Another Time* (1988). Critics' analyses of these films revealed that in my little book I had put my finger on a painful wound that was soon to burst open.

When the war ended and the country became politically more open, protests were heard from women who had endured economic pressure and shortages, life under bombs and rockets and the martyrdom of their dear ones, while many of them had had to assume the role of the breadwinner in the absence of their men. At the same time, women who were interested in the film industry tried to make up for their absence in front of the camera by working behind it. They first announced their presence in TV, in such roles as assistant directors, designers, stage managers, reporters and documentary-makers. Gradually, with fortitude and perseverance in the face of insults and coercion, they managed to open the gates of the seemingly closed and male-dominated citadel of the film industry.

In the late 1980s and early 1990s, works by several female Iranian filmmakers aroused the curiosity and sometimes the admiration of international critics. The debate on the subject of the image of women in Iranian cinema, which had been introduced but left unresolved, now resumed in a wider spectrum. The way women filmmakers chose to object to the unrealistic image of women in Iranian cinema was by making films themselves. Such filmmakers were confident of their professional expertise, and had a strong vision of the future for women. They showed in their work that, despite all the limitations, proscriptions and prescriptions that make the production of an acceptable film little easier than a miracle, it was possible to make better films and present women in a more realistic way.

The international reception of that approach finally persuaded their male colleagues to reappraise their own works. Films such as *Sara* (Daryush Mehrju'i, 1992) and *Zinat* (Ebrahim Mokhtari, 1994) showed that the community of Iranian filmmakers had put its seal of approval on the need to accept the reality of Iranian society. Sara is a woman who refuses to remain passive when her husband is unable to deal with his own financial problems. Zinat is a medical worker in a remote village who faces the

9. Rakhshan Bani-Etemad's *The Blue Scarf.*

hardships of living in those surroundings and confronting the reaction of the local population to a woman taking charge of their medical needs. Through her own efforts, she earns the villagers' trust and is elected to the local council. More than anything else, the film is valuable in that it portrays the life of not one but many Iranian women in similar positions.

Today, Iranian films have risen to the level of international acceptance and adopted a different approach, with an attitude to women that is far more progressive than attitudes before the Revolution. The new approach allows Iranian women to challenge representations of their place in society. Rakhshan Bani-Etemad's *Narges* (1992), *The Blue Scarf* (1994) and *The May Lady* (1998), and Tahmineh Milani's *Two Women* (1999) are signs of this challenge. In *Narges*, two women fall in love with one man and are left to work out the problem. *The Blue Scarf* is about a woman worker whose striking personality attracts the attention of her boss. *The May Lady* tells the story of a working woman – a filmmaker – called on to choose between total devotion to her son and her wish to remarry. *Two Women* challenges the myth of marriage as the sole destiny of a woman, and shows how a bad marriage can destroy a woman's life. Now, compare these with Mehrju'i's *Leyla* (1997) and Iraj Qaderi's *Tootia* (1998). *Leyla* is the story of a married but childless woman who, presumably complying with what is expected of any good woman in her situation, finds another more fertile woman to marry her husband and receives a note of approval for her good work. *Tootia* has a more complicated plot: the heroine is a working woman who inevitably – as traditionalists tell us – neglects her duties by refusing to give up her job and become a full-time housewife and mother in the service of her husband; by doing so, she spells out her own and her husband's doom. The moral of the story is clear enough: women should stay at home and leave men to handle the evils that lurk in every nook and cranny of the outside world.

Today, Iran is about to experience important changes, in the areas of civil society, culture and the arts. Women – for centuries or even millennia denigrated as 'half-perfect' creatures and doomed to chains and slavery – are gradually breaking out of their restrictive shells to declare their presence everywhere. The Iranian film industry, having ignored women's lives for almost 50 years, is purging itself of the notions of chaste and unchaste dolls in order to paint a real and realistic portrait of women and their presence.

Iranian women's dress cannot and should not prove a barrier to their activity both in front of and behind the camera. The headscarf should not go so far as veiling human identity. Women's participation in the film sector is a rational imperative which cannot be glossed over by fabrications of history or religion, or the realities of the present age.

Notes on Chapter 11

1.   'Women in films for this year's ten-day Dawn Festival', *Donya-ye Tasvir*, May 1999.
2.   Shahla Lahiji, *Sima-ye Zan dar Asar-e Bahram Beyza'i, Film-saz va Film-nameh-nevis* (Tehran, Rowshangaran, 1367/1988).

12

Children in Contemporary Iranian Cinema: When we were Children

Hamid Reza Sadr

The history of Iranian cinema in the 1980s and 1990s has been radically marked by the major social and political events that the country has experienced, such as the Revolution, the occupation of the US embassy and the war with Iraq. Each of these has had a profound impact on the way cinema developed in Iran and on the kinds of film made, with respect to Islamic rules, anti-Western attitudes and propaganda aims. These events have also isolated the majority of Iranians from any direct connection with outsiders. In the political struggle between the Iranian government and Western powers, ordinary Iranians were perceived as rough, ruthless and outlandish people lacking in humanity. At this time, cinema was the only medium that tried to portray a different image of Iran.

One conscious prerequisite for the creation of heroes or heroines on the screen is the existence of social stereotypes. The new epoch in Iran brought very different stereotypes and put forward a new series of characters as models; some of these were portrayed through children. The representation of children in Iranian cinema obviously has a long and complex history, shaped mainly by family structures and the rules of melodrama. In this chapter I am concerned with the importance of childhood on screen during the golden age of the post-revolutionary years. Exploring the depiction of children in Iranian cinema through these years, I analyse some key images and hidden aspects.

What Character? What Reality?

Ask people in Iran what Iranian character or national character actually is, and you will get a variety of answers. When I watch Iranian films, I ask myself, 'Is this our national character?' For example, are constancy and faithfulness among our distinguishing features? If so, constancy sometimes means deviating from the norm, so does this not violate the very meaning of national character? One could draw up a list enumerating all Iranian values which should not be transgressed.

Children have been cast in Iranian films as majestic statues of men and women, and sometimes as everyone's alter egos. They have almost been parodies of reports about Iran in the world's media during the last two decades. Iranian cinema was identified as presenting a more civilized way of life than was to be found in other media. A few directors changed Iranian cinema and the outside world's view of Iran. International film festivals acclaimed a kind of new wave. Its devotees were accustomed to films that would be non-commercial, with a new form and vision.

We may understand why children came to the forefront of Iranian cinema after the Revolution by recalling some of the most important features of this cinema. The main features included the dropping of the majority of actors and actresses from the pre-revolutionary industry, and the banning of sex, singing and dancing. Accordingly, Iranian films constitute a fascinating reflection of these regulations and limitations, but they are also close to a faithful reflection of social reality. Reality is a slippery concept at the best of times, however, and our understanding of it is more or less subjective. The best example has been Abbas Kiarostami's commitment to cinematic realism – how he presents reality in his films and allows his audience to interpret it.

The Iranian directors whose films have been shown outside Iran – from veterans such as Kiarostami and Amir Naderi to newcomers such as Mohsen and Samira Makhmalbaf – were theoretically pledged to realism, yet the reality they served up came in a form far from raw. This was partly because it was filtered through the new filmmaking regulations, sometimes because it was used as an educational tool, and sometimes because of these directors' interest in developing cinema as an art.

In addition, these films were further distinguished from indigenous commercial productions of the period by the contemporaneity and topicality of their subject-matter, their focus on lower-class milieux and their casting of unglamorous minor actors or even unknown non-professionals. Yet Iranian cinema apparently presents a curious contradiction. On the one hand it can be seen as a complete divergence from real life, and on the other it can and must be seen as a true reflection of the bizarre reality which actually characterizes contemporary Iran, like Rakhshan Bani-Etemad's *May Lady* (1998), Samira Makhmalbaf's *The Apple* (1998) or Kiarostami's *And Life Goes On...* (1991).

An Old Tradition

The 1980s was a period when many interesting films based on children came to the screen; some, such as *Pixote, Survival of the Weakest* (Hector Babenco, 1981), *Salaam Bombay!* (Mira Nair, 1988), *Pelle the Conqueror* (Bille August, 1988), *Toto the Hero* (Jaco van Dormael, 1991), *Ponette* (Jacques Doillon, 1997), *Tito and Me* (Goran Markovic, 1992) and *Silences of the Palace* (Moufida Tlatli, 1994) were internationally successful. However, children did appear in films before this; a unique tradition of filmmaking based on children as both audience and subjects was known in Iran from the late 1960s. A governmental organization, the Centre for Intellectual Development of Children and Adolescents (CIDCA), was founded in 1969 to make films and publish books. Starting out as a producer of short films and animations, CIDCA had few directors and animators, but the early results were astonishing in comparison with Iranian commercial films. In 1969 CIDCA produced seven films, including Kiarostami's *Bread and Alley*, an 11-minute short about a small boy who wants to go home through an alley and must confront a stray dog. The begining of Kiarostami's journey with children, this is a slow-paced, experimental work, which draws on both documentary and sub-generic strands. In the same year, Bahram Beyza'i also made a 28-minute film for CIDCA, *Uncle Moustache* (1969), in which an old man, annoyed at children playing football under his window, has to reach a compromise with them.

During the 1970s, CIDCA continued the rapid and steady growth which had characterized it since its foundation, and became established as a major producer of films for children. CIDCA released seven to ten films a year, by now totalling about 60 films; many won festival awards, especially for animation.

CIDCA never seriously tried to screen its films to regular audiences, and was criticized for its elitist orientation and intellectualism. Not until after the Revolution were CIDCA films screened in the theatres. Accordingly, they may be seen to depart quite radically from the conventions and production values of the studio system of the 1960s and 1970s. More naturalistic photography, closer to documentary than to studio-made fiction films, was achieved by location shooting and the use of available light

After the Revolution, CIDCA had financial problems, but continued its activities on a smaller scale. In the 1980s, it produced some feature films concerned with realism or social problems and based on children's dilemmas, including Kiarostami's *Where is the Friend's House?* (1987) and *Homework* (1988), and Beyza'i's *Bashu, The Little Stranger* (1988), which are among the classics of contemporary Iranian cinema.

This trend of filmmaking – looking at ordinary life with non-professional actors – was reinforced by Kiarostami's huge success outside Iran, but CIDCA models were its main source in Iranian cinema. Ebrahim Foruzesh's *The Key* (1987), made for CIDCA, became one of the most successful films in international festivals. A four-year-old boy must look after his infant brother when their mother leaves home to go shopping. All the action is based on the boy's efforts to find the key to the main door – the camera never leaves the little home. This film was very simple, but every event and situation was considered as a part of a puzzle which exists in Iranian society. The title of Foruzesh's latest film, *The Little Man* (1997), about a 12-year-old farmer's son who decides to help his mother by using an abandoned plot for gardening, is indicative. Mohammad Ali Talebi's *The Boot* (1993), another CIDCA production, has a similar theme: a mother who works in a factory leaves her little daughter with one of her friends who has an injured son. The two children can't get along peacefully, but find a way to become friends.

Through Different Eyes

From the early 1980s, we see a reversion to different understanding of realism, in which themes were explored mainly through the eyes of the young, a new generation confronting a new world. This was a new era, and filmmakers now had to deal with different aspects of the contemporary

Iranian way of life. Many directors turned to low-budget productions in real locations. Gradually, portrayals of children in short stories of village life, or on occasional excursions to the big city streets, came to dominate Iranian cinema. They depicted the historic changes in Iran over the previous two decades, particularly as experienced by Iranian people.

Using children in films facilitated the development of Iranian cinema and the role it played in reflecting, interpreting and above all representing Iranians. One of the distinctive features of Iranian films has been the use of innocent and hard-working children to convey symbolically certain apparently abstract ideas in a realistic way. Few people outside Iran remember the bloody, eight-year war with Iraq, but they may recall the children in Iranian films of the war – attractive, idealized, their innocent faces peering from the screens as they moved on, a long way, far from home. Sometimes it was seen as lost innocence in a world full of politicians.

The first Iranian film of the early 1980s to be welcomed in international festivals – because of its lack of dogma – was Amir Naderi's *The Runner* (1986), in which a young, lonely, homeless boy runs for his life. In Naderi's *Water, Wind, Earth* (1989), too, a young hero also fights against cruel nature. Iranian cinema received further impetus from Kiarostami's *Where is the Friend's House?* in which a little boy in a rural area tries to find his classmate's house, and we see the reactions of adult characters through his eyes. In *Bashu, The Little Stranger*, Beyza'i sent his young, homeless hero from the war-stricken south of Iran to the peaceful north where nobody could understand his language. In *Snake Fang* (1989), Massoud Kimia'i depicted the harshness of life in a big city like Tehran for a young boy whose own city had been devastated by war. Once again, a homeless immigrant fights to survive.

Children undeniably dominated the popular medium of TV. One of the most successful Iranian TV serials, Kiumars Pourahmad's *The Stories of Majid* (1990), about a hard-working orphaned boy with a sense of humour, was very popular, and Pourahmad also made feature films with the same actor and character.

No surprise, then, that the first Iranian film to be nominated for an Oscar (for Best Foreign Film) was one called *Children of Heaven* (Majid Majidi, 1997). A typical Iranian film, with the same familiar innocent children, had made it to Hollywood. In this film, a young brother and sister share a pair of shoes to go to school, one in the morning and the other in the afternoon. The film exaggerates the poverty of the family, yet it impressed the Academy members.

10. Majid Majidi's *The Children of Heaven*.

This is not to suggest that Iranian films about children, as a genre, display the degree of stylistic coherence that would allow for easy categorization. The evidence of the films themselves is complicated. Some seem to be clearly indebted to existing film genres and popular forms of entertainment. Others may be more aptly described as 'art cinema'.

Small Problems, Big World

Films about children bring many new aspects of Iranian society to the screen, including the alienation of children and youth, unemployment, violence and broken families. The heroic themes of the war, current in the films of the 1980s, have been replaced by the small-scale problems of everyday lives. The seven-year-old girl in *The White Balloon* (Jafar Panahi, 1995), who loses the money she was given to buy a goldfish and pursues a determined quest to recover it, is the quintessence of the Iranian film child. Incredibly serious, with a completely irresistible face, she is much too naive; but like her fellows, her move from passivity to extreme activity is clear. She can project her will into the audience, instinctively unaware of her power. A year after *The White Balloon* won a prize at the Cannes Film Festival, it became one of the most profitable foreign films in the US and Europe.

Children liberate plots by introducing non-essential actions – generally loafing around on the street or in a rural area. Usually the world is seen from a child's point of view. Sometimes the children's discourse realizes itself in their resistance to or confrontation with the adult characters of the story. These films pay much attention to the family, but do not proclaim it to be the basic cell of society or the ultimate source of love, support or morality. Rather, the family is depicted as a mass of tensions and conflicts. The viewer is invited to compare the adult characters with these hard-working children. The children acquire a tone of elevated romanticism that their parents never have. Parents cannot understand their children's language, and display an absolute indifference; when mother or father are present, they are most often looked at from the children's point of view. Parental sacrifice is replaced by filial sacrifice. These prevalent themes of hard-working children and the increasing relegation of childhood to the margins of adulthood suggest the importance of young adults in Iranian society in the last two decades.

The family, as an ideological cornerstone of Iran society, embodies a range of traditional values, such as love of family, love of mother and father and love of country. These concepts are intertwined, and we may see the child as a microcosm containing all the issues characteristic of society at large. In so many Iranian films, from box-office hits to art-house films, a family serves the crucial purpose of inserting, within the film's narration, the established values of competitive, repressive and hierarchical relationships. The presence of the family in Iranian films has served to legitimate and naturalize these values; therefore children's suffering reflects these social relationships. The sense of uncertainty about the smooth functioning of the social environment, present at the level of style through children's journeys, can be seen in the treatment of social institutions at the thematic level. *The Apple* is based on a true story of parents who imprisoned their twin daughters from their early days.

The absence of family in children's films can be interpreted as a comment on dominant social values. Many cynical films showed the dark side of family and society. Majid Majidi's *Baduk* (1992), a dark film about social reality set on the border between Iran and Pakistan, where drug smugglers take advantage of young boys, was quite successful at the box office and in film festivals. At the end, the film finds a political tone, narrating the story of young girls sold to Arab sheykhs.

In Abolfazl Jalili's *Dan* (1998) – based on a true story – the parents are never concerned for their child. Dan, a nine-year-old boy, does not have a

11. Jafar Panahi's *The White Balloon.*

birth certificate, which means he can't go to school or find a job. Like children in other films, he decides to look for his identity. This is a portrait of a small, vulnerable human being doing his best to cope with unfathomable rules. Parallel to the boy's story is that of a girl who yields to a forced marriage of convenience to help her family survive. She is somehow the boy's other half and reflects another facet of the misery of such young boys. Jalili's heroes show the ordeals of juvenile delinquents in jail in *Scabies* (1988), and delve into an abstract world in *Dance of Dust* (1992). *Scabies* – another true story – one of the most disturbing Iranian films, is a wrenching portrait of a boy's nightmarish existence in a crime-ridden atmosphere, and was never screened in public.

So films in which children appear have became more and more varied. They include slapstick comedies such as Mohammed Reza Honarmand's *Thief of Dolls* (1989), about a brother and sister fighting with a witch, and Mas'ud Karamati's *Patal and Little Wishes* (1990), about a brother and sister who take the role of their parents with disastrous results; both films were box-office hits. In these commercial films, the brother and sister behaved like a married couple, but were freer than any adult couple on screen. The girl, without veil or scarf, could easily accompany her brother/man in every situation, because they were children and were introduced as brother and sister. A number of melodramas by female directors that succeeded at the box office, such as Pouran Derakhshandeh's *Sweet Bird of Fortune* (1987) and Tahmineh Milani's *Children of Divorce* (1989), were based on children as victims, and made an impression on all categories of audience.

But the role of children was more important than simply to provoke sympathy. They went far beyond melodrama.

Gender and Children

Very occasionally a vivid male or female character appeared on screen. Many restrictions limited the showing of adult emotions in films, and love was hidden from the audience. Children were freer than adults; they could go anywhere and do more or less anything.

The first Iranian musical film after the Revolution was Mohammad Ali Talebi's *City of Mice* (1985), based on a successful TV animation series for children, but Kambozia Partovi's *Golnar* (1988) was the first musical with real characters. The young girl Golnar was different from any other Iranian female stars. Lost in the jungle, she sang and danced with animals freely, in a way which had not been seen before in post-revolutionary films. When the film became a box-office hit, it set a precedent for using children in order to make entertaining films. The traditional order of gender relations was eliminated because, while sex is a taboo in Iranian cinema, children are sexless, completely innocent of sexual knowledge, and appear to be free. Therefore, when people asked themselves what could be more important than love, children showed a platonic way of loving. This means that children have played a major role in depicting manifestations of love in the last two decades of Iranian cinema.

Reality and Symbolism

Accounts of the history of Iranian cinema are dominated by the critical centrality of a cluster of films made between the mid-1980s and the mid-1990s, commonly categorized as Iranian 'poetic realism'. It is clear, however, that the term cannot be traced back to a consciously planned, publicly circulated manifesto of a movement. On the contrary, the term is a descriptive category which has evolved through critical discourse. The films are relatively few, no more than 40 or 50 over a period in which domestic film production figures were much larger. Yet discussion of these films has been substantial and has engaged in a complex range of theoretical, methodological and historiographic debates.

Evidence of the commercial success of these films inside Iran is varied: a few were hugely successful hits and a number were disastrous flops. But the films were made at a particularly sensitive time in the history of con-temporary Iran, as the country emerged from eight years of bloody war with Iraq. In the immediate post-war years, films of poetic realism came mainly from Kiarostami, and CIDCA films provided an immediate response to the desire to get away from physical violence. The children in these films denounced the horrors of war or dealt with themes central to friendship. Moreover, in their social and geographical inclusiveness, they represented a bid to redefine the co-ordinates of national and cultural identity.

Children are usually like real characters and represent ordinary people; they relate to ideas about what people are – or are supposed to be – like. This idea was emphasized in Iranian cinema by using amateur actors with their amateurish way of acting. However, they had extraordinary dignity, as in *Bashu, The Little Stranger* and *Where is the Friend's House?* Unlike film stars, children were also real people. The audience could accept their dignity as easily as they would accept the dignity of a common individual. Because children have an existence in the world independent of their film appearances, we can believe that they are more real than other characters. This guaranteed the reality of the values they embodied.

One of the consequences of the growth of this notion was that we had two distinct conceptions of what we were, of our 'selves'. We could believe in the existence of knowable and constant selves – most people think they understand children or are like children at heart – and that these selves were not theoretically distinct from our social roles and our way of presenting ourselves to others. On the other hand, there was, in a way, an increasing anxiety about the validity of this autonomous, separate identity; only as children could we be ourselves. Poetic realism in Iranian cinema was built around the central image of childhood, and was inescapably social com-mentary, yet it must not offend the audience. Using children solved this problem by converting opinions expressed in the films into expressions of their being. They converted the question 'why do people feel this way?' to 'how does it feel to have such feelings?'

Paradoxically, the continuing interest of poetic realism in Iranian cinema lies precisely in that it was neither a straightforwardly homogeneous nor a unitary phenomenon, but successfully crossed the boundaries between high-brow and low-brow, tradition and modernity, engagement and pleasure. Perhaps the most compelling achievement was that children eased the problem of judgement – which would politicize the medium – by projecting it onto the realm of personal experience and feeling. Unlike film stars, who embody and dramatize the flow of information, and hence depoliticize modes of attachment in their audience, children represent the real world. They promote a privatization and personalization of structural determinants and a mass consciousness in the audience. Their personal troubles tend not to remain personal: they mark audience awareness of itself as a class by reconstituting social differences in the audience into a new polarity of collective experience.

The devaluation of enthusiasms and the open personality called into life a generation of non-actors. Perhaps the most rewarding experience offered by the children was in their non-acting style; the best performances of these two decades of Iranian cinema were given by non-professionals. Non-professionals were themselves, they were subtle and genuine, their lives resembling their characters' lives. Their plain acting combined the authenticity of everyday unattractiveness, the normality of the real person – a face in the crowd – with strong individuality. Their faces had a significance, the impressions of an intense inner life. The performance of Babak Ahmadzadeh in *Where is the Friend's House?* is mesmerizing, and the look of Adnan Afravian in *Bashu, The Little Stranger* is compelling. They played with such enthusiasm that they touched audiences nationwide.

In 1997, following the election of a reformist president by the votes of young adults, a new era in Iran has begun, bringing new themes and stories to Iranian films. We hope they will reveal on screen our hidden obsessions and secret inner lives, invisible from the outside – along with the lives of Iranian characters about whom hardly anything is yet known. At least those children are now grown up. Or are they?

13

Marking Gender and Difference in the Myth of the Nation: A Post-revolutionary Iranian Film

Nasrin Rahimieh

Bahram Beyza'i's 1985 film *Bashu, The Little Stranger* (first shown in 1988) has received attention both in and outside Iran for its candid depiction of post-revolutionary Iranian society and the Iran–Iraq war.[1] Although the film's title puts the boy Bashu at the centre of the story, the film itself gives equal prominence to a female character, Na'i, who becomes Bashu's primary interlocutor, in spite of the numerous differences that separate them. Bashu comes from the south of Iran and is a member of the Arab ethnic minority; his primary medium of communication is Arabic. Na'i, who lives in the northern province of Gilan, belongs to another ethnic group and speaks Gilaki, a local dialect of Persian. Neither Bashu nor Na'i is fluent in Persian, the national language of the country to which, however tenuously, they both belong. Through the difficulties Na'i and Bashu encounter in communicating with each other and overcoming their mutual anxieties about linguistic and ethnic differences, the film exposes the manner in which the construction of Iranian national identity has insisted upon the erasure and elision of gender, language and ethnicity. Taking the geographic polarities of north and south as its point of departure, the film introduces images of a country which is far from uniform and unilingual. The film's inclusion of ethnic minorities in its frame of vision helps to problematize the myth of a linguistically, racially and culturally unified Iran. The interesting intersections of this critique of Persian ethnocentrism with the problematics of gender and power will be the focus of my reading of the film. Before proceeding to my analysis, however, I first provide a brief sketch of the plot for readers unfamiliar with the film.

The story revolves around Bashu, a young boy from the Persian Gulf region, who is orphaned when missiles hit his village and kill his father, mother and sister. He hops into a truck that happens to be passing through his village during the shelling. Unknown to him, the truck is travelling to the Caspian region in the north. When Bashu finally emerges from his hiding place in the back of the truck, this time frightened by dynamite explosions used in the construction of a tunnel, he flees into rice fields and is discovered by two children, who alert their mother, Na'i, to the stranger's presence. Na'i, who has never seen anyone from the south, is startled by Bashu's darker skin colour, and can only assume that he has been hiding in a coal-cellar. After attempting to chase him away, she takes pity on him and leaves him some food. She overcomes her fear, draws him closer and finally, against the advice of other villagers and relatives, who are equally suspicious of Bashu's 'blackness', she brings him into her farmhouse. It proves almost impossible for them to communicate, as his Arabic has little in common with her Gilaki. Little by little, Na'i teaches him a few words in Gilaki, and one day in the course of an encounter between Bashu and other village boys she finds out that he has learned Persian at school.

Persian, the standard language of Iran since legislation in 1935, is the only means through which educated Iranians of diverse ethnicities can communicate with each other. This legislation coincided with a rise in nationalism. In its most fervent moments, this same nationalist spirit vilified Arabic language and culture, which, beginning with the Islamic conquest of Persia in the seventh century, changed the linguistic, religious and cultural map of Iran. That the pre-Islamic Persian empire already comprised many different ethnicities and languages is a point lost to modern nationalists, whose single-minded zeal for Persian also ignores Iran's existing diversity. This obsession has never been completely divorced from certain strains of racial intolerance. An integral part of the arch-nationalist agenda has been to cleanse Persian of Arabic 'contamination' in order to return the language to its Indo-European roots.

In the remote setting of Na'i's village, the artificiality of Persian – or its function as a 'paper language'[2] – is emphatically brought out. Na'i, who has received no schooling, is by and large barred from Persian; Bashu, who has

12. Bahram Beyza'i's *Bashu, The Little Stranger.*

access to Persian, has equally tenuous psychological ties to it. He speaks it haltingly, and his knowledge seems to be limited to words and phrases he has learned at school. In fact, he has to be coaxed into speaking Persian by the village boys, who betray their own linguistic alienation by prompting Bashu to 'speak like a book'. For these children, both Gilaki and Arab, seem to intuit the extent to which their identity as Persians is a construct.

In return for Na'i's kindness, Bashu lends her a hand in running the farm – which her husband's departure in search of work has made more arduous. Meanwhile, Na'i has informed her husband of Bashu's presence through letters dictated to one of the villagers. When Bashu finds out that Na'i's husband is opposed to his staying with them, he runs away. Na'i seeks him out, brings him back to her farmhouse and informs her husband that Bashu will remain with them. The film ends with Na'i's husband's return and the discovery that he has lost an arm, apparently at the front. The war with Iraq is not explicitly mentioned, but in response to Na'i's cries of anguish, her husband points out that there was no other work for him. The work at hand – the protection of the rice fields – constitutes the ending of the film and, like all other members of Na'i's family, Bashu is swept into action.

If Bashu succeeds in negotiating a place in his new community, it is primarily through Na'i's agency. And yet, this female agency is conditioned throughout the film by the linguistic and cultural barriers that separate the two central characters. Na'i's attempts to draw Bashu into her family and the village community are thwarted by her lack of knowledge of Bashu's language and, on a different level, by her difficulty in communicating Bashu's humanity to the other villagers. Although she is not linguistically cut off from the other villagers, who also speak Gilaki, she is nevertheless frustrated by their ethnocentrism. Not only are they suspicious of the new-comer, whose very appearance relegates him to the status of alien, they are also ill at ease when Na'i usurps power by deciding to shelter and protect Bashu without proper consultation with the sources of authority, her husband or his relatives.

What Na'i and Bashu have in common is their status as peripheral to the existing linguistic, social, and cultural systems of signification, which isolate and vilify difference. In order to create a space in which to co-exist, Na'i and Bashu must rethink the very codes and norms that consign them, as woman and other, to the margins. Their condition is best described in terms adopted by Julia Kristeva in her theory of semiotics: *le sujet-en-procès*, the subject in process/on trial, or the subject-in-the-making,[3] 'the subject as a speaking, meaning-producing and meaning-deforming desiring being'.[4] Kristeva's play upon the double meaning of the French word *procès* can be aptly extended to the fate of Bashu and Na'i: the *trial* to which they are subjected is also the *process* through which they modify the signifying system within which they find themselves. In the course of their encounter, they are forced to confront their own ethnocentric blindspots and to re-examine their naturalized modes of interaction. If they do not radically change a symbolic system intolerant of difference, be it in gender, linguistic or ethnic identities, together they pose an ethical challenge to it.

It is significant that the film is set in Gilan and uses Gilaki as its primary means of verbal exchange. The choice of a dialect is indicative of the centrality of language and ethnicity to the film's critique of Iranian social structures. Gilaki may not be completely incomprehensible to Iranian spectators, but, by replacing Persian and its centralizing and unifying tendencies, it acts as an agent of displacement. Removing the audience to a remote village in Gilan and subjecting it to the local idiom makes possible experiments with other shifts in power and authority. This is not to suggest that *Bashu* revolutionizes the notion of a fixed linguistic identity, but rather that it raises questions about the assumption that Iranian identity is inextricably bound to the dominant language of the nation, Persian. By problematizing this bond, the film text participates in the kind of unveiling Homi Bhabha describes in *Nation and Narration*: 'the image of cultural authority may be ambivalent because it is caught, uncertainly, in the act of "composing" its powerful image.'[5]

The contradictory and ambivalent discourse of nationalism laid bare in *Bashu* also brings to light the problematic position occupied by women in the 'imagined community'[6] that makes up Iran. In Na'i's utterances and in her exchanges with other women in the village we discern how women are situated in their community, how they talk about themselves and how they are talked about. If I dwell on this particular aspect of the film – women's relationship with and place in language – it is to illustrate how the 'natural' link between the woman and the stranger equates women and alterity only ultimately to trouble the notion of alterity as the cornerstone of the construction of subjectivity. In other words, I see Na'i as not only instrumental in Bashu's integration into the village, but also a focal point for the film's questioning of patterns of socialization. By drawing upon the work of critics such as Kristeva and Luce Irigaray, whose theories of subjectivity have brought together elements of linguistics, psychoanalysis and gender studies, I hope to show how the film explores the intersections of gender, subjectivity, ethnicity and language in an attempt to carve out a space in which to posit new ways of seeing, hearing and perceiving the self and the other.[7] If the film's more radical ventures into new gender boundaries are ultimately thwarted, the new ambiguities that emerge allow us to see how even a critique of nationalism fails to correct the type of subordination of gender to nation that Radhakrishnan interrogates:

> Why is it that nationalism achieves the ideological effect of an inclusive and putatively macropolitical discourse, whereas the women's question – unable to achieve its own autonomous macropolitical identity – remains ghettoized within its specific and regional space? In other words, by what natural or ideological imperative or historical exigency does the politics of nationalism become the binding and overarching umbrella that subsumes other and different political temporalities?[8]

As we shall see, Bashu's ambiguous ending risks replacing one totalizing discourse with another: viewers might be asked to rethink national identity, but they are also presented with a return to family structures. This alternative has resonances of binarisms of self and other which the film otherwise problematizes.

The initial encounters between Na'i and Bashu underline the extent to which self-identity is contingent on the recognition and existence of alterity.

Na'i's first glimpses of Bashu lead her to question his colour: '*Chi bamalasti, anqadr chark-e chaghandari?* [What have you rubbed on yourself to make yourself so dirty?]'.[9] Because she cannot conceive of otherness, she assumes that Bashu's complexion is unnatural. The absence of a common colour so unsettles Na'i that she instinctively chases him away. Throwing stones at him is symbolic of her attempt to keep the self intact and uncontaminated; so also is the forced bath she gives him in order to make him white. Na'i's field of perception has thus far been limited to self-reflexive referents, but Bashu's intrusion opens up new categories which demand revisions of the earlier modes of perception. For instance, when Bashu emerges from his bath unchanged, Na'i is forced to admit, '*Sefid nibeh, ki nibeh* [No, he won't become white]'. This is the first stage of a recognition on the part of Na'i that Bashu's complexion, like his language, must be accepted as indelible marks of his difference.

The transition that Bashu's arrival inaugurates can be described as constituting a shift from mimesis to alterity. In his *Mimesis and Alterity*, Michael Taussig observes:

> Pulling you this way and that, mimesis plays this trick of dancing between the very same and the very different. An impossible but necessary, indeed an everyday affair, mimesis registers both sameness and difference, of being like, and of being Other. Creating stability from this instability is no small task, yet all identity formation is engaged in this habitually bracing activity in which the issue is not so much staying the same, but maintaining sameness through alterity.[10]

That alterity has disturbed the balance between sameness and difference, and the stability of the identities of those villagers who have come into contact with Bashu, is clearly delineated in a scene in which we see Na'i's daughter, Gulbesar, looking at herself in a mirror she is holding in her hands and then turning and looking at Bashu, who is sleeping a few steps from her. The child's need to reconfirm, by consulting her own image in the mirror, that the colour of her skin is different from Bashu's, points at once to her curiosity about the newcomer and her incomprehension and fear of his visible difference. It is this fear that prompts her to get up and run away when Bashu wakes up. Ironically, Bashu is as startled as Gulbesar; she is the symbolic mirror in which he looks but does not find the similarities and the points of reference he is seeking. They run away from each other because their field of vision has suddenly and inexplicably allowed the alien to slip in. They have been forced to confront the illusion of seeing themselves replicated in the images of others.

This visual inscription of alterity is immediately translated and reinforced in the verbal domain, when Na'i attempts to engage Bashu in an exchange ranging from his physical appearance to his inability to speak:

'*Gab bazan bidinam chi zaban dari? Nukuneh zughal chah jan birun bamoyi? Siah ki isi, lal ham ki isi, ismam ki nari. Har adamizadi ismi dareh. Uniki ism nareh ghul-e sahrayeh* [Say something so I can know what language you have; surely you haven't come from a coal-cellar? You're black, you're dumb, you have no name. Every human being has a name. Anyone with no name is a wild monster].'

This reveals a level of recognition of his otherness: although she wants him to speak, she has already conceived of a category of 'monstrosity' into which to place him. Bashu's silence, like the darkness of his skin, only confirms the list of negative attributes with which Na'i believes him to be endowed. All those things that he is not and does not have move him further and further away from the human race. Her conclusion that only monsters lack names brings into focus the centrality of the process of naming in human socialization: to have a name is to be integrated into a family and social structure. The ethnocentricity of Na'i's conceptualizations is foregrounded in her assumption that to be human one must speak *her* language and have *her* skin colour.

Through the veil of Na'i's initial certainty about the values with which she is familiar, we begin to catch glimpses of her own conditional power and her later attempts to break through the limitations which the linguistic and social order impose on her subjectivity. When she asks Bashu what he is called and is met once again with silence, she proceeds to initiate him into the process of naming and identification. Beginning with herself, she says: '*Mi pe'er mi nam-e bana Na'i* [My father called me Na'i]'. With this assertion she confirms the supremacy of the name-of-the-father in the symbolic: her own entry into the linguistic and the social order was mediated through the authority of the father. Interestingly, however, she now shifts the relations of power and gender in the naming of her children: '*Aydanah dukhadam Gulbesar, oydanah Oshin* [I called this one Gulbesar, that one Oshin]'. Referring to her children as 'this one' and 'that one' may seem rather impersonal, but it does underline the artificial and contractual nature of naming and socialization. The sense of distance in her utterance also makes it possible for her to usurp the position of authority she has just acknowledged as belonging to the father. It is she, not the absent father of the children, who has done the naming. This is a far from unambiguous claim to power: Na'i asserts herself only after she has given due recognition to patriarchy. Moreover, she makes these statements to a 'stranger' who does not understand her language. In a sense, she is merely talking to herself. Her voice is an echo, analogous to the mirror her daughter holds in front of herself to dispel any self-doubt to which Bashu's intrusion may have given rise. But this inner dialogue gives us insight into the position Na'i would like to occupy in the linguistic and social order.

Soon after the attempt to discover Bashu's name and identity, Na'i is required to externalize these same perceptions. In response to her aunt's inquiry about what news she has had from her husband, she admits: '*Dast-e tanha bobostam, khaleh jan* [I've been left alone, Auntie]'. The Gilaki expression refers literally to the hand she has been denied. Her husband's absence is here linked to the work of running the farm: she needs a hand – his – in carrying out her duties. In the next portion of the exchange, she extends this dilemma to her children: '*A zakan pe'er khaiyedi* [These children want a father]'. In this part of her response, she is repeating a formula about the importance of a father to the children. It is a necessary part of her social interaction to reflect upon the absence of her husband and its implications for the family unit. By talking about his search for work, Na'i also clearly distinguishes between the work done by men and women. While the work she carries out in his absence is limited to the farm, her husband is in the larger sphere of the world beyond the farm. This is yet another concession to the patriarchy which rules women's lives even when its own representatives are not on the scene.

It is interesting to note that Na'i's husband remains nameless both in this exchange and throughout the film. But his namelessness does not have the same implications as Bashu's does in the earlier parts of the film. While Bashu is denied any possible link to a community as long as he is nameless, Na'i's husband's position in the community is so well entrenched that his name does not need to be evoked. His identity and presence are continually marked through the specification of the type of familial relationships that determine the link between him and others. When the news of his return reaches Bashu, the village boy who gives him the news refers to him as '*mard-e Na'i* [Na'i's man]'. In Gilaki, as in many languages, '*mard*' means both 'man' and 'husband', and the boy is clearly using it in the second sense. But in another sense he is her man, the one who defines and determines her existence. A name for him would be almost superfluous.

That this statement is delivered by a child is a reminder of how the sexual and social hierarchies embedded in language are passed from one generation to another. The child is conveying good tidings to Bashu; the return of Na'i's husband signifies a return to the established patterns of the past. And yet, the statement also implies that power must again shift back from Na'i to her husband. It is this shift that Bashu intuits as a threat to his own position: he picks up a stick, prepared to chase away the intruder who has come to upset the carefully negotiated balance.

In the end, Bashu does not need the stick to defend himself and his adopted family, precisely because he has acquired a language. Speaking to Na'i's husband in Persian – not Gilaki – he is able to communicate with him and reinstate himself in the family unit. The final segment of the film, beginning with the argument between Na'i and her husband and Bashu's arrival on this scene, switches between Gilaki and Persian. Interestingly, it is only Bashu and Na'i's husband who speak Persian to each other, arriving at an understanding that lays bare the structures of domination on which their future interactions are to be founded. When Na'i's husband identifies himself as '*pedar* [the father]', Bashu extends his hand to him and asks him to shake hands. Evoking a parallel to the earlier scene in which Na'i tells her aunt of the missing metaphorical hand of her husband, Bashu's gesture now confirms that Na'i's husband has physically lost his hand and can therefore not completely occupy his former position. This is already spelled out by Na'i, who, shortly before Bashu's arrival, points out: '*Pas hala keh ichi fada'i, ichi biafteh bi? Hala ki ti rast-e bal-e fada'i shayed u ti rast-e bal bibeh* [Now you've lost something, don't you want to gain something? Now you've lost your right hand, let him be your right hand]'. Bashu runs to Na'i's husband and embraces him, sealing his metaphorical transplantation onto the body of the family, represented by its highest source of authority – the husband. As they all run into the rice fields to chase away the birds, we are given a vision of a unified family, albeit an ethnically diverse one. But behind this apparent wholesomeness is the nagging reminder that Na'i has compromised her own authority. On one level, she succeeds in bringing Bashu into her family, but, on another level, she has had to do this with the help of a language which requires her to step into the background and leave the negotiation of power to men.

This is the kind of compromise to which Irigaray sees women being subjected within the inherent phallocentrism of language and social interaction:

> The way [the between-men culture] is structured excludes what the other sex brings to its society. Whereas the female body engenders with respect for difference, the patriarchal social body constructs itself hierarchically, excluding

difference. Woman-as-other has to remain the natural substratum in this social construction, a substratum whose importance remains unclear in relational signification.[11]

Na'i, the woman-as-other, is the one who facilitates the bond between her husband and Bashu by once again reinforcing how central his 'hand' is to their lives together. The film's literalization of this metaphor translates Na'i's gender-bound position within language from verbal into visual. Even though it is she who arrives at the new organization of the family, she has to deliver her message in a discourse encoded with her own submission to male power. Na'i's apparent exclusion from decision-making and her subordination to her husband are forcefully underlined in one of her sister-in-law's earlier reprimands regarding Bashu's stay at the farm. She accuses Na'i of not having consulted someone in higher authority: '*Akheh salah-u maslahati. Bozorgtar ti sar-e jor nisabu, aman ki isabim* [After all, you should have consulted. If there was no superior for you to consult, we were here]'. On a literal level, this utterance works as a graphic reminder to Na'i that a 'superior' authority stands over her head. Ideally this source of authority would have been her husband, but in his absence his relatives could have stepped in to relieve her of the responsibility of making decisions.

There is no better instance of Na'i's dependence and conditional power than the letters to her husband that she dictates to a neighbour. She delivers her message in Gilaki and the neighbour translates and transforms her sentences into Persian and writes them down on paper. It is interesting to note how communication in writing is automatically equated with Persian. Na'i and her husband, who would normally address each other in Gilaki, have to rely on Persian in order to exchange letters. The imposition of Persian modifies the meaning of the letters: while describing Bashu for her husband, she says: '*Ita siah rekeh. Du vajab bishtar sar u shaneh nareh. Hato khial kuni zughal chah jan farar bukudeh* [He is a black boy. His head and shoulders measure up to two hands' length. You would think he has run away from a coal-cellar]'. When rendered into Persian this last sentence becomes: '*Guyi az zoghal chah birun amadeh* [You would think he has come out of coal-cellar]'. The difference between emerging from a coal-cellar and running away from one may at first seem minute – it does not essentially change the fact that Bashu's appearance and origins remain mysterious. The Persian version does, however, tone down the urgency detectable in Na'i's believing Bashu to have escaped from a coal-cellar. Her suggestion that Bashu has run away and had to use a coal-cellar as his shelter makes him into a helpless child in need of protection, while the scribe's translation undermines this need. Na'i attempts to shift the focus away from his racial difference to his needs as a child, much in the same way as she later equates Bashu's 'hand' with her husband's. Whether the nuances are stressed or explained away, the point remains that Na'i is dependent upon someone else to communicate with her husband. Na'i herself is highly conscious of this dependence, as illustrated throughout the film.

The scene where the neighbor reads out the response to this letter is a case in point. Na'i's husband makes no mention of Bashu; Na'i notices Bashu's disappointment, grabs the letter from her neighbour's hand, and pretends to read from it:

> '*Amma dar bare-ye an tazeh vared keh esmash Bashu ast. Qadamash mobarak bashad. Antur keh shoma* binivishtid *baraye khodash mardi ast. Khial-e man rahat ast ke shoma ra tanha nemigozarad. Anja kheyli kar hast. Agar man nistam, aqallan u hast. Khub ast jaye man bashad va shoma ra* komak ahval *bashad. Salam mara be Bashu beresanid* [But regarding the newcomer whose name is Bashu. He is most welcome. According to what you wrote, he is quite a man. I am reassured that he does not leave you alone. There is much work there. If I am not there, at least he is. It is good that he has replaced me and can help you. Give Bashu my regards].'

'*Komak ahval*' is the Gilaki equivalent of the Persian 'he helps you' but, like '*binivishtid*', is unidiomatic in Persian. The Gilaki interferences remind us, over and above our knowledge that she cannot read, that Na'i is the true author of this passage. Her struggle with Persian is for Bashu's benefit even though he is well aware of Na'i's inability to read letters. However, Bashu rewards Na'i with a smile, indicating that he too has registered the depth of her message. By stepping outside Gilaki into Persian, the language of power, Na'i has pointed to her willingness to create the necessary authority to allow for Bashu's existence in the midst of her family.

That Na'i equates Persian with authority is more clearly emphasized when she finds Bashu in the shed, to which he has run away, having taken to heart Na'i's husband's disapproval of his stay. When she first sees him, she addresses him in Gilaki: '*Chereh ayah khufteyi? Magar tu jay nary khaneh kharab? Viriz bushu ti ja sar bukhus* [Why are you sleeping here? Don't you have a place, you wretch? Get up and go back to your bed]'. But she ends her command with a Persian translation, '*Bar khiz boro sar-e jayat bekhab* [Get up, go to sleep in your own bed]', intended to deliver the final force of her message. Here again, she uses the language she knows Bashu identifies with authority and formality.

In Na'i's final resort to Persian, instead of using her neighbour to write to her husband, she dictates her letter to Bashu, authorizing him as her son: '*In nameh ra pesar-e man minevisad keh nam-e u Bashust* [This letter is being written by my son, whose name is Bashu]'. In this instance Persian both facilitates the already complicated communications between Na'i and Bashu and legitimizes Bashu's position within the core of Na'i's family. The status she has bestowed upon him provides the illusion of normality: he is now her adopted son. The bond between them is marked in Na'i's admission that '*Nani keh mikhorad az kari keh mikonad kamtar ast, va an nan ra man az loqmeh-e khodam mideham* [The bread he eats is much less than the work he does, and that bread I give from my own portion]'. This image of Bashu and Na'i sharing her portion of the food suggests the corporeal merging of the body of the mother and the child that relativizes the absence of a biological maternal link as a crucial 'natural' missing element in the bond between Bashu and Na'i. It is precisely because Na'i resists granting supremacy to the symbolic order that she is able to replace the biological with the social and ethical. In other words, she defies and modifies the structures dictated to her by her society and culture. Her challenge to the existing social order is spelled out in the last sentence of the letter she asks Bashu to write to her husband: '*U mesle hame-ye bacheha farzand-e aftab va zamin ast* [Like all children, he is the child of sun and the earth]'. By placing Bashu among all other children and linking them to a pre-symbolic natural order she obviates the need to establish Bashu's origin: as a child of the sun and the earth, he is not in need of a father to give him a name and an identity. This does not mean that Na'i fully subverts the norms and principles upon which her society is founded. On the contrary, she carefully negotiates a middle ground between total dependence upon – or total rejection of – the paternal and the patriarchal. Her utterances and actions appear to embody the kind of pragmatic recognition that Kristeva argues will enable women to bring about a revolution in language and culture:

> Let us refuse both these extremes. Let us know that an ostensibly masculine, paternal identification, because it supports symbol and time, is necessary in order to have a voice in the chapter of politics and history. Let us achieve this identification in order to escape a smug polymorphism where it is so easy and comfortable for a woman to remain; and let us in this way gain entry to social practice.[12]

It goes without saying that this entry into social practice is far from easy. In fact, as Na'i's example illustrates, it is sometimes made possible at the expense of female subjectivity.

Na'i's negotiation of power is successful because she understands the prevailing hierarchies well enough to mimic the existing structures. As Irigaray has postulated, this mimicking does, nevertheless, have a subversive potential women which can deploy to their advantage:

> To play with mimesis is thus, for a woman, to try to recover the place of her exploitation by discourse, without allowing herself to be simply reduced to it. It means to resubmit herself – inasmuch as she is on the side of the 'perceptible', of 'matter' – to 'ideas', in particular to ideas about herself, that are elaborated in/by a masculine logic, but so as to make 'visible', by an effect of playful repetition, what was supposed to remain invisible: the cover-up of a possible operation of the feminine in language. It also means 'to unveil' the fact that, if women are such good mimics, it is because they are not simply resorbed in this function.[13]

Na'i does this by challenging the binaries of male/female, white/black and culture/nature from within. For instance, she does not perceive the separation between nature and culture as rigid, nor does she simply place herself on the side of one or the other. All the time she is trying to find a language in which to communicate with Bashu and to integrate him into a community, she remains close to other non-verbal means of communication. She reproduces animal and bird sounds and is particularly adept at detecting the presence of animals in the rice fields. Here the subversive element of mimicking is laid bare; Na'i's imitation of the sounds is what chases the birds and animals away. In a similar mimicking of the gender-specific roles dictated to her by language and social convention, Na'i explores possibilities for change. It is such moments that the representation of Na'i's interactions with a 'little stranger' capture on the screen. The woman and the stranger need each other to unsettle the beliefs and customs of an established community. They must together become the outsider, the embodiment of the other side of the self, in order to put the self and the other into dialogue with each other. That such a dialogue must cut across ethnic and linguistic boundaries is underlined in the film's juxtaposition of Persian, Arabic and Gilaki. Only such cross-breedings can make possible revisions of the categories of race, ethnicity and national identity.

The precarious nature of these encounters is emphasized in Na'i's careful placing of herself between tradition and change, and in the restoration of the old, albeit extended and restructured, family unit at the end of the film. In the final analysis, the potential for subversion is subordinated to questions of survival. Na'i is not socially or economically free to extend her acts of subversion to all realms of village existence. She nevertheless succeeds in overcoming her own fear of Bashu's difference and making the villagers reconsider their ethnocentrism and xenophobia.

What Na'i and Bashu communicate to Iranian audiences is a need to rethink the space assigned to the marginalized and minorities. The film points out that the comfortable and easily identifiable expressions and idioms that situate us within language also have the power to define and limit us. The Iranian viewer is subjected to the very linguistic alienation which Bashu and Na'i suffer. With the exception of the segments of dialogue in Persian, the film requires that Iranian viewers suspend their linguistic familiarity and, in effect, occupy a position not unlike the one in which Bashu finds himself after his arrival in Na'i's village. The film clearly insists on the type of linguistic defamiliarization that might translate into only a partial comprehension of the exchanges. But this incomprehension is at the very centre of the critique the film delivers to its Iranian viewers, who have to rethink the assumption that all their compatriots speak standard Persian.

In the subtitled version of the film, the experience of partial comprehension happens on a different level. Viewers drawing primarily on the subtitles nevertheless register the irrational fear and anxieties that prompt the villagers to shun the black-skinned outsider. In this sense, the visual grammar of the film is as integral as the verbal to the challenge it levels at the myth of a unified and homogeneous Iranian identity.

The Iran posited in *Bashu, The Little Stranger* is anything but uniform. It is a country incapable of facing its fear of the other within. The enemy against which war is waged is indistinguishable from the Arab-speaking minority living on the border with Iraq. Moreover, the destruction caused by the war is inscribed as much on the self as on the other. Both Bashu and Na'i's husband are subjected to loss. Na'i's husband loses an arm, while Bashu loses all the members of his family. The national conformity demanded of these Iranians dismembers them. Against this idea of the nation, the film posits the hybrid linguistic and social order Na'i and Bashu create together. But their new system of communication works particularly well in the absence of Na'i's husband, the figure of authority. His return dictates that Na'i must vacate the position she has carved out for herself and hand over the negotiation of power to her husband and Bashu, the newly integrated male member of the family. This is a particularly ironic ending, for the film succeeds in its critique of Persian nationalism through the agency of a woman whose final resubmission to patriarchal family replicates the patterns of subordination the film lays bare in the discourse of nationalism.

Notes on Chapter 13

1. See Hamid Naficy's commentary in 'A decade of Iranian cinema: 1980–1990', the programme of the film festival sponsored by the UCLA Film and Television Archive and FCF.

2. Gilles Deleuze and Félix Guattari, *Kafka: Toward a Minor Literature*, Dana Polan (trans.) (*Theory and History of Literature* 30) (Minneapolis, University of Minnesota Press, 1986), pp. 16–27.

3. For a comprehensive overview of this concept, see Julia Kristeva, *Revolution in Poetic Language*, Margaret Waller (trans.) (New York, Columbia University Press, 1984), pp. 19–164.

4. Elizabeth Grosz, 'Julia Kristeva', in Elizabeth Wright *et al.* (eds), *Feminism and Psychoanalysis: A Critical Dictionary* (Blackwell, Oxford, 1992), p. 194.

5. 'Introduction', in Homi K. Bhabha (ed.), *Nation and Narration* (London, Routledge, 1990), p. 3.

6. For this formulation, I draw upon Benedict Anderson's study of nationalism: *Imagined Communities: Reflections on the Origin and Spread of Nationalism* (London, Verso, 1983) – though, like Partha Chatterjee in *Nationalist Thought and the Colonial World: A Derivative Discourse?* (London, Zed Books, 1986), I find limitations in the application of Anderson's concepts to third world nationalisms. Most pertinent to my study is that, unlike Anderson's claim that '[t]he dreams of racism actually have their origin in ideologies of class, rather than in those of nation' (p. 136), I find a direct relationship between Persian nationalism and ethnocentrism and racism.

7. I am conscious of the fact that my use of these theoretical concepts might be interpreted as a form of 'Westomania' (*Gharbzadagi*), a term publicized in the 1960s by the Iranian writer and social activist Jalal Al-e Ahmad to refer to a whole range of social, cultural and political subjugation of Iranians by the West. Yet, like Leila Ahmed, I maintain that the prohibition of such cross-referencing in the name of preserving specificity and authenticity is isolationism at its worst: 'After all and in sober truth, what thriving civilization or cultural heritage today, Western or non-Western, is not critically indebted to the inventions and traditions of thought of other peoples in other lands?' (*Women and Gender in Islam: Historical Roots of a Modern Debate*, New Haven, Yale University Press, 1992, p. 237). This same spirit of intercultural engagement, espoused by the film, drew me to *Bashu, The Little Stranger* and prompted me to return to Gilaki, the language from which I was separated by the standard Persian my education imposed on me.

8. R. Radhakrishnan, 'Nationalism, Gender, and the Narrative of Identity', in Andrew Parker, Mary Russo, Doris Sommer and Patricia Yaeger (eds), *Nationalisms and Sexualities* (New York, Routledge, 1992), p. 78.

9. To avoid erasing the linguistic differences marked in the film, I have chosen to provide a transliteration of all Gilaki and Persian utterances, followed by my own translation into English.

10.   Michael Taussig, *Mimesis and Alterity: A Particular History of the Senses* (New York, Routledge, 1993), p. 129.

11.   Luce Irigaray, *Je, Tu, Nous: Toward a Culture of Difference*, Alison Martin (trans.) (New York, Routledge, 1993), p. 45.

12.   Julia Kristeva, 'About Chinese Women', in Toril Moi (ed.) *The Kristeva Reader* (New York, Columbia University Press, 1986), p. 156.

13.   Luce Irigaray, 'The Power of Discourse and the Subordination of the Feminine', in Margaret Whitford (ed.), *The Irigaray Reader* (Oxford, Blackwell, 1991), p. 124.

14

Afterword[1]

Laura Mulvey

I should make clear that my approach to Iranian cinema is necessarily that of an outsider. However, as a film critic and theorist, and particularly as a cinephile, over the last few years I have become more and more interested in the films of the new Iranian cinema as they slowly gained visibility in Europe. Abbas Kiarostami has been the most visible of all, and his films have interested me above all others. In the spring of 1999, I agreed to write an article about Kiarostami for *Sight and Sound* after *The Taste of Cherry* (1997) won the Palme d'Or in Cannes and was released in a West End London cinema.[2] Several papers given at the conference explicitly criticized 'Western cinephiles' and their enthusiasm for new Iranian cinema – most particularly for Kiarostami's films. I realize that I conform almost exactly to this profile and I would like, therefore, to try to make a contribution to the debate from this critical perspective.

Azadeh Farahmand raises the issues clearly in her chapter, in which she focuses specifically, and relevantly, on the 'Kiarostami case'. She argues acutely that when 'first-world' critics take up 'third-world' cinema there are, simultaneously and interlocked with each other, both national and international dimensions to the problem. At the heart of the debate lie the complex politics of international film festivals. From a positive perspective,

254

these festivals allow films that do not have international distribution circuits at their disposal to make connections with the few art-house distributors and exhibitors who can bring them to audiences on a country-by-country basis – such as Artificial Eye in London, which is the British distributor of several Iranian films. On the other hand, as Farahmand argues, the festival circuit has thrived on a particular kind of artistic, director-based cinema that depends on a succession of 'new waves'. And, as she points out, festivals are more inclined to welcome novelty than ask political questions about its origins. So an oppressive regime, working with strict censorship, is no barrier to the production of films that fit this market. In fact, she says, with an explicit indictment of festivals, the Iranian film production context and Kiarostami: 'the political escapism in Kiarostami's films is a facilitating, rather than a debilitating, choice, one which caters to the film festival taste for high art and restrained politics.'

These criticisms reflect and articulate important intellectual and political questions that should not be avoided in the particular context of the international distribution and reception of Iranian cinema. But they also raise general issues about the critical appropriation of new cinemas in, as it were, a cultural vacuum, without adequate understanding of the circumstances under which they have been produced and then circulated abroad. This position seems to assume either that all current Iranian cinema is tarred irrevocably with a totalitarian brush or that the ignorance and enthusiasm of the European cinephile audience disqualifies these films from foreign distribution. While taking these criticisms to heart, I would like to use this opportunity to offer some comments and suggest, specifically, that events such as this conference, as well as the essays in this book, all contribute to a greater political and cultural understanding of new Iranian cinema. The problem of the cultural vacuum may perhaps be addressed through the circulation of critical knowledge, discussion and debate.

But there are also internal reasons for the enthusiastic reception of new Iranian cinema in Europe – it is probably important at this point to differentiate between Europe and the US. European cinephilia has been in disarray for some time. The austerity of Iranian post-revolutionary cinema, beyond the case of Kiarostami himself, allows a space for form, for style and for thought about the cinema that has only sporadically been achieved here over recent years. This formal and intellectual cinema creates the 'cinematic' space of interaction and exchange between spectator and screen that defines art cinema. Art cinema and its audience may well, of course, be elitist in their mutual address and recognition, but that is the tradition out of which festivals and the art circuit have grown since the 1950s. Not only is the rich tradition of European art cinema in decline, perhaps terminal – with the possible exception of the French and the Dogma school in Denmark – but its last representatives have greater and greater difficulty in finding international distribution. In the UK, for instance, European art cinema has by and large been driven out by the so-called American 'independents', highly psychologized, often amusing, but very rarely cinematically innovative. And it is often suggested that the Hollywood, special-effects-dominated blockbuster has given rise to a nostalgia, certainly among cinephiles, for a cinema that is celluloid-based and film-referenced. This is not to say, at least categorically, that the US no longer produces worthwhile cinema at all, but rather that its reach has become so pervasive, its inward gaze so obsessive, that the cinephile – old-fashioned perhaps – longs for escape.

Escape: this is, of course, another aspect to the problem. While there is no point in denying an element of the exotic in attraction between cultures, it may also be important to remember that this exoticism was there for, say, a British audience encountering Antonioni or Godard in the 1960s, and is certainly not exclusive to 'third cinema'. And the sense of strangeness, of the unfamiliar, is just as much to do with an encounter with a surprising cinema as with the screening of unfamiliar landscapes and remote peoples. I would like to emphasize this point. The exotic alone cannot sustain a 'new wave'. A new cinema is only of lasting interest if it articulates questions and raises problems that are of aesthetic significance in their own right. However, in the case of the post-revolutionary Iranian cinema, political issues emerge that may perhaps have an element of strangeness and surprise that adds to its interest for critics both inside and outside the country. What, if any, is the relationship between the ideology of the Islamic Republic and the success of its cinema (beyond, that is, the well-documented state support for the art end of its production)? It is a collection such as this, and the conference which led to it, that enable such questions to become actual points of discussion, to contextualize the films and to provide a new dimension for understanding and interpreting them.

If the cinema has always allowed people to travel in their imaginations, it has also always been a travelling medium. Conferences and publications such as these offer the possibility of relocating 'travelling' films within their cultural, political and production contexts. These contexts are, of course, all too often missing when the films are first screened. But the kind of criticism and discussion we have seen here makes an invaluable contribution to the 'texture' of understanding, so that films that travel abroad can begin to convey more explicit meanings and resonate beyond the appeal of the exotic. Nasrin Rahimieh's chapter about Bahram Beyza'i's *Bashu, The Little Stranger* (1988) perhaps provides a useful example of what I mean. A film that is actually about a lack of a common language and the difficulty of communication inevitably faces any audience with a challenge. As Rahimieh points out, the film asks an Iranian audience to reflect on specific, recognizable cultural differences and difficulties within the nation itself. Foreigners, or those who lack the necessary language, therefore, cannot hope to understand the film thoroughly. But while this might reduce the film's political significance and flatten its nuances, the kind of problems it addresses are comprehensible, even if on an intuitive rather than an informed level. However, the next time I see *Bashu*, my understanding of the film will be transformed in the light of Rahimieh's discussion. I will still be unable to understand its spoken languages, but I will be able to follow their implications and its political message. As films do travel, and will continue to do so, discussion and criticism are essential for them to find a serious place in 'world cinema'. It is through these means that they can reach beyond the immediacy of fashions or the appeal of the exotically different.

But underlying these issues of encounter and context is a key issue about the nature of the cinema itself and how it has been renewed and re-articulated by the Iranian New Wave. So, turning to the other side of the coin, to the outsider's encounter with a 'travelling' cinema, I would like to try to evoke why these films might have a particular significance for someone concerned with the cinema, its aesthetics and its 'specificities'.

Throughout its history, the cinema has raised questions about ways of seeing. Unlike any other medium, the cinema is able to construct and inflect the way a spectator relates to its images. As a result, the question of 'how', the question of form, takes on a particular importance alongside 'what', the question of content. There is obviously a danger of formalism and essentialism here. However, whether a particular film or type of cinema specifically acknowledges this or not, cinema is 'about' seeing and the construction of the visible by filmic convention. What is represented is inevitably affected. The history of cinema has also been marked by a division between a mass, popular form – dominated above all by Hollywood – and 'art cinema' or the 'avant garde'. The dialogue and dialectics between the two are nearly as old as the cinema itself and are particularly relevant here. I hope most people will agree that the problems of 'what can be represented?' and 'who can see what?' are close to the heart of the new Iranian art cinema. These questions, in the Iranian context, necessarily raise questions about state censorship and regulation. But they also chime with the debates, in the context of the commodity culture of advanced capitalism, about how a political cinema might use an avant-garde aesthetic against the overblown images of the society of the spectacle. These are problems that have been of long-standing interest to film theory and, more recently, to feminist film theory.

In the first instance, my own commitment to feminism, feminist film theory and its cinema might well seem to be at odds with my interest in post-revolutionary Iranian cinema. This is a paradox that I would like to emphasize and explore. Islamic censorship reflects a social subordination of women and, particularly, an anxiety about female sexuality. But it then produces, as a result, a 'difficulty' with the representation of women on the screen which has some – unexpected – coincidence with the problems feminists have raised about the representation of women in the cinema. In the spirit of polemic, I argued in 1975 that the aesthetics of Hollywood cinema was constructed out of a way of seeing that was assumed to be 'male', the object of which, relentlessly exposed as image for male desire, was assumed to be female.[3] Of course, this argument is simplified and rhetorical but it provided the basic grounds from which I could imagine a new cinema, which would be built negatively and in opposition to the codes and conventions of Hollywood. It is here that feminist 'negative aesthetics' of the 1970s, a kind of 'iconoclasm from below', chimes strangely with the results of censorship, a 'regulation from above' that characterizes post-revolutionary Iranian cinema.

Of course, the authors of Islamic censorship regulations had no interest in film aesthetics or the traditions of avant-garde cinema that so heavily influenced feminist film theory. Both sides, however, were wary of the overt sexualization of femininity associated with Hollywood and its world domination. And focusing on the 'problem' of representing women on the screen, and creating a series of taboos or difficulties around this represent-ation, opens up a void which allows questions about the cinema itself to emerge. To put the argument crudely, the sexualization of cinema holds in place certain codes, conventions and ways of seeing. Once this dependence is undermined, the cinema has to question itself as a mode of representation, and return, self-consciously, to its own processes of signification. Such an emptying out of the usual forms of cinematic attraction can then reveal the cinema itself: its aesthetics and its forms find a space to flourish and discover a new visibility. On the most obvious level, pace is a key element here. The characteristic film of the Iranian New Wave shrinks in scope and expands in time, moving away from dramatic plot, action or romance into scaled-down events and location-based stories of great simplicity. With a shooting style that tends to avoid close-ups or shot-countershot, the camera takes on an equivalently greater importance, and its relationship to what it sees enters into the picture, breaking down the cinema's conventional transparency. The collapse of cinematic narrative convention opens up a space and a pace in which the elements of cinematic form acquire visibility in their own right. To summarize, the issue goes beyond the question of image as such. Although, from this perspective, the censors' approach to cinema is simplistic and one-dimensional, the taboos imposed erase many established conventions and ways of seeing, and create a new challenge for the cinema. The need to rethink and reconfigure affects not only gender image and relations but, as a logical extension, editing, staging, ways of storytelling, processes of identification and so on. Just as the first wave of pre-revolutionary directors sought to find their own neo-realism, the Revolution has, even if accidentally, generated the conditions in which innovation becomes an essential element in cinematic practice.

Extending the argument beyond that of aesthetics, film theorists have suggested that the cinema provides a key metaphor for the construction of identity and subjectivity. Again, ways of seeing are important here, but so too are questions about identification. Hamid Naficy has demonstrated convincingly that a different understanding of the gaze underlies the Islamic discourse of veiling and Western feminist concepts of voyeurism. Once again, as I suggested above, relevant cultural analysis and nuances illuminate difference and divergence. My point here is perhaps only a small one and is intended simply to draw attention to the relation between the 'problem' of woman's representation on the screen and the 'problem' of cinema as mode of representation. But Naficy also makes an extremely important point that coincides with the old aspirations of feminist film theory. A new cinema needs to be built with women behind the cameras, figuring out – as creators of cinematic images themselves – new representations of women which would not be, in Shahla Lahiji's terms, those of chaste or unchaste dolls. Now that women are emerging as filmmakers in sufficient numbers, Iranian cinema may explore new ways of seeing and of telling stories. And a film such as Samira Makhmalbaf's *The Apple* (1998) is a sign that this may be already happening.

To conclude, I would like to say something about Kiarostami's cinema and why it might be that films with little or no overt political content may still raise important issues for the politics of cinema. While Kiarostami has played an important role in defining the aesthetics and formal characteristics of the Iranian New Wave cinema, his films reach out towards key questions about the nature of cinema as a medium. To my mind, this is the main reason why his films have had such an impact on Western cinephiles and film theorists, who found themselves contemplating once again a cerebral, conceptual cinema of a kind that has more or less completely disappeared in their own countries. In particular, Kiarostami explores the narrow line between illusion and reality that is the defining characteristic of the cinema. Avoiding an either/or approach, his interest lies in boundaries and in the tension between the cinema's ability to register and print the actual image in front of the lens and its ability to transform and transcend it. This 'what is cinema?' approach to filmmaking affects the spectator's relation to the screen. Here, issues to do with the gaze and ways of seeing are extended beyond ideological content into a wider demand to question the nature of the image itself. To ask the spectator to think – and to think about the limits and possibilities of cinematic representation – is to create a form of questioning and interrogative spectatorship that must be at odds with the certainties of any dominant ideological conviction – in the case of Iran, of religion. Uncertainty is built into Kiarostami's cinema, and this is what differentiates it so definitely from the cinema of, say, Majid Majidi, which is ultimately a cinema of faith and certainty.

As I have argued before, uncertainty needs and breeds curiosity. This point allows me to end with a return to the beginning of my argument. Kiarostami's films emerge into the outside world, as discussed above, into something like a cultural vacuum, and have necessarily to be watched, by the film festival spectator, for instance, in a spirit of uncertainty and curiosity. But as Kiarostami's films are themselves actually built on an aesthetic of uncertainty and curiosity, this approach is simultaneously socially desirable and cinematically necessary. Although the film theorist may find important and fertile ground for further analysing the cinema, curiosity should also lead back to questions of social understanding, to finding ways to fill in the gaps of ignorance and cultural divergence, supplied, for instance, by Naficy's analyses. And curiosity should also extend to the history of this cinema, its indigenous development and its influences. There are also more general questions about the relationship between revolution and revolutionary cinemas which, in turn, lead to questioning the place of cinema as a site for the construction of subjectivity and identification and, thus, its crucial role at a time of ideological rupture. The kinds of discussions which have been initiated here bring Iranian cinema into contact with the theoretical and historical dialogue of film history and work towards a demythologization both of the post-revolutionary cinema and of a director such as Kiarostami.

I have insisted on the importance of Kiarostami's conceptual attitude to the cinema, but his films do also raise issues of cultural understanding and misunderstanding. The state of uncertainty in which he leaves his spectators, and the need to question the status of the images of the screen, breed a broader desire to understand the culture in which these films can be made. There is a politics of representation at stake here, but also a politics of cultural specificity at a time of increasingly encroaching cultural homogenization. And, for me perhaps most importantly of all, the pleasure of Kiarostami's cinema is to be found in the process of deciphering rather than in the fascination of spectacle.

Notes on Chapter 14

1.   This afterword is an elaboration of my concluding remarks at the end of the 1999 conference. I am grateful to the organizers of the conference for inviting me to speak.
2.   Laura Mulvey, 'Kiarostami's uncertainty principle', *Sight and Sound*, June 1998, pp. 24–7.
3.   Laura Mulvey, 'Visual pleasure and narrative cinema', *Screen* 16 (3), 1975, pp. 6–18.

Filmography

English Titles

Abi and Rabi (*Abi va Rabi*, Ovanes Oganians, 1309/1930)
America is Destroyed (*Amrika Nabud Ast*, Hoseyn Aqa Karimi, 1360/1981)
And Life Goes on... (*Va Zendegi Edameh Darad...* Abbas Kiarostami, 1370/1991)
The Apple (*Sib*, Samira Makhmalbaf, 1376/1998)
Athar's War (*Jang-e Athar*, Mohammad Ali Najafi, 1358/1979)
Avenue A.B.C...Manhattan (Amir Naderi, 1997)
Baduk (Majid Majidi, 1370/1992)
Bashu, The Little Stranger (*Bashu, Gharibeh-ye Kuchak*, Bahram Beyza'i, 1367/1988)
Battle of Algiers (Gillo Pontecorvo, 1965)
Battle of Chile (Patricio Guzman, 1976)
Besieged (*Dar Mohasereh*, Akbar Sadeqi, 1360/1981)
Beyond the Clouds (Phil Agland, 1994)
Birth of a Butterfly (*Tavallod-e Yek Parvaneh*, Mojtaba Ra'i, 1376/1998)
Blackboard (*Takhteh Siyah*, Samira Makhmalbaf, 1378/1999)
Blood-rain (*Khunbaresh*, Amir Qavidel, 1359/1980)
The Blue Scarf (*Ru-sari Abi*, Rakhshan Bani-Etemad, 1373/1994)
The Boot (*Chakmeh*, Mohammad Ali Talebi, 1371/1993)
The Border (*Marz*, Jamshid Heydari, 1360/1981)
Boycott (*Baykot*, Mohsen Makhmalbaf, 1364/1985)
Bread and Alley (*Nan va Kucheh*, Abbas Kiarostami, 1348/1969)
Bread and Poetry (*Nan va She'r*, Kiumars Pourahmad, 1372/1994)
The Bus (*Otobus*, Yadollah Samadi, 1364/1985)
Captain Khorshid (*Nakhoda Khorshid*, Naser Taqva'i, 1365/1987)
The Chess of the Wind (*Shatranj-e Bad*, Mohammad Reza Aslani, 1355/1976)
Children of Divorce (*Bache-ha-ye Talaq*, Tahmineh Milani, 1368/1989)

Children of Heaven (*Bache-ha-ye Asman*, Majid Majidi, 1375/1997)
City of Mice (*Shahr-e Mush-ha*, Mohammad Ali Talebi, 1364/1985)
Close-Up (*Nama-ye Nazdik*, Abbas Kiarostami, 1368/1989)
The Cloud and the Rising Sun (*Abr va Aftab*, Mahmood Kalari, 1376/1997)
The Color of Paradise (*Rang-e Khoda*, Majid Majidi, 1378/1999)
The Condemned (*E'dami*, Mohammad Baqer Khosravi, 1360/1981)
The Cow (*Gav*, Daryush Mehrju'i, 1348/1969)
The Crow (*Kalagh*, Bahram Beyza'i, 1356/1977)
The Cry of the Mojahed (*Faryad-e Mojahed*, Mehdi Ma'danian, 1358/1979)
The Cycle (*Da'ereh-ye Mina*, Daryush Mehrju'i, 1353/1974–1357/1978)
The Cyclist (*Baysikelran*, Mohsen Makhmalbaf, 1367/1989)
Dan (Abolfazl Jalili, 1377/1998)
Dance of Dust (*Raqs-e Khak*, Abolfazl Jalili, 1370/1992)
The Deer (*Gavaznha*, Massoud Kimia'i, 1354/1975)
Det Means Girl (*Det Yani Dokhtar*, Abolfazl Jalili, 1372/1994)
The Devotees (*Janbazan*, Naser Mohammadi, 1361/1982)
Dialogue with Wind (*Goft-o-gu ba Bad*, Bahram Beyza'i, 1377/1999), part of
    Stories of Kish
Diary of a Lover (*Tagebuch Eines Liebenden*, Sohrab Shahid-Saless, 1977)
The Divine One (*Malakut*, Khosrow Haritash, 1355/1976)
Divorce Iranian Style (Kim Longinotto and Ziba Mir-Hosseini, 1998)
Divorce Italian Style (Pietro Germi, 1962)
The Domain of Lovers (*Diyar-e 'Asheqan*, Hasan Karbakhsh, 1362/1983)
The Dossier (*Parvandeh*, Mehdi Sabbaghzadeh, 1362/1983)
Downpour (*Ragbar*, Bahram Beyza'i, 1351/1972)
The Eel (Shohei Imamura, 1997)
Elegy (*Marsiyeh*, Amir Naderi, 1354/1975–1357/1978)
The Emigrant (*Mohajer*, Ebrahim Hatamikia, 1368/1990)
Eyes Wide Shut (Stanley Kubrick, 1999)
The Fall of '57 (*Soqut-e '57*, Barbod Taheri, 1358/1980)
Far From Home (*Dar Ghorbat*, Sohrab Shahid-Saless, 1354/1975)
The Father (*Pedar*, Majid Majidi, 1374/1996)
Fear of Heights (*Höhenangst*, Houshang Allahyari, 1994)
Flying Towards Minu (*Parvaz be-su-ye Minu*, Taqi Keyvan Salahshur, 1359/1980)
Fortress in Fortress (*Hesar dar Hesar*, Mohammad Reza Honarmand, 1982)
Freeze, Don't Move (*Bi Harekat, Tekun Nakhor*, Amir Shervan); changed in
    1357/1978 to *The Thug and the Student* (*Jahel va Mohassel*); after the
    Revolution, to *Heroin* (*Hero'in*)
From Karkheh to Rhine (*Az Karkheh ta Rayn*, Ebrahim Hatamikia, 1371/1993)
Gabbeh (Mohsen Makhmalbaf, 1374/1995)
The Glass Agency (*Azhans-e Shishe'i*, Ebrahim Hatamikia, 1376/1998)
Golnar (Kambozia Partovi, 1367/1988)
Guardians of the Ayatollahs (Phil Rees, 1996)
The Guests of the Hotel Astoria (Reza Allamehzadeh, 1989)

Haji Washington (Ali Hatami, 1361/1982)
Hamoon (*Hamun*, Daryush Mehrju'i, 1368/1990)
Harmonica (*Saz-dahani*, Amir Naderi, 1352/1974)
Heroin (*Hero'in*), see *Freeze Don't Move*
Hidden Faces (Kim Longinotto and Clare Hunt, 1991)
Homework (*Mashq-e Shab*, Abbas Kiarostami, 1367/1988)
The Horizon (*Ofoq*, Rasul Mollaqolipour, 1367/1989)
A House Waiting (*Khaneh dar Entezar*, Manuchehr Asgarinasab, 1366/1987)
I Don't Hate Las Vegas Anymore (Caveh Zahedi, 1994)
In Limbo (*Barzakhi-ha*, Iraj Qaderi, 1361/1982)
The Jar (*Khomreh*, Ebrahim Foruzesh, 1370/1992)
The Jungle Messenger (*Peyk-e Jangal*, Hasan Hedayat, 1361/1982)
Justification (*Towjih*, Manuchehr Haqqani-parast, 1360/1981)
The Key (*Kelid*, Ebrahim Foruzesh, 1365/1987)
Lady (*Banu*, Daryush Mehrju'i, 1371/1992)
Leyla (Daryush Mehrju'i, 1375/1997)
The Little Man (*Mard-e Kuchek*, Ebrahim Foruzesh, 1376/1997)
A Little Stiff (Caveh Zahedi with Greg Watkins, 1992)
The Living Document (*Sanad-e Zendeh*, Asghar Bichareh, 1359/1980)
Long Live (*Zendeh Bad*, Khosrow Sina'i, 1359/1980)
The Lor Girl (*Dokhtar-e Lor*, Ardeshir Irani, 1312/1933)
Lovers of the Arctic Circle (Julio Medem, 1999)
Manhattan by Numbers (Amir Naderi, 1993)
The May Lady (*Banu-ye Ordibehesht*, Rakhshan Bani-Etemad, 1376/1998)
Maybe Another Time (*Shayad Vaqti Digar*, Bahram Beyza'i, 1366/1988)
The Mirror (*A'ineh*, Jafar Panahi, 1375/1997)
The Mission (*Ma'muriat*, Parviz Sayyad, 1983)
Moment of Innocence (*Nun va Goldun*, Mohsen Makhmalbaf, 1375/1996)
The Mongols (*Moghol-ha*, Parviz Kimiavi, 1352/1973)
The Monster Within (*Hayula-ye Darun*, Khosrow Sina'i, 1362/1984)
Mr Hieroglyphic (*Aqa-ye Hiroglif*, Gholam Ali Erfan, 1359/1980)
Nargess (Rakhshan Bani-Etemad, 1370/1992)
Nasuh's Repentance (*Towbeh-ye Nasuh*, Mohsen Makhmalbaf, 1361/1982)
The Need (*Niyaz*, Alireza Davudnezhad, 1370/1992)
The Night of Power (*Lailat ol-Qadr*, Mohammad Ali Najafi, 1358/1979)
Nightsongs (Marva Nabili, 1984)
Not Without my Daughter (Brian Gilbert, 1991)
The Nuclear Baby (*Nowzad-e Atomi*, Jalal Fatemi, 1990)
O Deer Saviour (*Ya Zamen Ahu*, Parviz Kimiavi, 1349/1970)
OK Mister (Parviz Kimiavi, 1358/1979)
Once Upon a Time Cinema (*Naseroddin Shah, Aktor-e Sinema*, Mohsen Makhmalbaf,
    1370/1991)
Out of Limits (*Kharej az Mahdudeh*, Rakhshan Bani-Etemad, 1366/1988)
P Like Pelican (*P Mesl-e Pelikan*, Parviz Kimiavi, 1351/1972)

Patal and Little Wishes (*Patal va Arezu-ha-ye Kuchek*, Masud Karamati, 1368/1990)

The Pear Tree (*Derakht-e Golabi*, Daryush Mehrju'i, 1376/1998)

The Peddler (*Dast-forush*, Mohsen Makhmalbaf, 1365/1987)

Pelle the Conqueror (Bille August, 1988)

Pixote, Survival of the Weakest (Hector Babenco, 1981)

Ponette (Jacques Doillon, 1997)

Qeysar (Massoud Kimia'i, 1348/1969)

Rain and the Native (*Baran va Bumi*, Rakhshan Bani-Etemad, 1377/1999), part of *Stories of Kish*

The Report (*Gozaresh*, Abbas Kiarostami, 1356/1977)

Report of a Death (*Gozaresh-e Yek Qatl*, Mohammad Ali Najafi, 1365/1987)

Roses for Africa (*Rosen für Afrika*, Sohrab Shahid-Saless, 1991)

The Runner (*Davandeh*, Amir Naderi, 1365/1986)

Salaam Bombay! (Mira Nair, 1988)

Salaam Cinema/Cinema, Cinema (*Salam Sinema*, Mohsen Makhmalbaf, 1373/1995)

Sara (Daryush Mehrju'i, 1371/1992)

Satan (*Sheytan*, Akbar Sadeqi, 1359/1980)

Scabies (*Gal*, Abolfazl Jalili, 1367/1988)

The Scent of Yusef's Shirt (*Bu-ye Pirahan-e Yusef*, Ebrahim Hatamikia, 1374/1996)

The School We Went to (*Madreseh'i keh Miraftim*, Dariush Mehrju'i, 1367/1988), re-titled from *The Yard Behind Adl-e Afaq School*

Seeking Refuge (*Este'azeh*, Mohsen Makhmalbaf, 1362/1983)

The Senator (*Senator*, Mehdi Sabbaghzadeh, 1362/1984)

The Sentry (*Didehban*, Ebrahim Hatamikia, 1367/1988)

Shinjuku Boys (Kim Longinotto and Jano Williams, 1996)

Silences of the Palace (Moufida Tlatli, 1994)

A Simple Event (*Yek Ettefaq-e Sadeh*, Sohrab Shahid-Saless, 1352/1973)

Snake Fang (*Dandan-e Mar*, Massoud Kimia'i, 1368/1989)

The Snowman (*Adam Barfi*, Davud Mirbaqeri, 1373/1994–1376/1997)

The Soldier of Islam (*Sarbaz-e Eslam*, Aman Manteqi, 1359/1980)

Someone Else's Death (*Marg-e Digari*, Mohammad Reza Honarmand, 1360/1981)

Still Life (*Tab'iat-e Bi-jan*, Sohrab Shahid-Saless, 1354/1975)

The Stranger and the Fog (*Gharibeh va Meh*, Bahram Beyza'i, 1354/1975)

The Suitors (*Khastgaran*, Ghasem Ebrahimian, 1989)

Sweet Bird of Fortune (*Parandeh-ye Kuchek-e Khoshbakhti*, Pouran Derakhshandeh, 1366/1987)

Tales of Kish (*Qesseh-ha-ye Kish*, 1377/1999), comprising shorts by Bahram Beyza'i, Mohsen Makhmalbaf, Naser Taghva'i, Abolfazl Jalili, Rakhshan Bani-Etemad, Daryush Mehrju'i

Talisman (*Telesm*, Daryush Farhang, 1365/1986)

Tall Shadows of the Wind (*Sayehha-ye Boland-e Bad*, Bahman Farmanara, 1357/1978)

Tara's Ballad (*Cherikeh-ye Tara*, Bahram Beyza'i, 1357/1978)

The Taste of Cherry (*Ta'm-e Gilas*, Abbas Kiarostami, 1376/1997)

The Tempest of Life (*Tufan-e Zendegi*, Esma'il Kushan, 1327/1948)

The Tenants (*Ejarehneshin-ha*, Daryush Mehrju'i, 1365/1986)
Thief of Dolls (*Dozd-e Arusak-ha*, Mohammed Reza Honarmand, 1368/1989)
Through the Olive Trees (*Zir-e Derakhtan-e Zeytun*, Abbas Kiarostami, 1372/1994)
The Thug and the Student (*Jahel va Mohassel*) see *Freeze Don't Move*
A Time to Love (*Nowbat-e Asheqi*, Mohsen Makhmalbaf, 1369/1991)
Tito and Me (Goran Markovic, 1992)
Tootia (Iraj Qaderi, 1998)
Toto the Hero (Jaco van Dormael, 1991)
Two Sightless Eyes (*Do Cheshm-e Bi-su*, Mohsen Makhmalbaf, 1362/1983)
Two Women (*Do Zan*, Tahmineh Milani, 1378/1999)
Uncle Moustache (*Amu Sibilu*, Bahram Beyza'i, 1348/1969)
Uprising (*Qiyam*, Reza Safa'i, 1359/1980)
Utopia (Sohrab Shahid-Saless, 1982)
Walls of Sand (Shirin Etessam and Erica Jordan, 1994)
Water, Wind, Earth (*Ab, Bad, Khak*, Amir Naderi, 1367/1989)
The Weak Point (*Noqteh Za'f*, Mohammad Reza Alami, 1362/1983)
Wedding of the Blessed (*'Arusi-ye Khuban*, Mohsen Makhmalbaf, 1367/1989)
Where is the Friend's House? (*Khaneh-ye Dust Kojast?*, Abbas Kiarostami, 1365/1987)
The White Balloon (*Badkonak-e Sefid*, Jafar Panahi, 1373/1995)
The Wind Will Carry Us (*Bad Ma-ra Khahad Bord*, Abbas Kiarostami, 1378/1999)
The Yard Behind Adl-e Afaq School (*Hayat-e Poshti-ye Madreseh-ye Adl-e Afaq*,
        Dariush Mehrju'i, 1359/1980)
Yazdgerd's Death (*Marg-e Yazdgerd*, Bahram Beyza'i, 1359/1981)
Z (Constantin Costa-Gavras, 1969)
Zayandehrud Nights (*Shab-ha-ye Zayandehrud*, Mohsen Makhmalbaf, 1369/1991)
Zinat (Ebrahim Mokhtari, 1372/1994)

Persian Titles

A'ineh – The Mirror
Ab, Bad, Khak – Water, Wind, Earth
Abr va Aftab – The Cloud and the Rising Sun
Adam Barfi – Snowman
Amrika Nabud Ast – America is Destroyed
Amu Sibilu – Uncle Moustache
Aqa-ye Hiroglif – Mr Hieroglyphic
'Arusi-ye Khuban – Wedding of the Blessed
Az Karkheh ta Rayn – From Karkheh to Rhine
Azhans-e Shishe'i – The Glass Agency
Bache-ha-ye Asman – Children of Heaven
Bache-ha-ye Talaq – Children of Divorce
Bad Ma-ra Khahad Bord – The Wind Will Carry Us
Badkonak-e Sefid – The White Balloon

Baduk – Baduk
Banu – Lady
Banu-ye Ordibehesht – The May Lady
Baran va Bumi – Rain and the Native
Barzakhi-ha – In Limbo
Bashu, Gharibeh-ye Kuchak – Bashu, The Little Stranger
Baykot – Boycott
Baysikelran – The Cyclist
Bi Harekat, Tekun Nakhor – Freeze, Don't Move (see *Jahel va Mohassel* and *Hero'in*)
Bu-ye Pirahan-e Yusef – The Scent of Yusef's Shirt
Chakmeh – The Boot
Cherikeh-ye Tara – Tara's Ballad
Da'ereh-ye Mina – The Cycle
Dandan-e Mar – Snake Fang
Dar Ghorbat – Far From Home
Dar Mohasereh – Besieged
Dast-forush – The Peddler
Davandeh – The Runner
Derakht-e Golabi – The Pear Tree
Det Yani Dokhtar – Det Means Girl
Didehban – The Sentry
Diyar-e 'Asheqan – The Domain of Lovers
Do Cheshm-e Bi-su – Two Sightless Eyes
Do Zan – Two Women
Dokhtar-e Lor – The Lor Girl
Dozd-e Arusak-ha – Thief of Dolls
E'dami – The Condemned
Ejarehneshin-ha – The Tenants
Este'azeh – Seeking Refuge
Faryad-e Mojahed – The Cry of the Mojahed
Gabbeh – Gabbeh
Gal – Scabies
Gav – The Cow
Gavaznha – The Deer
Gharibeh va Meh – The Stranger and the Fog
Goft-o-gu ba Bad – Dialogue with Wind
Golnar – Golnar
Gozaresh – The Report
Gozaresh-e Yek Qatl – Report of a Death
Haji Washington – Haji Washington
Hamun – Hamoon
Hayat-e Poshti-ye Madreseh-ye Adl-e Afaq – The Yard Behind Adl-e Afaq School
Hayula-ye Darun – The Monster Within
Hero'in – Heroin

Hesar dar Hesar – Fortress in Fortress
Jahel va Mohassel – The Thug and the Student
Janbazan – The Devotees
Jang-e Athar – Athar's War
Kalagh – The Crow
Kelid – The Key
Khaneh dar Entezar – A House Waiting
Khaneh-ye Dust Kojast? – Where is the Friend's House?
Kharej az Mahdudeh – Out of Limits
Khastgaran – The Suitors
Khomreh – The Jar
Khunbaresh – Blood-rain
Lailat ol-Qadr – The Night of Power
Leyla – Leyla
Ma'muriat – The Mission
Madreseh'i keh Miraftim – The School We Went to
Malakut – The Divine One
Mard-e Kuchek – The Little Man
Marg-e Digari – Someone Else's Death
Marg-e Yazdgerd – Yazdgerd's Death
Marsiyeh – Elegy
Marz – The Border
Mashq-e Shab – Homework
Moghol-ha – The Mongols
Mohajer – The Emigrant
Nakhoda Khorshid – Captain Khorshid
Nama-ye Nazdik – Close-Up
Nan va Kucheh – Bread and Alley
Nan va She'r – Bread and Poetry
Nargess – Nargess
Naseroddin Shah, Aktor-e Sinema – Once Upon a Time Cinema
Niyaz – The Need
Noqteh Za'f – The Weak Point
Nowbat-e Asheqi – A Time to Love
Nowzad-e Atomi – The Nuclear Baby
Nun va Goldun – Moment of Innocence
O.K. Mister – O.K. Mister
Ofoq – The Horizon
Otobus – The Bus
P Mesl-e Pelikan – P Like Pelican
Parandeh-ye Kuchek-e Khoshbakhti – Sweet Bird of Fortune
Parvandeh – The Dossier
Parvaz be-su-ye Minu – Flying Towards Minu
Patal va Arezu-ha-ye Kuchek – Patal and Little Wishes

Pedar – The Father
Peyk-e Jangal – The Jungle Messenger
Qesseh-ha-ye Kish – Tales of Kish
Qeysar – Qeysar
Qiyam – Uprising
Ragbar – Downpour
Rang-e Khoda – The Color of Paradise
Raqs-e Khak – Dance of Dust
Ru-sari Abi – The Blue Scarf
Salam Sinema – Salaam Cinema/Cinema, Cinema
Sanad-e Zendeh – The Living Document
Sara – Sara
Sarbaz-e Eslam – The Soldier of Islam
Sayehha-ye Boland-e Bad – Tall Shadows of the Wind
Saz-dahani – Harmonica
Senator – The Senator
Shab-ha-ye Zayandehrud – Zayandehrud Nights
Shahr-e Mush-ha – City of Mice
Shatranj-e Bad – The Chess of the Wind
Shayad Vaqti Digar – Maybe Another Time
Sheshomin Nafar – The Sixth Person
Sheytan – Satan
Sib – The Apple
Soqut-e '57 – The Fall of '57
Ta'm-e Gilas – The Taste of Cherry
Tab'iat-e Bi-jan – Still Life
Tagebuch Eines Liebenden – Diary of a Lover
Takhteh Siyah – Blackboard
Tavallod-e Yek Purvaneh – Birth of a Butterfly
Telesm – Talisman
Towbeh-ye Nasuh – Nasuh's Repentance,
Towjih – Justification
Tufan-e Zendegi – The Tempest of Life
Tutia – Tootia
Va Zendegi Edameh Darad ... – And Life Goes on ...
Ya Zamen Ahu – O Deer Saviour
Yek Ettefaq-e Sadeh – A Simple Event
Zendeh Bad – Long Live
Zinat – Zinat
Zir-e Derakhtan e Zeytun – Through the Olive Trees

Index of Films

General Index